FROM ROME TO
ROYAL PARK

From Rome to Royal Park

Gerald O'Collins SJ

Connor Court Publishing

Connor Court Publishing Pty Ltd

Copyright © Gerald O'Collins SJ 2015

ALL RIGHTS RESERVED. This book contains material protected under International and Federal Copyright Laws and Treaties. Any unauthorised reprint or use of this material is prohibited. No part of this book may be reproduced or transmitted in any form or by any means, electronic or mechanical, including photocopying, recording, or by any information storage and retrieval system without express written permission from the publisher.

PO Box 224W
Ballarat VIC 3350
sales@connorcourt.com
www.connorcourt.com

ISBN: 9781925138887 (pbk)

Cover design by Maria Giordano, photo by Fiona Basile, used with permission.

Printed in Australia

Contents

Preface	vii
List of Photographs	ix
1. Roman Afterthoughts	1
2. Joseph Ratzinger the Bridge	26
3. An English Interlude	53
4. Australian Re-entry	93
5. Lights and Shadows	123
6. Torturing the Language and Welcoming the New Pope	144
Appendix 1: *Spe Salvi* (Saved by Hope)	168
Appendix 2: Ecumenism in Advent	176
Appendix 3: The Congregation for the Doctrine of the Faith Explains and Comments	180
Appendix 4: One Little Word	184
Appendix 5: A Challenge for Theologians: Three Puzzling Positions	189
Appendix 6: Living the Sacrament of Matrimony	193
Appendix 7: Interpreting the Documents of Vatican II Integrally	199
Appendix 8: Six Obituaries	204
Appendix 9: The Living Word, the Living Tradition	225
Index of Names	231

Preface

'Is there life after Rome?', an American friend asked me in 2007. In 2006 I had left the Gregorian University and taken up a post as research professor at St Mary's University College (now St Mary's University), Twickenham. Eventually, in 2013, I would publish an account of thirty-two years of teaching (1974–2006) at the Gregorian University: *On the Left Bank of the Tiber* (Ballarat/Leominster: Connor Court/Gracewing). That volume told the story of three decades of busy life and work at an international university founded in the sixteenth century by a Basque and a Spaniard who were to become canonized saints: St Ignatius Loyola (1491–1556) and St Francis Borgia (1510–1572).

Life in Rome had been complex, intense, and very rewarding. But—to answer my friend's question—there was 'life after Rome'. This further volume of my memoirs takes up the story after I flew out of Rome in the summer of 2006. I remain resolutely happy to have made a clean break and not hung around the eternal city as a retired professor. I had enjoyed the time of my life, but hanging on might well have meant spiralling into senile self-destruction.

At the same time, scenes and episodes from the Roman years hover perpetually on the edge of my memory. Over and over again, I have to come to realize that *On the Left Bank of the Tiber* needs to be supplemented. Hence the first chapter of this book, 'Roman Afterthoughts', precedes 'An English Interlude'. That first chapter also incorporates some photographs from the April 2006 ceremony when the Australian ambassador to the Holy See and Ireland, Anne Plunkett, conferred on me an AC.

Three years of living in a small Jesuit community in Wimbledon and commuting most days to St Mary's College (2006–2009) closed when I presided at a wedding in the Farm Street church. Two days later in September 2009, I flew off to Melbourne and took up living again at the Jesuit Theological College (JTC) in Parkville (where I had already spent five years of my life, 1969–1973)

The JTC occupied a row of ten terrace houses, which were built in the 1880s and looked out on the elms of Royal Parade. Across the Avenue that bordered our generous backyards, Royal Park stretched away in both directions and teemed with currawongs, galahs, magpies, mudlarks, mynahs, parakeets, and other Australian birds. We lived where a line drawn across Royal Park from the Melbourne zoo to the University of Melbourne intersected with a line drawn from the Royal Children's Hospital to the Melbourne General Cemetery.

Will the JTC be my last pit-stop? The sum of my final years belongs to the mystery of divine providence. No matter when the last pit-stop comes, in the meantime I can give an account of what has happened to me, and how, from staging posts in the UK and Australia, I have understood the life of the world-wide Church and the world around me.

Time moves faster for me nowadays, and the witnesses to my life diminish. I remain most grateful to all those, both living and dead, who have shared the journey with me and in various ways supported me. With warm thanks this book is dedicated to the men and women committed to the ministry of education in the Diocese of Lismore.

Gerald O'Collins, SJ, AC
Jesuit Theological College, Parkville
Pentecost, 2015.

Photographs

Receiving AC from Anne Plunkett, April 2006	11
With Maurice Iemma, Anne Plunkett, and Malcolm Turnbull	11
With Australians at the AC ceremony	12
Leaving Rome, June 2006	12
Leaving London, September 2009	92
With group at the Jesuit Theological College, late 2009	94
With Michael Jones, chaplain on a visiting cruise ship, 2011	103
With George and Eileen Carey, 2012	111
With George Carey, 2012	111
Philip Freier and Graham Smith at launch of *A Midlife Journey*	135
With Moira Peters and Tim Fischer at launch of *On the Left Bank of the Tiber*	135
With Geoffrey Blainey at launch of *On the Left Bank of the Tiber*	136
With John Batt and Evarist Shigi at launch of *Ten African Cardinals*	136
With James Gobbo, December 2012	141

Photo Credits

The publisher and author thank Fiona Basile very warmly for the photo on the front cover.

For other photos we thank Fred Brenk, George and Eileen Carey, Catherine Hall, Michael Head, Michael Keenan Jones, Kevin Mark, Posey O'Collins, Elizabeth Parker, Catherine Pepinster, and Scott and Alisia Samson.

1

ROMAN AFTERTHOUGHTS

The second chapter of *On the Left Bank of the Tiber* recalled visitors to Rome. A whole book might have been dedicated to them. There were some whom I mentioned (for instance, Mother Teresa of Calcutta) about whom much more could be said. There were others who were not mentioned (for instance, Sir Zelman Cowen) but who should not be forgotten. Let me begin with Zelman, my brother Jim, and Mother Teresa.

Sir Zelman, Jim, and Mother Teresa

In 1990, the centenary of the death of John Henry Newman, two acclaimed figures from his Oxford college arrived to visit Pope (now Saint) John Paul II. Sir Zelman was retiring as provost of Oriel College (1982–90). Rev. Professor Ernest Nicholson was the incoming provost, and would serve as provost until 2003. As a Rhodes scholar, Zelman attended New College, Oxford, before becoming a fellow of Oriel (1947–50) and subsequently an outstanding professor of law and academic leader in Australia. He was appointed Governor General of Australia (1977–82), the second Jewish Governor-General after Sir Isaac Isaacs.[1] Internationally, Zelman loomed large as one of

---

1 Sir Isaac Isaacs was also the first Australian-born Governor-General of the Commonwealth of Australia (1930–36). A distinguished parliamentarian and the third Chief Justice of the Australian High Court, Isaacs was strongly opposed to political Zionism, and foresaw how the creation of the State of Israel would bring enduring hostility from hundreds of millions of Muslims. He expressed his moral, legal, and political objections in *Palestine: Peace and prosperity or war and destruction? Political Zionism: undemocratic, unjust, dangerous* (Melbourne: Ramsey Ware Publishing, 1946).

the most notable constitutional lawyers of his time. Ernest, born in Portadown, County Armagh, became a close friend of mine from the time he was chaplain and then dean at Pembroke College, our college in Cambridge. With numerous publications on the Old Testament, by 1990 he was long established as a leading biblical scholar.

Zelman and Ernest explained to me that they were in Rome to promote the cause of a famous Oriel man, John Henry Newman. Zelman was Australian and Jewish; Ernest came from the citadel of Protestantism in Northern Ireland. Back in Oxford, they were turning Newman's rooms into a shrine, with stained glass windows designed by the granddaughter of Field Marshal Douglas Haig. The Cowen-Nicholson project and visit to the reigning Pope caught my imagination as anything but a probable affair. 'College loyalties rather than religious differences', I thought, 'must count for everything.' They enjoyed a happy meeting with John Paul II, who expressed admiration for the heroic virtue and intellectual greatness of Newman. He regretted that no miracle had yet occurred which could lead to an official 'beatification', the major step on the way to being declared a saint or 'canonized'. In other words, Newman had so far 'failed his practicals'. Years later a cure was accepted as having come through the intercession of Newman, and he was duly beatified in September 2010—shortly before Zelman died in 2011 and Ernest in 2013.

(2) My brother Jim, his wife Rosemary ('Posey'), at times accompanied by their two children, James and Victoria ('Tori'), turned up in Rome regularly. One cold but clear Christmas morning when the smell of roasted chestnuts floated down the streets, Tori went with her parents to St Peter's Basilica and received her first Holy Communion from Pope John Paul II. During these visits I shared Jim and Posey with my local friends—not least, Frank and Orietta Doria Pamphilj. Memory supplies the picture of Orietta showing Tori some of the secrets of the Palazzo Doria, including a sliding bookcase behind which Orietta and her parents had hidden when German

soldiers raided their home in late 1943. The tall Italian princess strode down the corridors initiating a delighted Australian child into some of the mysteries of a gigantic Roman palace.

Jim was one of the busiest urologists of his generation. He contributed to the remarkable progress in treating the urinary system made during his four decades in that field of surgery. In the summer of 1989, Jim arrived to attend a medical conference sponsored by the Pontifical Council for Health Care. I was startled when he told me the theme of the conference: male impotence. He too had been surprised (and pleased) to find the Vatican inviting specialists like himself to share information about ways of dealing with impotence caused by operations on the prostate (about 60% of the cases of impotence). Then he learned from the Pontifical Council that the idea of the conference came from John Paul II himself. Knowing how marriages can be threatened and even wrecked when surgery makes a husband incapable of normal sexual relations, the Pope had brought together experts to discuss means for restoring such relations. John Paul II's loving concern for married people went beyond describing matters 'from first principles'—as he often did—to encourage practical solutions based on evidence and experience. My brother Jim was satisfied that the conference of specialists brought some progress in dealing with male impotence.

(3) *On the Left Bank of the Tiber* put on display the contribution that Mother Teresa made to the 1973 Eucharistic Congress in Melbourne when she spoke on peace in the town hall (p. 130). As well as being marvellously mystical, she could be practical and peremptory. On one visit to Melbourne she hailed a taxi and asked the driver: 'How long does it take to get to Broken Hill?' 'The best part of a day', he told her. 'Well, we better start right now', she told the startled driver as she and another nun stepped into the taxi.

In those days I sometimes celebrated the Eucharist for her sisters in a battered inner-city dwelling where they gave shelter and food to the homeless. One morning I had put on the vestments and was about to start Mass at 7 a.m., when in came Mother Teresa with a pretty, mini-skirted young woman. 'You will preach on religious life, won't you, Father?', she said to me. I had only five minutes in which to think up something useful to say. After Mass the young woman returned, now dressed in the white and blue colours of Mother Teresa's congregation and carrying the skirt, blouse, and other clothing which she had been wearing an hour before and which she now deposited in the arms of some relative or friend.

It was always compellingly clear what Mother Teresa wanted, no matter who she was engaged with. In Rome she called on Cardinal Agostino Casaroli, the Pope's admirable Secretary of State (1979–90), and asked for a place right in the Vatican where her sisters could live and care for the homeless. 'That's a beautiful idea', Casaroli said, 'but we don't have any suitable building to give you.' He was deluded into thinking that she would take no for an answer. Mother Teresa left his office and sat in the waiting room, 'doing a squat', as Indians say. Naturally she seized the attention of all the bishops and other officials going into the cardinal's office. 'Mother Teresa is sitting outside', they kept telling him. After an hour or so, the pressure proved too much. A frustrated Cardinal Casaroli burst into the waiting room and told her: 'Yes, we'll find you a place'. The shelter sits right on the edge of the Piazza del Santo Ufficio, a stone's throw from the *palazzo* housing what is now called the Congregation for the Doctrine of the Faith rather than the Holy Office. Mother Teresa's sisters and the homeless humanize the scene. I still puzzle over Cardinal Casaroli's initial refusal. On weekends he regularly visited a gaol for juvenile offenders, and as 'Padre Agostino' generously supported and encouraged the young men.

The Casaroli exchange typifies what it meant to be Mother Teresa. Some years later on a lecturing visit to San Diego, California, I learned that she had just been hospitalized there and brought back to life by a team of doctors. When she started recovering, she wanted to have the team come to her hospital room for the celebration of Mass. At once one of the doctors rushed off to the local bishop and told him about Mother Teresa's invitation, adding: 'The problem is that I'm Jewish. What should I do?' The bishop replied without hesitation: 'Do what we all do. Do what she tells you.' A day or so later the same bishop celebrated Mass in Mother Teresa's room. At the end she prayed silently for some minutes, and then fished out from under the sheets a contract prepared for the bishop's signature and authorizing her to open a shelter in San Diego. 'I was caught with my pants down', the bishop commented later.

Mother Teresa exemplified wonderfully well what an outstanding theologian, Karl Rahner (1904–84), wrote about human closeness to God: 'the closer we are to God, the more our individual personality is enhanced'. Unquestionably, Mother Teresa was very close to God. But that enhanced, rather than diminished, her personal characteristics.

Mother Teresa died in 1997, and, two years before he died, John Paul II beatified her in October 2003 on a morning made fresh by overnight rain. Over one hundred thousand pilgrims and tourists attended the ceremony in St Peter's Square. Several hundred homeless people were seated near the altar and afterwards shared a lunch served by the diplomatic corps. The media came in full force, partly to honour Mother Teresa and partly to use the occasion as a dry run for the coming death and funeral of Pope John Paul II. I was broadcasting on the BBC platform with Brian Hanrahan initiating my happy partnership with that TV presenter. (Two years later I was to join him repeatedly on the occasion of the death of John Paul II and the conclave that elected Pope Benedict XVI.) After Mother Teresa had been declared 'blessed', the Mass continued with the preparation of the gifts. Four lovely Indian ladies wearing saris and carrying lights began dancing up to the altar. Hanrahan turned to me and said: 'Father O'Collins, some people don't like this.' 'Brian, that's their problem',

I assured him. 'This is India's day in the sun. And what's more, I'm sure Mother Teresa wants me to say how much she approves of what they're doing.'

John Wilkins, Mel Gibson, and a Russian Archbishop

1. John Wilkins, the editor of the London *Tablet* from 1982 to 2003, became an enduring friend. On one of the big occasions which drew him to Rome, he reported my regular advice to visitors:

> Those travelling around Rome on the 64 bus, as the editor of *The Tablet* did recently, may find themselves subject to stern admonitions from the professor of fundamental theology at the Gregorian University, Gerald O'Collins. On one occasion, watching an American tourist preparing to board, O'Collins could not bear it any longer. 'Please, do you have your passport and travellers' cheques in that bag?' he asked the woman. 'Indeed', she replied, surprised. 'Then do me a favour—please don't carry it like that but sling it around your neck. Don't make things too easy for our boys and girls, the best pickpockets in Europe.' Once when travelling on the crowded bus which runs from the main station of Rome to St Peter's, O'Collins found himself near a demure nun in full habit. Two plainclothes police suddenly bundled her off at one of the stops. Beneath her ecclesiastical garb she was wearing jeans, with a series of hooks on her belt, to which she had fastened her very considerable takings. 'On the 64 bus', one gravely-spoken Vatican official told O'Collins, 'the pickpockets can rob you of your underpants and you won't notice till later.' Adopting a confessional mode, O'Collins announces: 'Any man who puts his wallet in the back pocket of his trousers is co-operating in sin. And when approached by little girls who pretend to sell you rosary beads, drive them off with obvious anger. This is morally in order, and need not be mentioned in your next confession.' So far *The*

Tablet's editor has always retained his trousers (*The Tablet*, 24 May 1997).

John had the nose of a first-rate journalist for smelling out a good and often controversial story. *On the Left Bank of the Tiber* tells how he involved me in reviewing critically *The Ratzinger Report* while it was still available only in Italian and had not yet appeared in English (pp. 200–02). John wanted an early shot fired across its bows.

Twelve years later John insisted that I send him a review of Jacques Dupuis' *Toward a Christian Theology of Religious Pluralism* (Maryknoll, NY: Orbis, 1997). On 22 November 1997 I had shared the gala occasion when the book was presented at the Gregorian University. The year was closing down and I had other pressing things to do, but John wanted the review. It appeared in *The Tablet* for 24 January 1998, and caught the attention of Cardinal Franz König, the archbishop emeritus of Vienna. He ordered a copy, read it carefully, and was in a position to defend Dupuis quickly and vigorously in a two-page article and a long interview when, in late 1998, Dupuis came under fire from the Congregation for the Doctrine of the Faith (hereafter CDF). *On the Left Bank of the Tiber* expressed my gratitude to the cardinal for joining me in speaking up for Dupuis (pp. 222–23). But I failed to mention that König would probably never have read Dupuis' book, had it not been for John's sixth sense.[2]

Toward a Christian Theology of Religious Pluralism developed an open-minded view of other living faiths. Dupuis always wrote knowledgeably and informatively; he showed a minutely detailed acquaintance with Christian and Hindu thought. Yet his book was heavy with theological language, and I did not think it would enjoy serious appeal for the

---

[2] Leaks from inside the second conclave of 1978, held when Pope John Paul I suddenly died, reported that, after a number of ballots, Cardinal König was on the point of being elected. He stood up and insisted, 'I'm too old. Please vote for someone else.' The 'someone else' proved to be Cardinal Karol Wojtyla who created history as Pope John Paul II. König, in fact, lived on until 2004 and remained thoroughly lucid to the end.

rank and file readers of *The Tablet*. But John's instincts were right; he wanted to alert the general public to what he suspected would prove, in the long run, a landmark in the theology of religions and, in the short run, a controversial volume that might draw fire from the CDF. John remained steadily loyal to Dupuis, inviting him to deliver *The Tablet* open-day lecture in October 2001 and constantly supporting him through editorials and articles in his journal.

John also proved immensely generous to me when I was writing *Living Vatican II: The Twenty-first Council for the Twenty-first Century* (Mahwah, NJ: Paulist Press, 2006). He not only came up with many challenging questions but also worked hard to improve the chapters that I sent him in draft form. The book was awarded 'best theology book of 2006' by the Catholic Press Association of USA and Canada. John should have been the co-recipient of the award. His eye for excellent and concise writing impressed me definitively when I sent him my obituary for Cardinal Carlo Maria Martini. Without destroying the themes I had researched and sketched, John drew on other sources, including an important one in Milan, and expressed everything with terse clarity. After Martini's death (31 August 2012), the London *Times* carried the obituary on 3 September 2012.

Right from the start of his twenty-one years as editor of *The Tablet*, John persistently alerted readers to an alarming development: the nomination by Pope John Paul II (or should one say imposition?) of too many bishops who failed to meet the pastoral needs of their dioceses. In this the Pope was aided and abetted by some members of the Vatican's Congregation of Bishops. *On the Left Bank of the Tiber* recalled several 'shadows' over the pontificate of John Paul II (pp. 152–60). That list of shadows should also have included some regrettable choices of bishops. Where Pope Paul VI had moved to 'liberalize' the hierarchies of Spain and the United States, John Paul II took things in the opposite direction. At times he neglected the proper gathering of information about episcopal candidates, and could select someone simply because he liked the look of him. Since he had lived for years under Nazi and Communist regimes, I expected him to prove more street wise. But he could be deceived by those who were unsuitable, sycophants, or worse.

Let me mention only two examples: first, the appointment of Wolfgang Haas as coadjutor bishop of Chur (Switzerland) in 1988 and his becoming sole bishop of the diocese in 1990. The second case is that of Cardinal Hans Hermann Wilhelm Groer, OSB, Archbishop of Vienna (1986–95).

With his dictatorial manner and ultra-conservative convictions, Wolfgang Haas quickly alienated the people and priests of Chur. The Vatican's 'solution', approved if not initiated by John Paul II, was first of all to parachute into the diocese of Chur two other bishops, who were given enlarged powers to keep Haas in check. Then he was appointed Archbishop of Vaduz, the capital of Liechtenstein, an diocese specially created for him in the hope that being a Liechtensteiner by birth he might behave better at home and be received more cordially by the locals. But even there the people and local parliament reacted angrily against the imposition of Haas (see *The Tablet*, 13 December 1997). Many commentators believed that Haas should never have been ordained a bishop in the first place.

In choosing (against some advice) Hans Hermann Wilhelm Groer, OSB, to succeed König as Archbishop of Vienna in 1986, John Paul II was apparently swayed by Groer's devotion to the Blessed Virgin Mary. Created a cardinal in 1988, Groer had to resign in 1995 after he was accused of having molested sexually a number of boys and young seminarians. Here at least the Pope accepted the evidence and removed Groer from office, even though he would not allow what the then Cardinal Joseph Ratzinger asked for: a full investigation into the whole affair. One or more Vatican officials persuaded the Pope to avoid that; they feared the bad publicity which such a probe could bring. In the case of Fr Marcial Maciel Degollado, John Paul II was reluctant to face the evidence that established the sexual crimes committed over many years by the founder of the Legionaries of Christ. He was brought to justice only after the election of Benedict XVI in April 2005.

John Wilkins was at his editorial best in pursuing the faulty episcopal appointments that cast a shadow over the pontificate of John Paul II. Some of the bishops chosen by the Pope have wounded seriously Catholic life in Austria, Ireland, and other countries.

(2) *On the Left Bank of the Tiber* recalled two young Jesuits, Patrick Gahizi and Innocent Rutagambwa who were martyred in Rwanda (p. 65). They were among the students—Jesuits call them 'scholastics'— whom I came to know very well at the International College of the Gesù, a Roman institution which I mentioned only in passing (p. 101) but where history could happen right under our noses. Memory evokes some of the visitors invited to lunch; they included the president of a Latin American country, Jesuits working in Siberia, and a Polish cardinal, Karol Wojtyla. Although I never lived in the college, I was twice prefect of studies there and used to eat at the Gesù once or twice a week right to the end of my years in Rome.

The staff of the college included Fr Joseph Barrett, a hefty, white-haired, and not always politically correct British Jesuit who served as treasurer. Joe had been a prison chaplain in the high-security Strangeways Prison (Manchester) and sometimes treated the scholastics almost as if they were convicts. His room displayed a notice detailing one's rights under British law if arrested by the police. 'You just never know; it might happen to you', he explained when I asked why he had put the notice on the wall.

As soon as he arrived in Rome to film *The Passion of Christ*, Mel Gibson called at the Gesù and asked to see an English-speaking priest. The young Italian porter, who recognized Gibson at once, put a call through to Joe's room. Joe came downstairs and was greeted by

Receiving AC from Anne Plunkett, April 2006

With Maurice Iemma, Anne Plunkett, and Malcolm Turnbull

With Australians at the AC ceremony

Leaving Rome, June 2006

the visitor: 'I'm Mel Gibson. Would you say Mass for me each day in Latin?' Joe, who did not have the slightest interest in films, had never heard of Gibson and replied with a blunt 'No'. Once upon a time he had happily celebrated in Latin, but now his eyesight was failing and he had memorized the essential English texts to enable him to continue saying Mass. Some scholastics, alerted by the porter, had drifted discreetly towards the front door. They were amazed and fascinated to hear Joe giving Gibson 'the brush off'. In the event the actor had no difficulty finding elsewhere someone who provided him with a daily Mass in Latin. Joe Barrett could give other visitors 'the brush off'.

Just down the street a British-style pub, 'The John Bull', was the scene of a mini-riot after an England-Italy football match. Earlier, shoppers and tourists in the Piazza di Spagna had been jeered and pelted with beer bottles by English visitors. Seventeen were arrested. Others ran to the Piazza del Popolo where they raised another storm of jeers and bottles, followed by more arrests. The rest moved down the Corso, turned into the Via del Plebiscito, and joined the English crowd already spilling out of 'The John Bull'. From his room in the Gesù, Joe heard the noise, stepped out of the college, crossed the street, and confronted the riotous mob. Seeing his clerical rig, they jeered at him all the more. 'Shut up', he commanded in a loud voice, and told them to 'knock it off and go home'. They had not reckoned on the compelling voice and imperious presence he had retained from his years as chaplain at Strangeways, negotiating with many more threatening insurrections. The drunken fans fell silent. Joe lifted his arms, gave the hooligans a lengthy blessing in Latin, and bade them to go in peace, which they did. *The Tablet* gleefully reported the incident, provided the heading 'Man of the Match', and carried a cartoon by Jonathan Pugh showing Italian police battling with hooligans and shouting: 'We need back up. Call Father Barrett' (25 October 1997).

One beloved visitor at the College and Church of the Gesù was the saintly Cardinal Eduardo Pironio, an Argentinian who headed the Vatican's office for members of religious institutes. Sometimes he came to ordain groups of young Jesuits to the diaconate. He was also the only high Vatican official to attend the packed funeral Mass in the Church of the Gesù after a government death squad in November 1989 murdered six Jesuits (plus their housekeeper and her daughter) in San Salvador (*On the Left Bank of the Tiber*, pp. 159–60).

Desperately in love with each other, Pironio's young parents had fled Italy for Argentina in order to get married. Their first child was born when his mother was only eighteen years of age. She became gravely ill and was bed-ridden for six months. When she recovered, the doctors said that her life would be in danger if she had more children. In her bewilderment she talked with an auxiliary bishop of La Plata, who calmed her down, celebrated Mass for her, and assured her that she would be protected. She proceeded to have twenty-one more children, the youngest being the future cardinal, and died at the age of eighty-two. The cause for the canonization of Eduardo Pironio has been introduced in both Rome (2006) and the Argentines (2007).

(3) When I began teaching fulltime at the Gregorian University in 1974, I found that Russian-speaking professors there and at other institutes in Rome were doing their best for Orthodox seminaries in the Soviet Union. They provided Bibles and other books in Russian, and a least two of them managed to teach courses in Leningrad and elsewhere. Some Orthodox students came to Rome on scholarships for further training.

After I was elected dean of the theology faculty in 1985, a Russian archbishop, together with his 'secretary' (obviously a KGB man), visited the Gregorian University to check courses and consider possible collaboration. The president of a theological academy in Moscow, the archbishop was pleasantly surprised to find that the Gregorian had no officially prescribed philosophy. We offered courses and seminars in analytic, Aristotelian, existentialist, idealist, Marxist, Thomist, and other forms of philosophy. He was not so happy to find that we had an institute of spirituality, which was separate from our theology faculty. 'Shouldn't all theology be spiritual?', he asked. I had to agree with him.

Sadly, after the fall of communism in Europe, official relations between the Orthodox and Catholics cooled. Any plans we had for the Gregorian to be engaged more closely with our counterparts in Russia were shelved. However, years later a theologian contacted me from Moscow and presided over two of my books being translated in Russian: first, *Believing in the Resurrection* and then one I had co-authored with Edward Farrugia, *A Concise Dictionary of Theology*, a work which has enjoyed three editions in English. I sometimes wondered whether this development came as a long-delayed 'thank you' for relations that had been initiated over twenty years earlier. The publishers in Moscow did something that no other publisher has ever done when translating into a foreign language any of my books. They asked for a preface that would introduce the two books to Russian readers.

Here is the preface I wrote to accompany the Russian translation of *A Concise Dictionary of Theology*:

> Right from the first edition of this dictionary, Edward Farrugia and I set ourselves to include entries that identified the theological and spiritual treasures of Orthodox Christians and—more widely—of all Eastern Christians. In particular, we were concerned with what has been contributed to spirituality, theology, and church life and worship by such writers as Nikolai Afanas'ev, Vasilij Bolotov, Sergii Bulgakov, Fyodor Dostoyevsky, Paul Evdokimov, George Florenskij, Vladimir Lossky, Vladimir Solov'iev, and Leo Tolstoy.
>
> Our central aim was to explain the origin and meaning of key words and phrases. By clarifying terminology and promoting accuracy in its usage, we hoped to play our part in

encouraging healthy growth in the theology of both Eastern and Western Christianity. We are most grateful for this new version of our concise dictionary, which makes it readily accessible to students, teachers, and a general readership in Russia and in other countries where Russian is spoken. May this translation help to advance theological study and the discipleship it aspires to serve and encourage.

For the translation of *Believing in the Resurrection*, I composed a similar, brief preface, telling Russian readers how delighted I was to appear in their language. Knowing how central Christ's resurrection is to the spirituality of Russians, I felt honoured at the thought of possibly contributing something to their understanding and living of Easter faith.

The Da Vinci Fraud

On the Left Bank of the Tiber dedicates pages to a painful episode that pressed against my last years in Rome, the controversy over the theology of religions developed by Jacques Dupuis (pp. 213–51). Around the same time, Dan Brown's *The Da Vinci Code* provided me with repeated invitations from individuals and groups in Europe and North America to lecture, write articles, and appear on TV. I would not have missed my engagement with him for anything, and do not want to airbrush him out of this chapter on Roman afterthoughts. Despite its bizarre claims and sloppy style of writing, the book proved the talk of the town and for two years remained on the best seller list. Published in 2003, it sold more than forty million copies.

First of all, a word about the genre to which it belongs. For the last two centuries, every few years a sensational book is published which promises to tell you who Jesus really was, and how for twenty centuries the official church concealed this genuine Jesus. To spice up the story, these books often introduce a hidden document which will reveal at last the sensational truth about Jesus. Often enough these books add the theme of a cover-up, with bureaucrats, at times corrupt officials in the Vatican, desperately engaged in a conspiracy to suppress the embarrassing document, which could bring to the attention of the world some explosive, ancient truth about Jesus.

At times such books 'reveal' another astonishing 'fact', a sexual relationship between Jesus and Mary Magdalene, either with or without the benefit of marriage. I am thinking here of *Holy Blood, Holy Grail* by Michael Baigent, Richard Leigh, and Henry Lincoln, which appeared in 1982, drew on earlier sources, and supplied Dan Brown with some of his material. That threesome argued that Jesus survived crucifixion, and retired with Mary Magdalene to France. Their offspring became the ancestors of various European dynasties, like the Hapsburgs and the House of Lorraine. There were so many historical mistakes in *Holy Blood, Holy Grail* that I could illustrate how Baigent, Leigh, and Lincoln needed to publish an errata slip in the shape of a companion volume.[3] Privately I was hoping that they might sue me, as I would have cherished a day in court listing all their errors. Baigent and Leigh brought a case, but it was against the publishers of *The Da Vinci Code* for plagiarising their book.[4] What of Brown's book?

It is a murder mystery, a religious exposé, and a romantic novel all in one. Many have found it a gripping read, a real page turner, which manages to maintain suspense about the identity of the mysterious 'teacher' and about the nature of the Holy Grail. But when you compare *The Da Vinci Code* with earlier works in the field, the only new

---

3 G. O'Collins and Daniel Kendall, 'On Reissuing Venturini', *Gregorianum* 75 (1994), pp. 241–65, at 253–55.
4 When in April 2006, Mr Justice Peter Smith, while recognizing that material in six chapters of *The Da Vinci Code* was largely drawn from *Holy Blood, Holy Grail*, rejected the claim of Baigent and Leigh that there had been copyright infringement. They took their case to the Court of Appeal where in March 2007 three judges dismissed the appeal and upheld the judgment of Mr Justice Smith. Baigent and Leigh faced legal bills of around three million pounds.

item is Brown's claim about Leonardo's 'Last Supper'. He proposes that the figure to the right of Christ is not John the beloved disciple, but Mary Magdalene. She bore Jesus a child and thus was the Holy Grail for his blood. According to Brown, in the most dramatic cover-up in history, the official Church suppressed the truth about Mary's relationship with Jesus and did its best to belittle and discredit Mary and all that she represented, or at least all that she represented in the gospel according to Dan Brown: the sacred feminine, fertility cults, and even goddess worship. But a secret society, the Prior of Sion, maintained the truth about Mary and Jesus. Some European royals belonged to their bloodline. Two youngish people in Brown's story turn out to the current descendants carrying the precious bloodline.

As I said, Brown goes beyond earlier books of this kind in only one point—by using or rather misusing Leonardo's painting of the Last Supper to support his thesis about a liaison between Mary Magdalene and Jesus. What do art experts think of Brown's reading of Leonardo's fresco? Professor Bruce Boucher of the Art Institute in Chicago wrote an article for *The New York Times* (3 August 2003) in which he dismissed Brown's interpretation as 'extremely eccentric'. When Florentine painters before and after Leonardo depicted the Last Supper, they represented St John as a handsome young man seated at the right side of Jesus. This figure in Leonardo's painting is the apostle John, not the bride of Jesus. In lectures I used to put this point less solemnly by asking: 'if that's Mary Magdalene, where's John? You can see that there are twelve figures at table with Jesus, and John was one of the twelve.' 'He must have gone out for a toilet break', was the whimsical suggestion from one of my audiences in Washington, DC.

Brown found it highly significant that there are glasses and no central chalice on the table for Leonardo's masterpiece. But, as Boucher pointed out, that is exactly what we find in earlier Italian representations of the Last Supper: glasses and no chalice. Boucher had much more to say about Brown's stunning ignorance of the history of art. Brown refers to Leonardo's 'enormous output of Christian art' and 'hundreds of lucrative Vatican commissions'. But Leonardo was notorious for his meagre production, finishing few works and spending very little time in Rome. In fact, there seems to be only one work by Leonardo in Rome, a picture of St Jerome in a Vatican museum. Michelangelo, however, did spend many years in Rome, and left numerous wonderful paintings and pieces of sculpture there—not to mention the cupola of St Peter's. I wonder whether Brown confused Leonardo with Michelangelo. He is capable of such breathtaking confusion and mistakes. His earlier book *Angels and Demons* pictures the hero slipping on coins in a central fountain of the Piazza Navona. Wrong fountain, old chap. You find the coins half a mile away in the Trevi Fountain. But let's leave Leonardo 'Last Supper' for other false details in *The Da Vinci Code*.

The book teems with historical misinformation. The claim that the Emperor Constantine shifted the Christian day of worship to Sunday is simply false. We know from St Paul and other New Testament writers that, soon after Jesus rose from the dead, Christians replaced Saturday with Sunday as their central day of worship. What Constantine did in March 321 was to decree Sunday to be a day of rest from work. He did not make Sunday the day of worship for Christians; it already was that from the first century. Brown also tells us that, under pressure from Constantine, the bishops at the Council of Nicaea in 325 declared Christ to be divine: 'Until that moment in history Jesus was viewed by his followers as a mortal prophet, a great and powerful man, but a man nonetheless.' Would Brown please read St John's Gospel which has St Thomas calling Jesus 'my Lord and my God' (John 20:28). Decades before John's Gospel was finished, St Paul's letters repeatedly affirmed faith in Christ as divine. The Council of Nicaea in 325 did not invent faith in the divinity of Christ, but reaffirmed it once again in the Creed that we still use every Sunday.

When putting his case for goddess worship, Brown belittles the Jewish roots of Christianity. He assures us that 'virtually all the elements of Catholic ritual—the altar, communion [and so on] were taken directly from earlier pagan mystery religions'. Doesn't Brown know about the use of altars in ancient Jewish worship, in which much of the Christian ritual had its roots? Communion originated in the Jewish Passover, celebrated by Jesus and his disciples on the night before he died.

Apropos of Judaism, Brown introduces some stunning falsehoods about ritualistic sex in the Jerusalem Temple. Israelite men did not come to the Temple to enjoy a 'spiritual' experience by engaging in sacred sex with priestesses. That is a sheer fabrication. There were no priestesses offering sacred sex in the Temple. According to Brown, the Holy of Holies housed not only God but also his 'powerful female consort, Shekinah'. Now 'Shekinah' is a word not found in the Bible but in later Rabbinic writings. It denotes the closeness of God to his people, not to his (alleged) female consort. It is also breathtaking nonsense to allege that the sacred name, YHWH, was derived from 'Jehovah'. And 'Jehovah', according to Brown, was the ancient name for God, expressing an androgynous union between the masculine 'Jah' and an early name for Eve, 'Havah'. Well, what are the true facts? YHWH was the ancient, sacred name for God, which out of reverence the Israelites did not pronounce. 'Jehovah' was an artificial name for God created by some Christians in the Middle Ages. It was not an ancient name for God, and certainly not an ancient, androgynous name from which YHWH came.

On could press on and on pointing out the historical errors in *The Da Vinci Code*. The so-called Priory of Sion is central to the plot of the novel, as it begins with the murder of the priory's head. But the Priory of Sion was a modern fabrication, based on a series of forgeries committed by Pierre Plantard, a convicted confidence trickster who died in 2000. When in 1982 they published *Holy Blood*,

Holy Grail, Baigent, Leigh, and Lincoln accepted the forged documents as genuine. But then a BBC documentary and a series of books in the 1990s exposed the nonsense about the so-called Priory of Sion. Even Baigent, Leigh, and Lincoln could see that they had been duped. Brown should have known that. His details about the Priory of Sion were based on forgeries, but he needed to keep the nonsense alive.

A final example of the historical fabrications Brown endorses. The killing of alleged witches was a horrible crime. But the claim that the Catholic Church burned at the stake five million witches is bizarre. That kind of savagery could have depopulated Europe. Experts give instead the statistic of around fifty thousand victims for the three centuries when witch hunts were carried out by Catholics and Protestants in Northern Europe and elsewhere. About 20% of the victims were men, and not all alleged witches died by being burnt at the stake. But it suits Brown's purpose to multiply the figure by one hundred and come up with five million women burnt by the Catholic Church.

To sum up. Brown added no fresh evidence to previously discredited attempts to establish that Jesus was married to Mary Magdalene and fathered one or more children by her. Brown did not unveil any astonishing new truth. But he did reveal enormous gaps in his own education, and a willingness to endorse historical lies and errors. The truth did not matter to him. What mattered was creating the most successful fiction for the market.

Instead of unveiling the real Mary Magdalene, Brown disguises and belittles her. In all four Gospels she is the prominent figure in the stories of Jesus' resurrection. She stands by the cross at his death, witnesses his burial, returns to the tomb on Easter Sunday, discovers it to be open and empty, meets Jesus himself now gloriously alive, and then announces to the male disciples the wonderful news of the resurrection. One can understand the tributes paid to her by early Christian writers like Leo the Great and Gregory the Great. They called her the apostle to the apostles and the new Eve proclaiming not death but life to the men. Brown's idea that the official Church ran a smear campaign against Mary Magdalene may go down well with some readers but remains nonsense. It would have been a very strange smear campaign since it encouraged the faithful to celebrate her feast on 22 July, blessed lovely old colleges that bear her name at the University of Oxford and University of Cambridge, and built beautiful churches in her honour in Paris, Rome, and across the Christian world. Back in the 1920s my mother visited Paris, went to the Madeleine, and prayed through the intercession of St Mary Magdalene that she would have a son and that he would be ordained a priest. I am the result of that prayer, and remain very grateful to Mary Magdalene and my mother.

After all my criticisms, I still have to face the question: why did *The Da Vinci Code* enjoy such enormous success in English and then in the translations (into French, modern Hebrew, Italian, and so forth)? One might answer that it offers a good piece of escapism, an intriguing cocktail that mixes religion, conspiracy, sex, murder, and mystery. We have a different answer from someone who reviewed the Hebrew translation, Professor Aviad Kleinberg of the history department of the University of Tel Aviv. He pointed out some of the gross historical errors and lies, dismissed the writing as moving from cliché to cliché, and then faced the question about the mega-success of *The Da Vinci Code*. He wrote in the *Haaretz Daily* (7 November 2003): 'it seems that the reason for the success of the book is neither the sophistication of the riddles in it, nor the very modest quality of the writing. What thrills many of the readers is its pretension to a revealing and daring interpretation of authentic materials from Christian history and religion. *The Da Vinci Code* purports to reveal a Catholic conspiracy and show us its underpinnings.' Professor Kleinberg then doggedly lists a litany of historical mistakes and fabrications: for instance, the claim that the descendants of Jesus married into the Merovingian royal dynasty. This claim is based on a figure called Giselle de Razes who is supposed to have married King Dagobert II in the seventh century. But Giselle de Razes never existed; she was invented in the twentieth century. Kleinberg then asks: 'what more can be said'? Just that I feel sorry for the charming heroine in *The Da Vinci Cade*. She was often treated as ingenuous and even ignorant. Two wretched men spent many pages of the novel lecturing at her and bombarding her with what are often falsehoods. I hope she changed her mind and never kept the rendezvous with the so-called hero in Florence. She deserved a much better relationship than that.

At the risk of providing an overdose about *The Da Vinci Code*, let me add a footnote about the section where librarians shelve it: historical fiction. Those who write novels about totally fictional characters enjoy considerable freedom concerning events, dialogue, scenery, and the rest. J. R. R. Tolkien took such freedom when developing his fantasy adventures: *The Hobbit* (1937) and *The Lord of the Rings* (1954–55) He set his stories in Middle Earth, an imaginary land occupied by hobbits and further mythical creatures.

But those authors, like Dan Brown, who write about Jesus and other persons who belonged to human history and left well-documented lives, write under the constraints of the available evidence. To be sure, they can and should invent dialogue, add further characters to the cast of their novels, as well as attending to psychological interactions, weather, and so on. But readers expect authors of historical fiction to remain faithful to the known, central facts. They will not be amused to find the assassination of Julius Caesar shifted from Rome to Alexandria. Nor would they look with favour on an author who took the liberty of inventing a secret marriage between Queen Elizabeth I and Philip II of Spain. Writers of historical fiction may not play fast and loose with history.

By an opening page named 'Fact', Brown laid claim to be using reliable documents about the Priory of Sion housed in the Bibliothèque Nationale in Paris, documents that had long been exposed as forgeries by the time he wrote and published his novel in 2003. He ended his claim to 'Fact' by alleging that 'all descriptions of artwork, architecture, documents and secret rituals in this novel are accurate'. Only the gullible and ignorant can accept Brown's 'Fact'.

When an Italian publishing house, Rizzoli, came to put out an Italian translation of *The Da Vinci Code*, they simply omitted the page on 'Fact'. In its place, they inserted a statement to the effect that in this novel any resemblance to characters living and dead—read Jesus, Mary Magdalene, Leonardo, and others—is purely coincidental. Should we put this change down to the historical conscience of an Italian editor? Or was the change dictated by the fear that someone might bring an action on the basis of an old Italian law penalizing writers who deliberately mislead the public? If the page on 'Fact' had remained in the book, it would have been a tempting target for such a prosecution.

Let me give the last word to Richard Hammond, known throughout the world for his programme *Top Gear*. In 2006, a few days before the film of *The Da Vinci Code* appeared in British cinemas, BBC One broadcast at prime time 'Richard Hammond and the Holy Grail', a beautifully shot documentary on his travels in search of the Holy Grail, the cup from which Jesus drank at the Last Supper. Hammond's journey took him to places that feature in the novel such as the Temple Church in London and Rosslyn Chapel in Midlothian. He toyed with various meanings that could be given to the Holy Grail. They stretch from the traditional view (which believes an ancient goblet from the Middle East preserved in Valencia to have been used by Jesus at the Last Supper) to Brown's sensational secret about a sacred bloodline descended from Jesus. A scene when Hammond interviewed a psychic in Rosslyn and looked away with disbelief caught the spirit of this entertaining travelogue. The psychic, Brown, and others have their inane and groundless theories, but as far as

Hammond was concerned 'the Holy Grail' represents any noble human quest inspired by genuine values.

When making his travelogue, Hammond had also visited Rome and somehow managed to talk his way into the secret archives of the Vatican. (Did some officials there sense that he was an ally in rejecting dangerous nonsense coming from Dan Brown?). During his stop in Rome, he came with his zestful young crew to interview me on the roof of the Gregorian University, raising two questions. Could that chalice in Valencia be the cup from which Jesus drank? 'That's very, very unlikely, even if the cup did come from first-century Jerusalem', I commented, and added: 'Thousands upon thousands of people went there to celebrate the Passover, and they used a very large number of goblets'. His second question touched on the motives of those like Brown who fabricate eccentric explanations: 'What drives them to do that?' 'Richard, it's their quest for money, not truth. Money is their Holy Grail.'

When the film of *The Da Vinci Code* and 'Richard Hammond and the Quest for the Holy Grail' appeared almost simultaneously, I found Hammond's way of taking on Brown the more effective because it poked fun but not in a blatantly aggressive fashion. The travelogue left the film miles behind, because, unlike the film, it was, from a visual point of view, stunningly attractive.

A dramatic postscript occurred fairly soon, when Hammond was involved in a terrible car crash that almost killed him. Sadly some of the supporters of *The Da Vinci Code* and other zany accounts of the Holy Grail, who had been angered by Hammond gently ridiculing their 'explanations', showed themselves satisfied by the near-fatal accident that he had suffered. Did they think that some divine Power had punished Richard for his disrespectful put down?

2

JOSEPH RATZINGER THE BRIDGE

The first two volumes of my memoirs evoked various memories of Joseph Ratzinger. Living next door to Professor Ratzinger and his sister Maria helped shape an idyllic summer spent at the University of Tübingen, but that summer quickly seemed a world away (*A Midlife Journey*, pp. 346–48). For thirteen years he belonged to my past, except for one incident: his veto as Archbishop of Munich on Johann Baptist Metz being appointed to the Catholic theology faculty at the University of Munich. The veto preoccupied Metz and distracted him from contributing his chapter to a book I co-edited (*On the Left Bank of the Tiber*, p. 32). After John Paul II called Cardinal Ratzinger to Rome in 1981 and appointed him the Prefect of the Congregation for the Doctrine of the Faith (CDF), our paths crossed regularly.

When John Paul II visited the United Kingdom in 1982, the Archbishop of Canterbury, Robert Runcie, welcomed him at Canterbury Cathedral and later came to Rome to return the visit. Ratzinger and I were both guests at a small dinner party in the Anglican Centre on that occasion. During the meal I could not help noticing the frosty relationship between Orietta Doria Pamphilj and Ratzinger. Her open-minded attitudes did not sit well with him. There seemed little love lost between the Italian princess and the German cardinal.

On the Left Bank of the Tiber recalls how Ratzinger marked important things I ended up doing with my life in Rome—not least during the controversy over Jacques Dupuis and his theology of religions. Even after I left Rome in the summer of 2006, as Pope Benedict XVI he naturally remained part of my story and has his place in this third volume of my memoirs.

Cardinal Ratzinger

On the Left Bank of the Tiber listed several misgivings about the theological views of Cardinal Ratzinger: his limited attention to divine revelation and human evil, his unease with biblical scholarship, and his opposition to liberation theology (pp. 195–98). Those pages should have opened, however, by expressing appreciation for the valuable insights he contributed to the teaching of the Second Vatican Council (1962–65) and to the indispensable, five-volume *Commentary on the Documents of Vatican II*, edited by Herbert Vorgrimler (1967–69). Francis Moloney rightly praises the breadth of vision shown when Ratzinger reflected on Scripture, tradition, and theology in what he wrote for Vorgrimler's work in collaboration.[5] In the *Gregorianum* 89 (2008), pp. 233–311, Jared Wicks retrieved, introduced, translated, and evaluated positively six texts that the young Ratzinger produced (for Cardinal Josef Frings and others) and that fed into the Vatican II debates and the final crafting of the sixteen documents. In *My Journal of the Council*, Yves Congar, the outstanding theological expert at Vatican II, mentions much of Ratzinger's input at the Council and not least his contribution to the drafting and revising of the final text of the Decree on the Church's Missionary Activity (*Ad Gentes*).

Yet, as is obvious, all that praise belongs to the younger years of Ratzinger, and I retreat from endorsing the view that, after he took up his Vatican appointment in 1981, we had a theological giant on our Roman hands. That title applies rather to Cardinal Walter Kasper, who came to Rome in 1999 as number two at the Pontifical

---

5 F. J. Moloney, 'Vatican II and "The Study of the Sacred Page" as "The Soul of Theology"', in Mark O'Brien and Christopher Monaghan (eds.), *God's Word and the Church's Council: Vatican II and Divine Revelation* (Adelaide: ATF Theology, 2014), pp. 19–39, at 36–38.

Council for Promoting Christian Unity and, from 2001, its President until 2010. Before he was appointed Bishop of Rottenburg-Stuttgart in 1989, his production as a theology professor included enduring masterpieces such as *Jesus the Christ* and *The God of Jesus Christ* (the former on Christology and the latter on the Trinity, with both books translated into several languages). As bishop he continued to serve as the editor of the third edition of the prestigious, eleven-volume *Lexikon für Theologie und Kirche* (1993–2001).

That Kasper was called to the Vatican in the declining years of Pope John Paul II astonished me. In 1993 he had joined Karl Lehmann (the Bishop of Mainz and also the president of the German Bishops' Conference 1987–2008) and another bishop in publishing a pastoral letter urging that the divorced and remarried, under certain appropriate conditions, should be allowed to return to the sacraments. This letter was not well received by Cardinal Ratzinger and Pope John Paul II, and yet six years later Kasper was appointed to the Vatican. Undoubtedly he had won their esteem for what he had achieved since 1994 as co-chair of the International Commission for Lutheran-Catholic Dialogue. The Pope and Ratzinger supported and applauded the outcome of that dialogue: the 1999 Joint Declaration on Justification, a huge landmark in post-Vatican II relations with other Christian churches and communities. But Kasper was to take his distance from Cardinal Ratzinger by interpreting the Church as primarily local rather than universal and by criticizing the CDF's document of 2000, *Dominus Iesus*. In particular, Kasper was disturbed by its failure to respect the unique position of the Jewish religion. He feared that it might destroy bonds that he and others had worked so hard to develop. Later, when as Benedict XVI, Ratzinger lifted the excommunication on Bishop Richard Williamson, a Holocaust-denier—to which we return below—Kasper spoke of a 'management error in the Curia'. After retiring as President of the Pontifical Council for Promoting Christian Unity, Kasper produced an outstanding book on divine mercy, cited with approval by Pope Francis within days of his election in March 2013. *On the Left Bank of the Tiber* slots Kasper repeatedly into the narrative (pp. 114, 174, 192, 236–37).

Before moving to the pontificate of Benedict XVI, I want to comment further on Cardinal Ratzinger's attitude toward biblical scholarship and then reveal how he might have contributed to *The Cambridge Dictionary of Christianity*.

In a two-volume work that he began writing in 2003 and so two years before he was elected to the papacy, *Jesus of Nazareth* (London: Bloomsbury, 2007, 2011), Ratzinger showed, as Frank Moloney points out, 'his discomfort with critical biblical scholarship', and even claimed that such 'critical scholarship has nothing further to offer'. Moloney, perhaps somewhat too negatively, dismisses the two volumes as 'largely a pseudo-patristic appeal to believers on the basis of a selected reading of events from the Gospel'.[6] He argues further that any study of the figure of Jesus that 'disregards critical scholarship' cannot 'hope to produce a personal relationship with Jesus'.[7]

It is less than fully accurate to allege that the two volumes 'disregard critical scholarship'; notable scholars, like Martin Hengel and (in the bibliography) Moloney himself, make their appearance, although it is unclear that Benedict had read and learnt anything from Moloney. My own pastoral experience has shown how the volumes have, at least in some cases, produced and enhanced 'a personal relationship with Jesus'. But what would I say in detail, taking up, for example, volume one of *Jesus of Nazareth*, which even more than volume two became a best-seller everywhere? It sold more than two million copies across the world.

When publishing the first volume two years into his papacy,

---

6 Moloney, 'Vatican II', p. 25, n. 14.
7 Ibid., p. 38, n. 45. Peter Cornwell, when reviewing the first volume of Ratzinger's book, remarks that 'he takes swipes at the "alleged findings of scholarly exegesis"' (*Times Literary Supplement*, 25 January 2008, p. 30).

Benedict XVI stipulated that 'this book' was 'in no way an exercise' of his official magisterium but 'solely' a testimony to 'his personal search for the face of the Lord'. Through his position as head of the Catholic Church, the Pope seized the opportunity to spread around the world the good news that in the person of Jesus of Nazareth the Son of God has come among us and shares with us abundant life here and hereafter.

Even though the Pope began writing *Jesus of Nazareth* only two years before his election to the papacy, some sections read like beautifully crafted biblical homilies that have been preached and polished over many years. This is how his presentation of the Lord's Prayer, the parables, and principal images in John's Gospel (water, vine and wine, bread, and shepherd) strike me. They read like the products of long study, prayerful meditation, and preaching. Whatever their precise origin, these three chapters could prompt a more profound preaching of several major themes in any portrait of Jesus, as well as a richer, personal reading of the Gospels.

After eloquent pages on the seven petitions of the 'Our Father', the Pope highlighted ways in which three parables, the Good Samaritan, the Prodigal Son (which he more accurately calls the Parable of the Two Brothers and the Good Father), and the Rich Man and Lazarus, show how 'divine light shines through in the things of the world'. They convey a knowledge of God 'that makes demands on us'. Over and over again he illustrates the 'topical relevance' of the parables. He transposes, for instance, the parable of the Good Samaritan into the dimensions of the world scene, recognizing how the people of Africa, in particular, have been 'robbed and plundered' through 'the cynicism of a world without God in which all that counts is power and profit'.

Contemporary, recent, and ancient biblical scholars and other authors enter the bibliography and the text itself. The long chapter about the Sermon on the Mount moves through the beatitudes to discuss with Rabbi Jacob Neusner the identity of Jesus as being himself the new Torah. The beatitudes not only synthesize the programme of the kingdom but also give us a self-portrait of Jesus. Behind preaching purity of heart, the search for justice, and the rest, we find the uniquely authoritative claims of the Preacher himself. Summarizing the Sermon on the Mount for his Jewish interlocutors, the Pope concludes: Jesus 'has brought the God of Israel to the nations, so that all the nations now pray to him and recognize Israel's Scriptures as the word of the living God. He has brought the gift of universality which was the one great definitive promise to Israel and the world.' This 'faith in the one God of Abraham, Isaac, and Jacob, extended now in Jesus' new family to all nations', is the supreme 'fruit of Jesus' work'.

The book is shaped by the conviction that we can truly know Jesus through the Gospels and that in him we see the human face of God. The Pope argues that lesser portraits of Jesus as, for instance, merely a wandering prophet or a reforming rabbi, do not do justice to the historical evidence, and do not explain why such a relatively harmless figure could be condemned to crucifixion and then go on to have an enormous and lasting impact on millions of people. This book has an apologetic purpose, alongside its pastoral and spiritual message. Only God can demand of us what Jesus asks. The divine identity of Jesus is no optional extra.

The Pope asks for 'goodwill' from his readers, but adds: 'everyone is free to contradict me'. Contradicting him would be unjustified, but some quibbles are in order. First, I thoroughly agree that our historical knowledge of Jesus is indispensable, above all because God has persistently acted in history and in Jesus has personally entered our history. In various books (e.g. *Foundations of Theology*, *Fundamental Theology*, and *Rethinking Fundamental Theology*) I have repeatedly argued that historical knowledge belongs essentially to Christian faith. I also agree that some biblical scholars have produced 'the impression that we have very little certain knowledge of Jesus'. But only some. The Pope needed to acknowledge the work of such experts as Richard Bauckham, Raymond Brown, Brendan Byrne, James Dunn, Joseph Fitzmyer, Daniel Harrington, Luke Timothy Johnson, John Meier, and Bishop Tom Wright—to name only a few who do not give that impression. They encourage us to join the Pope in 'trusting the Gospels', because we hear in and through the Gospel texts the reliable testimony of eyewitnesses and their associates.

Second, apropos of liturgy, the Pope expresses his deep concern that 'modern liturgists want to dismiss' the 'social function of Sunday as a Constantinian aberration'. Evidently he has read or heard one or two liturgical scholars who maintain that Emperor Constantine made a mistake in March 321 by declaring Sunday a day of rest from work. But so far in my life I have never heard or read a single liturgist who defends such a misguided view.

Third, it was important to be reminded of the way in which the Eastern Christians have deepened our outstanding of Jesus' baptism. But I wonder what they would think of this account of what happened at the Jordan: 'Jesus loaded the burden of all mankind's guilt upon his shoulders, and bore it down into the depths of the Jordan'. Western Christians also might wonder about evidence from the texts of the Gospel that might support this view of what Jesus consciously did before entering the Jordan.

Fourth, when describing how Jesus freely accepted death to expiate human sin and inaugurate a new family under God, the Pope could appeal to reliable testimony from the accounts of the Last Supper. One can convincingly argue that Jesus did interpret his imminent death in that way. But did he do so precisely in the light of the Suffering Servant of Isaiah 53? Certainly early Christians did so. But it is not clear that, when facing death, Jesus consciously identified himself with the suffering and dying Servant of God. Isaiah 53 will return below, when we come to Benedict XVI's reasons for changing the words of institution at the Eucharist from 'for all' to 'for many'.

All in all, at least in volume one, *Jesus of Nazareth* achieved its central purpose by showing a wider public how the divine Sonship of Jesus was 'the source from which his action and teaching and suffering sprang'. It was also a moving testimony to what Jesus meant to Joseph Ratzinger, who came to publish this work as Benedict XVI.

Before moving to reflect on his pontificate, I wish to add a footnote about *The Cambridge Dictionary of Christianity* (eventually published in 2010). When Daniel Patte began organizing this mega-reference volume around 2003, he enlisted me as an advisor. I vigorously encouraged the principle of inviting well known church leaders to contribute key articles. One name I mentioned, in particular, was that of Archbishop Rowan Williams. In the event others wrote the entries about 'Anglicanism'. Patte brought up the name of Ratzinger and suggested asking him to contribute three articles: 'The Roman Catholic Church and Its Theology', 'The Second Vatican Council', and 'Tradition: A Roman Catholic Post-Vatican II Perspective'. I hastily offered to write these entries myself, as well as taking on two others ('Biblical Theology' and 'Redemption'). Patte would have invited Ratzinger to write the first three articles, but, rightly or wrongly, I believed that I could do a more appropriate job. Of course, the cardinal might have turned down the invitation, and the three articles might then have been offered to me.

Pope Benedict XVI

On the Left Bank of the Tiber reported the exchanges on the BBC platform between the presenter (Brian Hanrahan), myself, and a younger priest immediately after the Cardinal Deacon stepped out the balcony high above St Peter's Square and named the new pope (pp. 170–71). 'Oh, no', the younger priest blurted out at once. Afterwards

I tackled him: 'Tom, why did you say that?' 'It was the prophecy of Malachy', he explained. It was perhaps because he was Irish that he took too seriously a cryptic phrase attributed to St Malachy which allegedly predicted the new pope as '*gloria olivae*' (the glory of the olive). Tom anticipated the election of the genial Cardinal Ennio Antonelli of Florence. Tuscany abounded in olive groves. Where else would John Paul II's successor come from?

An eleventh-century bishop, Malachy belongs to recorded history, but his brief 'prophecies' surfaced for the first time in 1595, and are generally reckoned to be forgeries. But being vague and concise, they remain open to generous explanations. In our case, some find a genuine fulfilment, since the new pope took the name of St Benedict of Nursia, and the Olivetans form one branch of the Benedictine Order. (They draw their name from an ancient hermitage on Monte Oliveto, situated in Tuscany and not far from Siena.)

There was more to Hanrahan's opening words to me than I recognized on 19 April 2005: 'Father O'Collins, Pope Benedict is 78 years of age. Do you think he will retire at 80?' The question revealed the instincts of an insightful journalist. As it turned out, Pope Benedict did resign, but only shortly before his 86th birthday. This resignation had been predicted in his despatches to the Australian government by the Honorable Tim Fischer, who served as ambassador to the Holy See (2009–2012) and told his story in *Holy See, Unholy Me—1000 Days in Rome* (Sydney: ABC Books, 2013).

On the Left Bank of the Tiber quoted the closing words of the vividly attractive homily preached by Pope Benedict at his inaugural Mass (p. 171). From the first weeks of his papacy, he impressed the Roman public by homilies and sermons that were clear, brief, and thoroughly intelligible. Too often John Paul II's words were too abstract and went right over their heads (pp. 146–48). Let me begin by paying tribute to things his successor said and wrote, starting with a particular area of his preaching.

In 1988 the then Cardinal Ratzinger published some meditations on the ordained priesthood, *Ministers of Joy*. The same deep joy constantly showed through a second collection, drawn from his first three years as pope, *Priests of Jesus Christ* (2009). The editor, Gerard Skinner, selected fifty pieces for this volume: ten entire homilies; 27 addresses (mostly extracts from them); a section on the Eucharist and the sacrament of holy orders taken from Pope Benedict's apostolic exhortation of 2007 (*Sacramentum Caritatis*); three messages for the World Day of Prayer for Vocations (2006, 2007, and 2008); relevant extracts from seven addresses and two homilies directed to a specific audience, seminarians.

As well as seminarians, the original audiences included clergy, bishops, those about to be ordained to the priesthood by Pope Benedict, religious, and, occasionally, wider groups. Most of the material was originally delivered in Italy: for instance, at Chrism Masses in St Peter's Basilica or during meetings with Italian clergy (either in Rome or in other dioceses). Some of the chapters came from the Pope's visits to Australia, Austria, Brazil, France, Germany, Poland, and the United States.

The themes that Pope Benedict handled covered the Eucharist, the sacrament of reconciliation, biblical meditation, the divine office, personal prayer, the pastoral ministry. evangelization, priestly holiness, and, above all, the close friendship with Jesus to which priests are called. He spoke about the Eucharist as 'a school of life', about priests knowing their people 'with the Heart of Jesus', about communion with the bishop and other priests in the presbyterate, and about much else (but not the pursuit of social justice) that enters or should enter into the life of ordained ministers.

The homilies, with which the volume begins, are outstanding models which invite imitation. In one homily, the Pope moves from the imposition of hands in the ceremony of ordination to reflect on 'the hands of the Lord' that take our hands and guide us. In another homily, he cites a story from Leo Tolstoy about changing clothes, and considers the vestments priests wear for the liturgy (from the amice to the chasuble) and the messages those vestments convey.

Pope Benedict's first encyclical, *Deus Caritas Est* (God is love), suitably dated 25 December 2005, appeared in early 2006. It had been nearly thirty years since the inaugural encyclical of a new pope had been published: *Redemptor Hominis* (Redeemer of Human Beings) in 1979. The media made much of *Deus Caritas Est*, even though some younger journalists seemed bewildered about criteria for selecting particular passages and interpreting the whole text. In a press office near St Peter's Square, one of them told me that he had just phoned his head office, only to be told: 'Wait for the movie'. Presumably the person in the head office was joking.

The second part of the new encyclical took up the practice of justice and charity in the life of the Church, which John Paul II had been elaborating as his life faded away. In a subsequent encyclical, *Caritas in Veritate* (Love in Truth) of 2009, Pope Benedict was to produce a longer, more persuasive social encyclical on such issues of globalisation, hunger and poverty, climate change, and social equity among nations. It was the first half of *Deus Caritas Est* that caught my attention; it proved a startling meditation on how *erōs* and *agapē*, which could be translated, respectively, as 'the love of desire' and 'altruistic love', differ and are united. When presenting his arresting teaching on how (a) love as need or love as receiving complements (b) love as benevolence and giving, the Pope quoted a surprising team of authors: not only the Scriptures—in particular, the Song of Songs—, St Augustine, St Gregory the Great, and Pseudo-Dionysius the Areopagite, but also Aristotle, René Descartes, Pierre Gassendi, Friedrich Nietzsche, Plato, Sallust, and Virgil.

When he turned to expound the story of Adam and Eve and the erotic attraction between the sexes, Pope Benedict cited something I had studied many years before in Plato's *Symposium*: the myth which pictured the human being as originally spherical, that is to say, complete, self-sufficient, not divided as male and female, and so without a sexual partner. Now, when 'split in two by Zeus, he longs for his other half, striving with all his being to possess it and thus regain his integrity' (no. 11). Benedict, while paying his respects to the 'love between parents and children', thrilled to 'love between man and woman' and called this love 'the very epitome of love; all other kinds of love seem to fade in comparison' (no. 2). Here, however, I prefer Isaiah (49:15) and St Thomas Aquinas, who acknowledged maternal rather than marital love as the great paradigm of unconditional love.[8]

The complementary nature of both human and divine love as not only giving (*agapē*) but also receiving (*erōs*) was a surprising choice of theme for Pope Benedict's first encyclical. I had expected that he would have highlighted human and divine beauty. This theme had come through the closing words of the homily he preached at his inaugural Mass on 24 April 2005: 'If we let Christ into our lives, we lose nothing, nothing, absolutely nothing of what makes life free, *beautiful* and great' (emphasis added). The Pope knew very well the works of St Augustine of Hippo, who had classically expounded beauty in his *Confessions*, *Expositions of the Psalms*, and elsewhere.[9] But human and divine beauty failed to surface much in Pope Benedict's eight years of teaching. It was to feature repeatedly in Pope Francis's apostolic exhortation of 2013: *Evangelii Gaudium* (the Joy of the Gospel) (e.g. nos. 167–68).

In 2007, Benedict XVI reached a double milestone: he celebrated his eightieth birthday and completed two years as Pope. By phone—as I was by then living in London—the Vatican Radio interviewed me and asked for a stocktaking on the papal performance. I highlighted two major landmarks: Benedict's visit to Brazil in May 2007, and his long letter that month to the Catholics in China.

---
8 *Summa theologiae*, 2a2ae. 27.1.
9 See e.g. Carol Harrison, *Beauty and Revelation in the Thought of Augustine* (Oxford: Clarendon Press, 1992).

In Brazil, the largest Catholic country in the world, he attended the Fifth General Conference of the Bishops of Latin America and the Caribbean (CELAM) that convened at the shrine of Aparecida from 13 to 31 May 2007—a conference at which Cardinal Jorge Bergoglio (to become Pope Francis in 2013) shone. He expressed strong concern for solid marriages and happy family life. He reached out effectively to his audiences by speaking in Portuguese. But he outraged the indigenous people of Latin America by asserting that the arrival of Christianity did not amount to 'the imposition of a foreign culture'. The president of Venezuela, Hugo Chavez, went on television to protest at the Pope's remarks: 'There was a real genocide here and, if we were to deny it, we would be denying our very selves'. Paulo Suess, an adviser to Brazil's Missionary Council, remarked that Benedict 'is a good theologian, but it seems he missed some history classes'. Subsequently, speaking to pilgrims in Rome, the Pope acknowledged that it was impossible 'to forget the suffering [and] injustices inflicted by the colonisers on the indigenous population'.

The Pope's long and truly ground-breaking letter to Catholics in China came out in several languages, including traditional and modern Chinese. It revealed a deep desire to normalize relations with the government of China and to secure unity between Catholics officially registered with the government and those who belonged to clandestine communities. The letter showed an openness and flexibility that in the post-World War II period had not always characterized Vatican stance towards China.

When I looked back over 2007 for Vatican Radio, I added a check list of five urgent causes for Christianity and the world that Benedict had continued to promote and support: (1) reaching out to Muslims; (2) building bridges to Orthodox Christians, especially the Russian Orthodox; (3) showing deep concern for Africa's suffering and calling on the G8 to cancel the continent's crippling debt; (4) urging a progressive ban on nuclear weapons that would eventually deliver our world from their presence; and (5), finally, revealing his deep concern about climate change and global warming and, in effect, telling the world: 'go green before it's too late' and 'being green is being pro-life'. This concern led him at the end of August 2007 to insist with a crowd of 300,000 young people gathered in Loreto that protecting creation is an urgent task. The Pope practised what he preached by installing solar panels on the roof of the Vatican.

Before finishing my interview for the Vatican Radio, I mentioned a couple of papal 'firsts' that featured in 2007. By publishing his *Jesus of Nazareth*, Benedict became the first pope to publish a book on Jesus, a book that was carried by bookstores in airports around the world and sold over two million copies. His encyclical *Spe Salvi* (Saved by Hope) of November 2007 stood out as the first encyclical any pope has ever published on the virtue of hope. It is discussed below in the opening appendix.

I could not finish the interview without mentioning a small item that meant a great deal to me. The Pope donated £3,000 to the Catholic chaplaincy at the University of Cambridge. To survive, Fisher House desperately needed an endowment fund, and Benedict's gift encouraged people to support financially and in other ways the work of the Catholic chaplain and his associates. Before being elected Pope, Benedict had in 1988 lectured at Fisher House and slept there—in the very same bed and room (called after his election to the papacy in 2005 'the papal chamber') that I occupied on several visits. In 1991 my brother Jim and his wife Posey also stayed in what was to be called 'the papal chamber'.

On two notable occasions BBC television involved me in the travels of Pope Benedict. When he visited New York and spoke to the General Assembly of the United Nations in April 2008, the BBC sent a car to bring me from where I lived in Wimbledon to their studios in White City. But the car came late and, when I arrived at White City, the papal address had already taken place. However, this meant that I could read the address at leisure and share more effectively in a discussion that took place on hour or so later. I recalled hearing Ratzinger lecture forty years earlier at the University of Tübingen, spoke of 'the Pope as professor', and singled out seven issues that he raised. (1) The international community must not close its eyes to 'grave and sustained violations of human rights'. (2) Global inequality calls for international action to reduce world hunger and save those who are literally starving. (3) Climate change requires common action to protect our planet. (4) A deeper search for 'ways of pre-empting and managing conflicts' involves 'exploring every possible diplomatic avenue'. (5) World leaders must seek peace by working for justice, human rights, and forgiveness. (6) Rights are universal, for everyone. (7) Dialogue between religions will serve the common good.

I expressed satisfaction over the Pope outlining general principles; it would not be hard to translate them into specific examples and support them with concrete data. I pointed out, for example, how easy it was to back up (2): nearly a billion people remained chronically hungry, as well as lacking safe drinking water. As regards (5), a more secure world would come only through promoting human rights and eliminating gross inequalities. If you seek peace, work for justice and human rights. Those who remain oppressed, economically and politically, will turn to violence.

The BBC also brought me to their studios in White City when Pope Benedict made his first pilgrimage to Africa by visiting Angola and the Cameroon in March 2009. He called for an end to years of horribly destructive wars and civil strife. With many African countries ravaged by AIDS, journalists raised the question of using condoms to prevent spreading the pandemic. Unlike several cardinals, the Pope would not accept that use, even as 'the lesser of two evils'. In my BBC interview, I recalled the progress made in Uganda, where the Christian churches encouraged radical changes in social attitudes and practice needed to check the spread of AIDS. With the slogan 'zero grazing', they called on men to be faithful to their wives. Only the naïve thought that, by simply distributing condoms everywhere, the tragedy of AIDS would be overcome. Nevertheless, I could not condemn husbands using condoms when they were already infected and did not want to infect their wives. 'Thou shalt not kill trumps everything', I proposed. For a week the BBC quoted that statement.

Unfortunate sayings and doings

Any honest weighing up of Benedict XVI's pontificate must include things he said and did that were doubtful, disappointing, or worse. Let me recall six such examples.

(1) In an address at the University of Regensburg (12 September 2006) he quoted some unfortunate remarks about Muhammad, which provoked angry relations from Muslims. He had cited a 14th century Byzantine emperor as saying that Muhammad brought 'only evil and inhuman things' to the world. Subsequently the Pope said that these words from Manuel II Palaeologus did not reflect his own personal views; he wanted only to encourage interreligious dialogue 'with great mutual respect'.

If Archbishop Michael Fitzgerald had seen the speech beforehand, he would have strongly urged Pope Benedict to omit the offensive section. But earlier that year Fitzgerald had been unfairly exiled to Cairo as papal nuncio to Egypt (2006–2012). Secretary (1987–2002) and then president (2002–2006) of the Pontifical Council for Interreligious Dialogue, he was one of the foremost Catholic experts on dialogue with Islam. What the Pope over and over again desperately needed were close advisers like Fitzgerald, who would say 'no' to him and eliminate in advance remarks that were insensitive or plainly mistaken. His Secretary of State, Cardinal Tarcisio Bertone, was a prelate of limited capacity and experience, and had a less than distinguished career as Ratzinger's secretary at the Congregation for the Doctrine of the Faith (see *On the Left Bank of the Tiber*, p. 206). Reportedly a group of German cardinals visited Benedict in his summer residence at Castel Gandolfo and begged him to find another secretary of state. But the Pope insisted on keeping Bertone at his side, even beyond the normal retirement age of 75.

Some time late in 2006, I pointed out to a journalist who had been present at Pope Benedict's address that Regensburg was an unfortunate city to quote anti-Muhammad sentiments. Right in the middle of the city a tall statue commemorates Don John of Austria, who was born there and eventually led the Christian forces to their victory over the Muslims at the Battle of Lepanto in 1571. 'None of us ever noticed that statue', the journalist commented ruefully. 'Otherwise', he added, 'it would have entered what we wrote'.

(2) Second, within Christian circles Pope Benedict displeased Anglican leaders by introducing a special 'ordinariate', which enables Anglicans to enter communion with the Catholic Church but retain Anglican features—in particular, by maintaining some parish structures and enjoying their own bishop. Supposedly the motivation for this move was to allow Anglicans to preserve their particular 'heritage'. It was hard to identify what that might mean concretely. All honour to the Book of Common Prayer, treasured by Anglicans but now replaced normally by modern texts. Some gems of the Anglican heritage have long ago entered the practice of many Christian churches: for instance, the Advent service of nine lessons and carols. Married clergy has been another, significant feature of the Anglican heritage, and numerous married Anglican priests (like my dear friend Matthew) who entered full communion with Rome have become ordained, Catholic clergy and function wonderfully well in the regular parishes. Another precious feature of the Anglican heritage has been a liturgical dignity that included an excellent proclamation of the Scriptures. When former Anglican clergy enter the ordinary structures of Catholic parish life, they encourage that excellence to

spread everywhere. The united but separate status of the Anglican ordinariate seems at best unnecessary and at worst divisive.

(3) Third, Pope Benedict gave a high priority to bringing back into Catholic unity a tiny, schismatic group, the Priestly Fraternity or Society of St Pius X, created by Archbishop Marcel Lefebvre in 1970 as a counter to the Second Vatican Council and its implementation. Lefebvre questioned or rejected key teachings of Vatican II, including freedom of conscience, religious freedom, ecumenical and interreligious dialogue, the common priesthood of the baptized, the collegiality of bishops 'with Peter and under Peter', and liturgical reform. Then in 1988 Lefebvre illicitly consecrated four bishops, to stand in witness against what he considered 'neo-Modernist' and 'neo-Protestant' tendencies even among the Roman Catholic hierarchy. Canon law meant that Lefebvre and the four bishops incurred automatic excommunication. In January 2009, and so after the death of Lefebvre (1991), in the hope that all members of the Society of St Pius X would return to full communion with the Catholic Church, Pope Benedict lifted the excommunication, but with little effect on the members of the Society. Under its superior general, Bishop Bernard Follay, it continues to reject the teachings of Vatican II, even if a few members have trickled back into Catholic communion.

The lifting of the excommunication caused international uproar, above all because one of the four bishops, Richard Williamson, took his revisionist views of history as far as Holocaust denial. His first publicly known denial that Jews died in Nazi gas chambers hit the press in 1989 during a trip to Canada and he repeated his denials on Swedish television in November 2008. In 2010 a German court was to fine him 10,000 euros for unrelentingly and very publicly challenging the reality of the murder of European Jews. Pope Benedict tried in vain to justify his lifting of the excommunication in a March 2009 letter to the bishops of the world.

A 2010 volume, no. 236 in the famous *Quaestiones Disputatae* series was edited by Professor Peter Hünermann of the University of Tübingen, and discussed issues of church governance and teaching raised by the Williamson affair. While respecting the pastoral responsibility of the Pope to bring back splinter groups, Hünermann and his fellow contributors clarified a range of issues involved in Lefebvre's schismatic movement. They also raised a number of critical questions about the direction of the Church under Benedict's leadership. They highlighted the roots of Lefebvre's movement in the antidemocratic and anti-Semitic milieu of the late-nineteenth century and early twentieth-century *Action Française*. Traditionalist ideology had shaped the theological outlook of Lefebvre and his associates who repudiated the Church's 'dialogue with the world', initiated by Pope John XXIII and Vatican II and spectacularly endorsed by John Paul II, right from his first encyclical, *Redemptor Hominis* (1979). The volume made it clear that the whole controversy concerned nothing less than a comprehensive struggle over Vatican II and its lasting meaning for the Church and the world.

Hünermann himself made a convincing case that there were no legitimate grounds for raising the excommunication of Williamson and of the other three bishops. He concluded that we faced an *Amtsfehler*, a mistake in the exercise of the papal office, which in the light of canon law should be considered invalid. By way of epilogue, Hünermann quoted, with deep dismay some reactionary and 'uncatholic' items from the 1997 catechism of the Society of St Pius X, and prayed that God would be gracious to the Church, the Pope, and all the bishops.

(4) Fourth, in a 2007 *motu proprio* (of one's own accord), largely as a gesture of reconciliation with the Society of St Pius X and their symathizers, Pope Benedict authorized for a wider use the 1962 Latin Missal or what is often inaccurately called the 'Tridentine Missal'. The Council of Trent (1545–63) called for liturgical reforms, but did not produce any missal; St Pius V did so in 1570. This missal for the Latin rite subsequently underwent minor modifications, right down

to the eve of Vatican II. For instance, in 1960 John XXIII removed from the Good Friday prayers a phrase about 'the perfidious Jews'. After Vatican II, the standard form of the Latin rite was issued as the *Roman Missal* of Blessed Paul VI, published in Latin in 1970 and then translated into the vernacular for use around the world. Normally priests celebrate the Eucharist in their own language, but they have every right, and need no official permission, to use the Latin text of the 1970 *Missal* whenever they judge this appropriate.

By his 2007 *motu proprio*, Benedict left Latin-rite Catholics confusingly divided by two missals: the pre-Vatican II *Roman Missal* of 1962 and the revised *Missal* of 1970. If he had acted 'collegially' and asked Latin rite bishops around the world for their opinion, it seems quite clear that the majority, even a vast majority, would have spoken against reintroducing the 1962 *Missal* as a licit alternative to that of 1970.

Pope Benedict and his advisers, when reintroducing the 1962 *Missal*, failed to think of rewriting its Good Friday prayer for the 'conversion' of the Jews. That version ran:

> Let us pray also for the Jews that almighty God may remove the veil from their hearts, so that they too may acknowledge Jesus Christ our Lord. Let us pray. Let us kneel.
>
> Almighty and eternal God, who dost also not exclude from thy mercy the Jews, hear our prayers, which we offer for the blindness of that people, so that acknowledging the light of thy Truth, which is Christ, they may be delivered from their darkness.

By authorizing for wider use the 1962 *Missal*, whether in its Latin form or in a vernacular translation, and hence this prayer for the Good Friday service, the Pope ignored the teaching of the Second Vatican Council. In particular, by retrieving the teaching of St Paul, Vatican II had affirmed the eternity of God's covenant with the Jewish people and, implicitly, the value of the Torah as a way of salvation for the Jewish people.

Many Jews appreciated the teaching of the Council and the subsequent, positive terms in which the post-Vatican II *Missal* of 1970 had revised the Good Friday prayer:

> Let us pray for the Jewish people the first to hear the word of God, that they may continue to grow in the love of his name and in faithfulness to his covenant. Almighty and eternal God, long ago you gave your promises to Abraham and his posterity. Listen to your Church as we pray that the people you first made your own may arrive at the fullness of redemption.

Having grown to appreciate this version, many Jews and their Christian friends were upset by Benedict authorizing a return to the pre-Vatican II language and theology of the 1962 *Missal*.

To avoid accusations of anti-Semitism, Pope Benedict responded to the criticism by issuing in early 2008 a revised version of the Good Friday prayer to be inserted into the 1962 *Missal*:

> We pray for the Jews, that our God and Lord enlighten their hearts so that they recognise Jesus Christ, the Saviour of all mankind. Eternal God Almighty, you want all people to be saved and to arrive at the knowledge of the Truth. Graciously grant that by the entry of the abundance of all peoples into your Church, Israel will be saved.

While avoiding explicitly denigrating language about the Jews, the Pope's revised version said nothing about the Jewish people being 'the first to hear the word of God', about the divine 'covenant' with which they were blessed, or about the 'promises to Abraham and his posterity'. One can understand why David Gifford, the chief executive of the Council and Jews, was 'saddened'. Benedict 'could have gone much further and built on the work of the Second Vatican Council'.

Rabbi David Rosen, chairman of the International Committee for Interreligious Consultations, expressed his disappointment. Where the teaching of Vatican II supported the 1970 *Missal* in praying for the salvation of Jews in general terms, the Pope's revised version of the Good Friday prayer wanted Jews to embrace Christian faith in Jesus.

A few years later I felt a certain irony in a photograph used for the front cover of my *The Second Vatican Council on Other Religions* (Oxford: Oxford University Press, 2013). It showed a group of religious leaders united by the cause of peace, with Rabbi Rosen standing next to Pope Benedict.

(5) Fifth, at the start of Advent 2011, a new English translation of the *Roman Missal* was introduced. At the express direction of Pope Benedict it replaced 'for you and for all' with 'for you and for many' in the words the priest says over the chalice at the consecration. What should we make of this switch from 'all' to 'many', or rather the reversal to 'many' after 'all' had been used in the liturgy for nearly forty years?

This was a change with which Eucharistic liturgies in other languages were 'threatened' by the Pope. (He resigned in 2013 before effecting this worldwide change. As far as I know, it came only in the English-speaking liturgies.) In the vernacular rendering of the Eucharistic Prayers revised (the Roman Canon) or introduced (the other Eucharistic Prayers) after the Second Vatican Council, the German, Italian, Portuguese, and Spanish translations all spoke of Christ's death 'for all' rather than 'for many'.

Where should we turn for help in translating and interpreting the words that Mark's Gospel (followed by Matthew, but not found in Luke and Paul) reports Jesus to have said over the chalice: 'This is my blood of the covenant, which is poured out for many'? In a letter to the German Bishops' Conference (24 April 2012) outlining his reasons for wanting the reversal to 'for many', the Pope drew attention to some relevant passages in the New Testament, as well as to a title for Jesus 'the new Adam'. Let us see the details.

In his Letter to the Romans, Paul declares that it was 'for all of us' that God allowed his Son to die (8:12). The apostles writes twice in another letter of Christ dying 'for all' (2 Corinthians 5:14–15).

The classic New Testament passage about Adam and Christ, the new Adam, comes in Romans 5:12–21. We can sum up Paul's argument this way. The disobedience of Adam had a universal, evil effect. Christ's obedience did much more than merely reverse the universal results of Adam's sin. When expressing the universal impact of Adam and Christ, the apostle (who writes in Greek) sometimes uses the term *'pantes'* or 'all' (verses 12 [twice] and 18 [twice] and sometimes *'hoi polloi'* or 'the many' (verses 15 [twice] and 19 [twice]). Paul's usage makes it obvious that the Greek terms are equivalent. He understands 'the many' to be 'all' human beings. This is quite unlike the situation in English, where 'many' or 'the many' is simply not synonymous with 'all'.

What led Paul to introduce 'the many', instead of simply using 'all' throughout that passage in Romans 5? Was it merely a matter of 'elegant' variation? Another explanation is possible. The apostle might well have envisaged a classic contrast between 'the one and the many'—in this case between the one (obedient) Christ and the many sinners, who are in fact all human beings.

Another text which Pope Benedict cited in his letter of April 2012 was 1 Timothy 2:6: Christ Jesus 'gave himself as a ransom for all'. Probably taken from an early Christian creed, this phrase understands the self-sacrificing love of Christ to benefit *'pantes'* or 'all'. A parallel statement in Mark's Gospel says that 'the Son of Man came to give his life as a ransom for many (*polloi*) ' (Mark 10:45). The two passages share the same meaning: Jesus gave himself or surrendered his life to set all human beings free from the slavery of sin. 1 Timothy corrects a misunderstanding into which unwary readers of Mark 10:45 might slip. It was 'for all' that Christ gave his life and not merely 'for many'.

But when we come to Mark 14:24 (which uses '*polloi*'), should we insist on translating 'the blood of the covenant poured out for many' and then explain that this means 'for all'? We face a Semitic idiom: the 'many' includes all and excludes none. The meaning is inclusive (the sum total which consists of many, or—in other words—the whole world), but not exclusive (many but not all). In short, the 'many' of Mark's text includes all, and excludes none. In English, it is then misleading to insist on 'many' when we know what is meant. 'All' is meant.

Here one should add that appropriate liturgical texts do not purport to be 'exact' translations, let alone literalist versions which insist on translating words and ignore meanings. The classic Latin liturgical texts echo, adapt, add to, and weave together biblical passages. Such texts are not offered as strict translations of the original Hebrew or Greek. They are primarily concerned with clearly communicating what is meant.

In the New Testament we find *four different versions of the words of institution.* The oldest turns up in 1 Corinthians 11:23–25, to which Luke 22:19–20 approximates but not word for word. Then Mark 14:23–24 is followed, again not word for word, by Matthew 26:26–28. Obviously when celebrating the Lord's Supper, the early Christian communities allowed themselves some freedom in the words they attributed to Jesus. No attempt was made to settle precisely the words that he used (in Aramaic) on the night before he died, with the aim of imposing that version uniformly.

Those who centuries ago fashioned the Roman Rite wove together words and phrases from the New Testament sources. The words of institution that we have inherited from them about the institution of the Eucharist do not correspond exactly to any one of the four original sources: Paul, Luke, Mark, and Matthew. Neither in the New Testament nor in later liturgical texts did fidelity to Jesus involve trying to establish the words he used and then rigidly following them.

Take, for instance, the words used in the English Missal up to 2011: 'this is the cup of my blood, the blood of the new and everlasting covenant. It will be shed for you and for all, so that sins may be forgiven.' All four New Testament sources speak of 'my blood' and of the 'covenant'; only Paul and Luke name this covenant as 'new'; and none of them call it 'eternal'. Mark and Matthew say that Christ's blood will be shed 'for many/all', and Luke that it will be shed 'for you'. Paul simply has Christ saying, 'this cup is the new covenant in my blood', without explicitly adding that this blood will be shed for anyone. The shedding of Christ's blood 'for the forgiveness of sins' is found only in Matthew's version of the Last Supper.

The history of the celebration of the Eucharist yields two central conclusions. First, the New Testament shows that the early Christians enjoyed a flexible openness in using four differing versions of the words of institution. Second, our Roman Rite claimed its own freedom by putting together the four versions and adding a few words of its own, as happened when it called the new covenant 'everlasting'. Neither here nor elsewhere did the Roman Rite aim at providing a literalist translation of the words of the Bible. It has always been in the business of communicating the profound meaning of what Jesus said and did for the salvation of all.

Fidelity to Jesus in the liturgy does not involve a woodenly literalist translation. What it does call for, from priest and people, is sharing with all their hearts in the celebration and joining their hearts with Jesus—an active participation made easy because the text clearly states the meaning of what Jesus intended and did at the Last Supper.

His words and actions showed that he was willing to shed his blood *for all people*.[10]

Mark and then Matthew wrote in Greek about Christ's death 'for many'. In today's English this meant that he died 'for all'.

The Second Vatican Council's constitution on the liturgy repeatedly endorses the principle that the texts and their meaning should be readily understood, and should not 'normally require much explanation' (no. 34). After forty years of hearing that Christ laid down his life 'for all', switching to dying 'for many' unfortunately requires such explanation. Otherwise people could easily be misled into thinking that Christ did not die for all. The reversal brought about by Pope Benedict to 'for you and for many' can too easily suggest that Christ died for some but not for others.

In his letter to the German Bishops' Conference, the Pope insisted that Jesus at the Last Supper showed that he understood himself as the Suffering Servant of Isaiah 53. Beyond question, early Christians thought of the crucified Jesus in those terms. But it is by no means historically clear that Jesus understood himself precisely in the light of Isaiah 53.[11] Benedict also alleged that an earlier scholarly agreement about Isaiah 53:11–12, and the 'many' (for whom the Servant suffers) meaning 'all' had 'collapsed'. It was news to the exegetes that their consensus about the Hebrew idiom meaning 'all' no longer existed. What had happened was that the Pope no longer accepted their consensus.

(6) A sixth and final example concerns an address to the Roman Curia on 22 December 2005. What Pope Benedict said at the beginning of the address led many commentators to believe that he was claiming that one should not use 'discontinuity' when speaking of the teaching and reforms of Vatican II. He did, in fact, contrast

---

10 See G. O'Collins, *Christology: A Biblical, Historical, and Systematic Study of Jesus* (Oxford: Oxford University Press, 2nd edn, 2009), pp. 67–80.
11 Ibid., pp. 78–79.

two contrary hermeneutics or ways of interpreting the Council: 'a hermeneutic of reform' over against 'a hermeneutic of discontinuity'. Many commentators apparently failed to read further and notice his closing remarks: 'It is precisely [in a] combination of continuity and discontinuity at different levels that the very nature of reform consists'. He was perfectly aware that the Council could not introduce various reforms in church teaching and practice without introducing some measure of discontinuity. So, after all, the Pope recognised a legitimate sense in which one can and should speak of 'discontinuity'.

While the Pope's closing remarks put things in a clearer and happier way, one question rarely, if ever, surfaced in what was written about that address. What kind of hermeneutic or mode of interpretation was he talking about? A merely speculative hermeneutic? Or what we might call a 'decisional' hermeneutic— a mode of interpretation that would shape what he and other Church leaders said and did about Vatican II's teaching and reforms? A 'speculative' or theoretical hermeneutic can never stand by itself, but is always reflected in the decisions that flow from it. Hence Pope Benedict's language of 'hermeneutic' invites the question: can we totally endorse what he said and did in putting the teaching and reforms of Vatican II into practice? He spoke about a 'hermeneutic of reform'. To what extent and in what ways did he practise it?

3

AN ENGLISH INTERLUDE

After leaving Rome in June 2006, I spent a semester as a visiting professor at Marquette University (Milwaukee), and joined in cheerfully celebrating the university's 125 years of existence (see *On the Left Bank of the Tiber*, pp. 289–90). The library housed archives from a fantasy writer, J. R. R. Tolkien, and a social activist, Dorothy Day. The Chapel of Joan of Arc crowned the lawn that stretched away behind the library. Much used for weddings, the medieval chapel had been transported, stone for stone, across the Atlantic from a part of France where the saint grew up. She may well have prayed in that chapel. Pacing the lawn at night, I could hear the clash of weapons as Tolkien's hobbits now fought under the standard of Joan of Arc. Was this a questionable flight of my imagination from the peacemaking and service of the poor and powerless inculcated by the life and teaching of Dorothy Day?

In mid-December I flew to London to take up my position as a research professor at St Mary's University College (now St Mary's University), Twickenham. Friends and relatives sometimes raised two questions: 'Why did you go to St Mary's and not to the Jesuit-run Heythrop College in central London?' 'In any case, is there life after the Gregorian?'

It was easy to answer the first question: 'Michael Hayes at St Mary's invited me, and my superior in Australia gave me the green light to spend three years in the School of Theology, Philosophy, and History of St Mary's.' At the same time, from the start to the finish of my three years in the UK, Heythrop provided me with a first-rate theological library and the setting for some lectures: from the three Cardinal Hume Lectures that I gave in March 2007 (on the salvation of those who follow 'other' living faiths) to the *Tablet* Lecture in September 2009 ('My dreams for the future of the Church'). As for the second question, it receives a resounding 'yes' in this chapter.

Living in Wimbledon

The small community that welcomed me at No. 9 Edge Hill belonged to a cluster of several communities which made Wimbledon a Jesuit enclave: the Sacred Heart parish, Wimbledon College, and several houses that provided a home for the scholastics and priests studying or teaching at Heythrop College (on Kensington Square and about an hour away by public transport). Trains (mainline and underground), buses, and one tramline (across to Croydon) move the young people who attend the numerous primary and secondary schools in Wimbledon, as well as thousands of visitors who arrive each year for the tennis.

When you walk out of No. 9 Edge Hill, turn left, and head up the steep rise, you pass the nineteenth-century parish church (built in late Decorative Gothic style) and the College before you end your climb at a busy road, the Ridgway, and cross to Wimbledon Common Southside, where William Wilberforce lived for a time and often entertained his friend William Pitt the Younger. An entry in Wilberforce's diary recalls, 'persuaded Pitt to church. At night walked ladies on the common'. A few doors away from the site of the Wilberforce home, you come to Southside House, where John Murray II fled to escape the rent-a-mob that surrounded his premises and home in Albemarle Street after he published Lord Byron's bawdy epic, *Don Juan*. Crossing the Common to the right, you reach the nunciature of the Holy See, where the Spanish nuncio and his (American) number two made me instantly welcome. A corner of the Common features an area known as 'Caesar's Camp', where Julius Caesar is supposed to have encamped on one of his two invasions of England (55 and 54 BC). The area was inhabited, perhaps as early as the eighth century BC, but it is almost certain that Caesar never stopped there.

Leaving No. 9 Edge Hill and turning right, I would come at once to the very busy Worple Road, which at the foot of the ridge runs parallel to the Ridgway at the top. A couple of doors along Worple Road I found the home of Dr John Marshall, emeritus professor of neurology at the University of London. He had been a member of the Pontifical Commission on Population, Family, and Birth (popularly known as 'the birth control commission') right from the time that Pope John XXIII first set it up in 1963. John had kindly supplied me with Appendix D for my *Living Vatican II: The 21st Council for the 21st Century* (Mahwah, NJ: Paulist Press, 2006): his 'voyage of discovery' from holding the traditional teaching that contraception is intrinsically evil to seeing that the traditional, official Catholic ban on artificial birth-control cannot be upheld. The overwhelming majority on the commission either shared his voyage of discovery or had already made it before they were appointed as colleagues. Yet, against their advice, Pope Paul VI repeated the traditional ban in his encyclical *Humanae Vitae* of 1968 (see *A Midlife Journey*, pp. 348–50, 355–56, 360, 368–69).

If I took Worple Road in the direction of Wimbledon Station, I came at once to a short side-street that led to what had been the grounds of the All England Lawn Tennis and Croquet Club. In the 1920s the club had moved to its present, spacious setting on the London side of Wimbledon. The original grounds were taken over for hockey and other sports by the girls of Wimbledon High School. The original, brick gates remained, along with the simple, rustic changing rooms. As I stood there one morning in 2007, I had the grounds to myself, as the girls had not yet poured in for their afternoon sport. Memories flooded back of Norman Brookes playing golf with my father on a course outside Melbourne (*A Midlife Journey*, pp. 44–46, 63). Known as 'the Wizard', he became the first non-Briton (and the first left-hander) to win the men's singles at Wimbledon exactly a century earlier. In 1907 he also joined Tony Wilding to win the doubles, as well as the Davis Cup. In the summer of 1914 he was back again at Wimbledon, won the singles and doubles, and sailed for the United States to win once again the Davis Cup. Standing at the gates of the courts where he played in Wimbledon, I looked across the grass, dreamt up the stands of ladies and gentlemen dressed in light clothes and entranced by Brookes's skill, and lifted my eyes beyond the fields to the busy railway line. It prompted the shift from these grounds. In the early twentieth century smoke from coal-burning trains could play havoc with white dresses and jackets.

One huge, human plus about moving to Wimbledon was the close presence of my cousin Monica Ellison and her husband John. They had featured importantly in my life after 1964 (see *A Midlife Journey*, pp. 312, 331, 350, 370, 403). Now I was living only a few hundred yards from them. To the right of Edge Hill, a narrow path threaded behind many houses and led diagonally up the ridge towards the Ellison home and beyond. That ancient path made the climb easy, and in spring and summer was heavy with the perfume of roses, lilacs, and other flowers. Sometimes when I returned as the last streaks of daylight were fading, foxes crossed the path, intent on raiding garbage bins for an evening snack.

Both Ellisons played roles in local Wimbledon affairs. Monica devised a 'Literary Walk' that alerted me, among other things, to the birthplace of Robert Graves and the visits of W. B. Yeats. He not only attended séances in Wimbledon, but also, many years later, at the age of sixty-eight found 'beatitude' in Burghley Road, in the arms of the controversial, thirty-four- year-old novelist, Ethel Mannin.

John, Monica, and I took brisk walks on the Wimbledon Common, often ending at 'The Hand-in-Hand' for some shepherd's pie and cider. Or else we drove across to the South Downs, rambled through the woods, and found a pub where we could sample the tasty ale of an independent brewery, 'Shere Drop'.

Without this being planned in advance, once established at No. 9 Edge Hill, I became an unofficial theologian in residence to the Sacred Heart parish. Before I arrived, the parishioners were debating vigorously the question of adding married deacons to the staff. In January 2007 a big audience heard me speak on 'Ministry in the New Testament and the History of the Church'. The focus spiralled out of control as several people turned the discussion towards tragic experiences they had suffered. One mother spoke of her daughter who had worked for convicts on parole, only to be murdered by one of them.

A June lecture for the parish proved less dramatic, when I presented the first volume of Pope Benedict's *Jesus of Nazareth*. The Pope's book reached me just as I had completed writing my own *Jesus: A Portrait* for publication in 2008 (by Darton, Longman & Todd in the UK and Orbis Books in the USA). I admitted to the Wimbledon parishioners that I had read Benedict's volume nervously and quickly, being anxious that he might have simply pre-empted the popular Jesus-book I had set myself to write. In fact, while there was some overlap, we differed notably, not least because I aimed to encompass the whole story in one volume rather than divide the material into two volumes as the Pope set himself to do.

When *Jesus: A Portrait* appeared a year later, the parish generously invited me to present the book by giving two lectures (8 and 15 April 2008). This gladdened the hearts of the publishers, especially as the book was sold through the parish bookstore. This parish presentation in Wimbledon turned into a dress rehearsal for subsequent lectures on the book that quickly followed: at the University of Birmingham (26 April), at the Milltown Institute in Dublin (17 May), and at St John's Seminary, Wonersh (12 June), as well as an interview for BBC

Radio Ulster (1 June)—along with presentations in Australia (during the July-August, Northern hemisphere, summer break) for the Yarra Theological Union in Melbourne, the Australian Catholic University campus in Ballarat, and Catholic Theological College in Adelaide. The 'selling' of *Jesus: A Portrait* included preaching on the book at the Farm Street church one Sunday (21 September) and closed with a day-long workshop at Aylesford Priory for the clergy of the Southwark Archdiocese (4 December) and another such workshop at Farm Street (17 January 2009).

Often initiatives of Pope Benedict shaped what I did as the Wimbledon parish's theologian in residence. In January 2008 sixty people came to hear me lecture on his new encyclical, *Spe Salvi* (see previous chapter and Appendix 1). Once again this proved a trial run for talking elsewhere. In February I spoke on the encyclical in Holy Apostles' parish, Pimlico, and St James's parish, Spanish Place.

Then the Pope declared 2008–2009 'the year of St Paul'—a decision that was widely welcomed by Catholics and other Christians. The Wimbledon parish invited me to lead a day-long workshop on St Paul, and forty people attended (17 January 2009). Once again this became the first in a sequence of engagements: a day's workshop ('What was Paul's Vision of Christ?') at St Beuno's Retreat Centre in North Wales (19 February); another workshop on the same topic at Aylesford Priory (23 February); a lecture on Paul for two hundred people at Oscott College, Birmingham (27 February); a day of recollection at Worth Abbey on 'Journeying with Paul through Lent to Holy Week' (11 March); a lecture ('What do we owe to St Paul?') at St Anthony's parish, Forest Gate (26 March); the same lecture ('What do we owe to St Paul?') at St Anne's on Sea, near Preston, (2 April); a lecture ('In Praise of St Paul') at St Joseph's parish, Bunhill Road, central London (6 June); and a lecture on the same topic to the Carmelite sisters in Preston (12 June). Finally, an article of mine ('In Praise of Paul') was published by Michael Hayes (ed.), *In Praise of Paul* (London: St Paul's Publications, 2009), pp. 17–26.

I was delighted to speak repeatedly on St Paul. Years before I had lectured in Cambridge, Massachusetts, on the apostle's letters during each of the five semesters spent as a visiting professor at Weston School of Theology (1968–72). In those heady and challenging days I clung to Paul as a truly authoritative guide to what Christian faith is about—as someone I knew, loved, and trusted. Over many years of lecturing on fundamental and systematic theology at the Gregorian University (1974–2006), I drew on his writing whenever appropriate. Now I had the chance of returning to 'my first love', and was delighted at the enthusiastic response of audiences up and down England and Wales to what I had to say about him during the Year of St Paul.

The Sacred Heart parish in Wimbledon was geographically large and included many Catholics, both active and 'resting'. Teams of young boys and girls, led by a tall and elegant Indian girl, provided abundant altar servers. Several men in their seventies and eighties meticulously served at a sung, Latin Mass on Sunday mornings. The parish had close to one hundred Eucharistic ministers, who did great service in bringing Holy Communion to the sick and the elderly. During my stay in the parish I led a day of recollection for seventy-five of these ministers at the Kairos Centre in Roehampton (8 March 2008). They were mostly women, but they included men like John Marshall. When he brought Holy Communion to a retirement home, the communicants gathered for a service before they received the Eucharist. With his loving, kindly manner, John would have made an ideal priest.

The parish profited from the activities of several groups, not least the presence of an international movement founded in France in 1945, the Teams of Our Lady. Made up of five to seven married couples, along with a spiritual adviser, they met each month to share, pray, and discuss the challenges of being Christian and married in our modern world. One couple, Luisa and Chris Elliott, became close friends. She taught Italian, and he was a medical general practitioner. But our contact did not centre on any chaplaincy work for 'the Teams' but rather on keeping my Italian alive through weekly sessions of reading and 'conversazione'. One book I read with Luisa, Carlo Levi's *Cristo si è fermato a Eboli* (*Christ Stopped at Eboli*), was a memoir, published in 1945, of his 'internal' exile (1935–36) under Mussolini's fascist regime to Grassano and Aliano, remote towns in Basilicata that history had bypassed. The memoir allowed me to grasp finally the terrible poverty, material and spiritual, from which some Italians had suffered for centuries. Just before moving from London to Melbourne, I was able to repay some of the generous kindness that the Elliotts had shown me by officiating when their son Charles married Amber Penrose in Farm Street church (12 September 2009). I could give the service an Australian voice—something appropriate since Sydney-born Amber drew a number of Australian guests to the ceremony. Alas, an aunt, Beryl Penrose, was too old to come all the way from Australia. Not quite at the level of Margaret Court and Evonne Goolagong Cawley, in the 1950s Beryl had, nevertheless, enjoyed her success in international tennis. She won the Australian Singles and Mixed Doubles, and reached the semi-finals in the French Open and at Wimbledon. I had been looking forward to sitting with her and hearing stories of Roy Emerson, Neale Fraser, and other legendary players, once we moved from the church to Claridge's Hotel for the wedding dinner.

A month before the wedding, I had preached at several Masses in the Sacred Heart church, Wimbledon, to say goodbye to the parish and leave them with a final message before I flew away to distant Australia. As the theme for those homilies I chose the Eucharist as the bread of life that satisfies our hungry hearts.

St Mary's Twickenham

By train it took me less than an hour from my room in Wimbledon to my office at St Mary's University College, Twickenham. A Gothic-style castle built by Horace Walpole in the eighteenth century, Strawberry Hill House had proved a most influential building in promoting the Gothic revival of the nineteenth century. This elegant and eccentric building on the banks of the Thames, a short distance from the rugby ground built later at Twickenham, passed to the Waldegrave family and in 1923 was bought to house St Mary's. Since then the College (now St Mary's University) has added various buildings, a chapel, and extensive sporting facilities.

After arriving at St Mary's a few days before Christmas 2006, I had my first 'public' engagement there on 13 February 2007 when the BBC interviewed me on the record of Pope Benedict. As the place for the interview they chose the fan-vaulted gallery of Strawberry Hill House. Was an eighteenth-century, Gothic-style setting the right place to speak about Benedict and do so for what was a preparation of his obituary? Now nearly ten years old, that interview has presumably long ago disappeared, with the BBC updating the obituary several times since then.

The head of the School of Theology, Philosophy and History, Michael Hayes, was no stranger to me and prominent among those Irish priests who have blessed my life. Before I left Rome in June 2006, he had already enlisted me in contributing to the journal he continues to edit, *The Pastoral Review*. At St Mary's, he and his colleagues did not ask much of me. After giving a lecture in March 2007 on *The Da Vinci Code*, which had ceased to be the all-consuming talk of the town but still commanded some interest, my 'duties' over the three years were slight. I examined one doctoral thesis, read a few major essays for Peter Tyler (fast becoming a world expert in Christian spirituality), shared in some lively staff seminars, and pressed ahead with research and writing. Along with me, Michael had recruited a few other 'golden oldies', now set free from full-time teaching and administration and able to concentrate on publishing. Our books and articles (appearing in scholarly journals and professional works in collaboration) lifted the profile of St Mary's, both academically *and* financially, with the government and general public. Offering us research chairs proved a wise and profitable investment.

During my early months at St Mary's, I saw through to publication with Oxford University Press a book that emerged from the 2003 conference in New York on redemption (see *On the Left Bank of the Tiber*, p. 296), from some courses at the Gregorian University, and from a staff seminar at Georgetown University (October, 2004): *Jesus Our Redeemer. A Christian Approach to Salvation* (2007). I dedicated it with gratitude to the students I had been privileged to teach at the Gregorian, and prayed: 'May this book offer some help towards understanding that faith in the Redeemer which was at the heart of their existence and which led some of them to suffer like him a violent death' (*On the Left Bank of the Tiber*, p. 65).

Life and experiences at the Gregorian prompted the choice of research towards my next book with OUP: *Salvation for All: God's Other Peoples* (2008). Working with Jacques Dupuis and reading other contributors to the theology of religions convinced me that none of them, no matter where they came on the spectrum of opinions, had grasped the full scope of biblical testimony about God's saving intentions towards all peoples. For that matter, no scriptural scholar had presented all this testimony; the one book on this topic, Giovanni Odasso's *Bibbia e religioni. Prospettive bibliche per la teologia delle religioni* (Rome: Urbaniana University Press, 1998) did not cover adequately both testaments. Hence I set myself to gather what the Bible, from Genesis to the Book of Revelation, witnessed about the universal divine benevolence. As I went through the Bible, my guiding principle was to draw from the latest *and most authoritative* commentaries. I told myself: 'if I am wrong, at least I am going wrong with the best biblical scholars'. The book added some chapters of theological reflection about the universal presence of Christ as divine Wisdom and the universal saving work of the Holy Spirit; it concluded by proposing that the Letter to the Hebrews illuminated the possibilities of saving faith for those of 'other' faiths. With affection I dedicated the book to the memory of Dupuis, 'a theologian of immense learning who always held that followers of other religions are persons to be encountered and not "cases" to be reduced to mere statements about them'.

A 2009 issue of an American quarterly, *Horizons*, featured a debate about the book, with four scholars evaluating *Salvation for All* and myself responding to their observations. Peter Phan of Georgetown University, in particular, laid out some searching questions. I was also grateful to Catherine Cornille of Boston College for confirming what I believed to be the case: this is 'the most comprehensive treatment to date of biblical resources which demonstrate God's universal work of salvation'.

The three years of research at St Mary's opened the way to a serious revision of *Christology: A Biblical, Historical, and Systematic Study of Jesus* (Oxford University Press, 2009) and to writing two further books for OUP: *Catholicism: A Very Short Introduction* (2008), and *Jesus Our Priest: A Christian Approach to the Priesthood of Christ* (2010). The former obviously followed on naturally from an earlier, much longer work that I had co-authored with Mario Farrugia for OUP: *Catholicism: The Story of Catholic Christianity* (2003). The latter had a slightly curious origin.

Published now in more than twenty-five languages worldwide, the 'Very Short Introductions' began in 1995 and have grown to a library of over two hundred volumes. They cover a wide variety of topics in history, philosophy, religion, science, and the humanities. I was delighted to find at least one other Australian contributing to this lively and informative series, my fellow graduate student from Cambridge in the late sixties, Germaine Greer. She produced a VSI on Shakespeare. The close 'supervising' of my work by those responsible at OUP explained for me the stunning success of the project. In the interests of being stimulating and even controversial, they wanted, for instance, more on the Spanish Inquisition (p. 26) and on the question of Pope Pius XII and the Jews (p. 46). Writing five years after the first edition of *Catholicism*, I was able to update some matters in my VSI—not least the passage of the papacy from John Paul II to Benedict XVI. Specifically the televised funeral of John Paul II, which up to three billion people watched around the globe, persuaded me to begin by recalling the service for the dead pope. It had put on display many of the distinctive features of the Catholic Church.

In mid-2007 I did something that had frequently filled my summer breaks at the Gregorian. I flew over to the USA and taught a course (on Christology or the doctrine of Christ) for a summer programme at Boston College. The following summer I was to return to the States to lead a retreat for priests and to teach a course in a summer school (not at Boston College but at another university). But those responsible for the two engagements managed, quite independently, to bungle the arrangements.

My initial irritation, however, soon gave way to a renewed sense of how God can write straight with crooked lines. Fr Michael Keenan Jones, the parish priest of St Lawrence's church in Huntington, Connecticut, e-mailed me to say: 'Why don't you come all the same? You can give a couple of lectures, and preach on St Paul. That should cover your airfare.' So I spoke to one hundred lay people on *Jesus: A Portrait*, gave another lecture to forty priests and deacons (on 'The Beauty of Jesus'), and preached at the six weekend Masses in St Lawrence's (on 'The Year of St Paul'). Some years earlier Mike had successfully defended a doctoral thesis with me at the Gregorian University, and went on to publish it in the *Tesi Gregoriana* series. Staying in Mike's presbytery I picked up again a copy of the thesis and suddenly realized: 'with some rewriting and expanding, this dissertation can be turned into a significant book. I should take this on; it's disturbing to see how very rarely the priesthood of Christ appears in recent theological writing.' 'The gap is not just there in recent theology', Mike observed. 'For some reason the whole Christian tradition doesn't offer much on his priesthood.' He paused and added: 'maybe people run away from this topic because of problems with those who share through ordination in Christ's priesthood'. He gave me the green light to set about recasting and enlarging the text. En route to finishing the ms in 2009, I tried out some of the ideas on audiences at St Patrick's College, Maynooth (12 February), Milltown Institute, Dublin (14 February), and Oscott College, Birmingham (27 February).

OUP had hardly received the completed manuscript, when I wondered whether Joseph Ratzinger had become an obsessive presence in my life. As Benedict XVI he had now declared 2009–2010 the 'year of the priest'. Yet it was consoling to think that 'you can't make too much of a good obsession'. In any case, his decision confirmed what drove Mike and myself: there should be much more reflection on the priesthood of Christ and those who share in it through baptism (all Christians) and ministerial ordination (relatively few).

One charming priest of the Westminster Archdiocese, Daniel Cronin, organized a work in collaboration, *Priesthood: A Life Open to Christ* (London: St Paul's Publications, 2009). The (nearly eighty) contributions came from the deceased John Paul II, Benedict XVI, nine cardinals, Archbishop Vincent Nichols, numerous other archbishops and bishops, the eloquent Dominican leader Timothy Radcliffe, and many other priests, including myself. Nichols hosted the launch in Archbishop's House, and Dan Cronin was at his wittiest best. He caricatured an earlier image of the parish priest as being a bus conductor: 'You take their money; you ring the bell; and you tell them where to get off.'

As an extension of his work for *The Pastoral Review*, to which I have continued to contribute constantly, Michael Hayes arranged conferences at St Mary's for clergy and laity. I first shared in that work by speaking at a conference for priests and deacons 18/19 June 2007: 'To Preach the Christ'. Afterwards it was gratifying to hear one priest say: 'I've been ordained twenty-five years, and never before have I been offered the chance of attending a conference on preaching. We need input on preaching'.

A more ambitious conference came a year later, 24–27 March 2008: on the legacy of Pope John Paul II. Michael took charge of the funding and organizing. I drafted the preface, wrote the opening chapter ('John Paul II and the Development of Doctrine'), and did much of the editing and indexing. We published ten of the contributions and three of the responses in *The Legacy of John Paul II* (London: Continuum, 2008). The quality of the chapters and responses was high; we managed to cover many of the major aspects of John Paul II's teaching. For me the outstanding paper came from Jared Wicks, on 'John Paul II and Lutherans: Actions and Reactions' (pp. 139–202). Initially he was not scheduled to contribute, but had suggested a world-class Lutheran scholar, who agreed to come but then fell ill. Jared stepped in and worked quickly to produce a landmark study on the late pope's relations to Luther and Lutherans. Jared's paper demonstrated the enormous benefit of working on a subject with which one is already very familiar.

On the back cover we quoted what Benedict XVI had said about the late pope: 'I consider it my essential and personal mission not so much to produce many new documents but to see to it that [John Paul II's] documents are assimilated, because they are a very rich treasure, the authentic interpretation of Vatican II.' When he visited the UK in September 2010, after I had left for Australia, Pope Benedict came one day to St Mary's for two meetings: the first with educators and students, and the second with representatives of other living faiths. On the occasion of that visit, Michael pressed into his hands a copy of *The Legacy of John Paul II*.

I had already used the words from Benedict about the late pope for the back cover of a book that I edited with two Jesuit friends from the University of San Francisco, Daniel Kendall and Jeffrey LaBelle: *John Paul II: A Reader* (Mahwah, NJ: Paulist Press, 2007). In a papacy that lasted for over twenty-six years (1978–2005), John Paul II left behind an enormous legacy. It included well over seventy thousand pages of teaching, found in encyclicals, apostolic exhortations, apostolic letters, homilies, addresses, letters, and other published texts. His teaching took up a wide range of themes—from the self-revelation of God, through the sacramental life of the church, relations with other Christians and the followers of other religions, to questions of social and sexual morality, and on to basic elements of the Christian spiritual life.

With Dan and Jeff, I wanted to ensure that the highlights of this teaching, especially where it broke new ground, would remain available for a wide audience. To make things more useful and accessible, we arranged what the Pope had written and said according to themes: from the divine self-revelation to the spiritual life of Christians. Within each of our twelve chapters (or, in some cases, sections of chapters) we followed where it was possible and appropriate, the chronological order in which the documents on which we drew were published.

Our reader cited only the official teaching of John Paul II. Hence it did not include any extracts from his poetry and such personal writings as *Crossing the Threshold of Hope* (New York: Knopf, 1994) and *Gift and Mystery* (New York: Doubleday, 1996). Nor did we draw from any documents published during his papacy by various offices of the Roman Curia, like *An Instruction on the Study of the Fathers* (published in 1989 by the Congregation for Catholic Education), *Dialogue and Proclamation* (published in 1991 by the Pontifical Council for Interreligious Dialogue and the Congregation for the Evangelization of Peoples), and the *Directory for the Application of Principles and Norms on*

Ecumenism (published in 1993 by the Pontifical Council for Promoting Christian Unity).

During his pontificate, John Paul II promulgated two codes of canon law: the *Code of Canon Law* in 1983 and the *Code of Canons of the Eastern Churches* in 1990. He also promulgated (in 1992) the *Catechism of the Catholic Church* as an official follow-up to the teaching coming from the Second Vatican Council. But, once again, our reader did not include any passages from either the *Catechism* of 1992 or the two codes of canon law. We already had an enormous amount of material to draw upon, even when we limited ourselves to the official teaching coming from John Paul II himself.

In making our choices we were guided above all by the question: What texts continue to illuminate and nourish most vividly belief and behaviour for Catholics and other Christians—and sometimes, indeed, for the followers of other religions? In most cases we picked significant extracts from John Paul's II's encyclicals and other published documents. In three instances we reproduced the full text: the words he broadcast by radio in May 1981 after he was shot in St Peter's Square (p. 230); the address (August 1985) in Casablanca to over 100,000 young Muslims on the religious and moral values common to Islam and Christianity (pp. 148–58); and the prayer he left at the Western Wall when visiting Jerusalem in March 2000 (p. 242). In all cases we indicated where to find the full texts of the documents: in the *Acta Apostolicae Sedis*, the *Osservatore Romano*, *Origins*, *The Pope Speaks*, published collections of the papal encyclicals and apostolic exhortations, and other sources.

As far as I know, this reader has not only been the first of its kind in the English-speaking world but also the only comprehensive John Paul II reader that exists in any language. Paulist Press generously undertook to publish the volume, even though it involved their paying the Libreria Editrice Vaticana several thousand dollars in royalties. I have never been so gobsmacked in my life when the Vatican Press demanded these royalties. I had expected that the LEV would be delighted that we were spreading the enlightening and life-giving, official teaching of the late pope. But a new policy had come into force, which obliged the Paulist Press and other houses to pay serious money when they published or re-published official papal teaching!

Before I left St Mary's and Wimbledon in late 2009, Dan and Jeff collaborated with me on another project, editing some lectures by Anthony de Mello, SJ, (1931–1987) on the *Spiritual Exercises of St Ignatius Loyola*. Before his sudden death in New York, Tony had become known throughout the world for his spiritual conferences and such books as *Sadhana: A Way to God*, *Song of the Bird*, and *The Way to Love*. In 1973 Tony had founded near Pune, India, the Sadhana Institute, a centre for training spiritual guides and directors of retreats. The third Sadhana group consisted of seven Jesuit priests and seven religious sisters.

From July to November 1975, Tony lectured to this group on the *Spiritual Exercises*. Two or three times a week he gave hour-long talks that were taped. Several members of the group then typed out the talks and gave the others a carbon copy. Thirty years later one of the participants, Fr Albert Menezes, SJ, made his copy available to us.

The pages were difficult to read: the typists had frequently used old ribbons, adopted single space throughout, and left very little room for margins. In any case a tropical climate had played havoc with the paper. There was no chance of scanning the text and transferring it directly to a computer. A grant from the Jesuit Foundation at the University of San Francisco enabled us to have the pages retyped entirely as a computer document.

Then we faced the task of editing the material. While preserving as much as possible the words and conversational style of de Mello, we inserted headings and set his talks out in readable paragraphs. He did not always follow the order of the *Spiritual Exercises*. Hence, where necessary, we rearranged the chapters to follow the order of the *Exercises* themselves. We also added endnotes to clarify terminology: for instance, the names Jesuits apply to their superior general in Rome ('the general'), their superiors in various parts of the world ('the provincials'), and students in training ('the scholastics'). We needed to explain as well some Indian and psychological terms. In particular, the talks of de Mello, himself a trained psychotherapist, adopted occasionally the language of transactional analysis ('parent', 'child', and 'adult'). Transactional analysis is an integrative approach to psychology and psychotherapy.

Perhaps the most time-consuming part in editing this manuscript consisted of verifying and giving precise references to different authors, both ancient and modern, when de Mello quoted them. Here and there we also inserted information to make his writing accessible to a wider audience.

In the opening lectures, de Mello commented on the 'Annotations' or introductory guidelines for anyone directing or doing the Exercises. The overriding aim is to make a journey through prayer and self-awareness that provides a context for becoming spiritually free and so able to seek, find, and follow the will of God in one's personal life. Such a process of 'putting order into our lives', de Mello reflected, 'means putting order into our love'. Hence he called doing the Exercises 'a crash programme for centring our hearts on God'.

In preparing the manuscript for publication as *Seek God Everywhere: Reflections on the Spiritual Exercises of St. Ignatius* (New York; Doubleday, 2010), Dan, Jeff, and I were blessed with the advice of Gary Jansen of Doubleday. He helped to have the book translated into Finnish, Indonesian, Korean, Polish, and Spanish. We dedicated it to the memory of Tony de Mello, a treasured and delightful companion in the Society of Jesus. We hoped that our book would illustrate something very dear to him, the enduring power of the Spiritual

Exercises to bring believers everywhere closer to God and to their fellow human beings.

Some months before the book was published, I put it to good use at a July 2009 conference held at St Mary's, 'Sources of Transformation: Revitalising Christian Spirituality'. Peter Tyler asked me to give a keynote address, 'A Transformative Blending: Anthony de Mello on the *Spiritual Exercises* of St Ignatius Loyola'. He and his colleague in spirituality, Edward Howells, had invited speakers not only from the UK but also from the USA and elsewhere. The star of the conference was Bernard McGinn of Chicago, *the* world expert in Western mysticism. Presenting my paper gave me the cheerful sense of sharing a scoop with a wider public. Tyler had to handle gently one speaker who, right before he was to deliver his paper, threatened to pull out unless his expenses were paid there and then. The fourteen papers were quickly published as *Sources of Transformation* (London: Continuum, 2010).

Speaking about Jesus to a Wider Public

Living in Wimbledon let me direct my energies also toward public lecturing, as well as leading various groups on retreat. Almost always, British Rail took me to my destination; each month or so I ordered on line a bunch of train tickets, with the handy reduction for a senior citizen.

Very often Jesus himself supplied the topic on which audiences up and down England, as well as in Ireland and Scotland, wanted to hear me speak. On 6 February 2007 I flew over to Belfast and, in their St Mary's University College, lectured one evening to a large audience of students and others on the question, 'Does it matter who Jesus is?' 'The others' included a few who had suffered internment without trial. A Margaret Beaufort lecture at University of Cambridge took the theme 'Jesus as Universal Wisdom' (19 April 2007). A few weeks later I talked about Jesus to the catechetical co-ordinators of the Westminster Archdiocese (3 May). Heythrop College had me back for a lecture on 'Jesus Our Redeemer' (15 May). Later that month I crossed London to lecture on the beauty of Jesus in the cathedral of the Brentwood Diocese (26 May). This engagement proved the start of numerous invitations from that diocese. The parish of Wells brought me down to Somerset to speak on 'Who is Jesus? Does it matter?' (7 June). Jesus and Christology remained the focus for a summer spent on the East coast of the United States: first at Seton Hall University's International Institute for Clergy Formation, where I gave five lectures on Christ's redeeming work (25–28 June), and then at Boston College's Institute of Religious Education and Pastoral Ministry where I taught a crash course in Christology (9–20 July).

Back in London after the summer, I delivered the 2007 Francis Clark Lecture at Maryvale Institute, Birmingham, on 'The Virginal Conception of Christ: Its Theological Significance' (29 September). A few days later I was on the train for Bristol and led a study day on Christology for the priests of the Clifton Diocese (2 October). Then in quick succession I discussed 'Who is Jesus? Does our answer matter?' at the Brentwood Religious Education Centre (4 October), the University of Liverpool (6 October), and the parish of Whitten, near Twickenham (11 October). The month did not end before I spent a day at Henley-on-Thames giving two talks to some Anglican bishops and their wives on the Christ-centred spirituality of John's Gospel (25 October). Our venue, Highmoor Hall, with its elegant interior and immaculate garden, turned out to be the loveliest small retreat house I have ever visited.

The year was not over before I was speaking on Jesus in further settings: first, on Jesus as universal wisdom to the theology department at Durham University (21 November). That trip to Durham included two sessions with the Catholic clergy on preaching Christ in Advent and at Christmas, talks that I repeated on 29 November for the clergy of Brentwood Diocese. The visit to Durham included a dinner at the Catholic chaplaincy where I was seated between two outstanding scholars and long-standing friends, Bishop Tom Wright and Professor James Dunn. The other guests spent much of the meal listening to a spirited conversation between the three of us about the Christology of the New Testament and other topics. Perhaps the subtext of the invitation they had received was becoming our audience. Back in London, the Friends of the Anglican Centre (Rome) brought me to the Jerusalem Chamber in Westminster Abbey to speak on Christmas carols and their ecumenical meaning (4 December). Inevitably the Christ Child figured centrally in what I had to say.[12]

Through January and February 2008 I remained constantly engaged with the mystery of Jesus Christ: two lectures for one hundred teachers of the Diocese of Salford on 'Rediscovering Christ at the Centre' (14 January); two lectures for priests of the same diocese on 'Preaching the Christ' (15 January); two lectures for head teachers of the Diocese of Clifton on 'Christ at the Centre' (18 January); six lectures for the bishop and priests of the Leeds Diocese on preaching the death and resurrection of Christ (12–15 February); five lectures on the same topic for the bishop and priests of Shrewsbury Diocese (19–20 February); two lectures for the bishop, priests, and deacons of the Brentwood Diocese (28 February). For their week of lectures, the Leeds Diocese took over the Old Swan Hotel in Harrogate, a spa town not far from Leeds itself and now transmogrified into a conference centre.

In December 1926, Agatha Christie, already famous for her murder mysteries, had put the Old Swan on the map by disappearing from her home and husband in the South and heading North to stay in that hotel under the name of her husband's mistress (and second

---

12 A substantial part of the lecture was eventually published as 'Ecumenism in Advent', in *The Pastoral Review* 6/6 (November-December 2010), pp. 56–58.

wife). She did not hide away in her room, but sang with the hotel band and played billiards with other guests. A massive police search failed to find her. But, after she had been missing for eleven days, a banjo player at the hotel recognized her. Her husband was fetched, and there was a short-lived period of public reconciliation. Vanessa Redgrave and Dustin Hoffman starred in the Warner Brothers 1977 film, *Agatha*. At the Old Swan the room occupied by Agatha Christie was carefully marked, and stills from the film were prominent along the corridors. For the aficionados of Agatha Christie, the Old Swan offered a ritual experience approaching a pilgrimage.

As Holy Week drew closer, I spoke to the members of the Wellspring Community, Strawberry Hill, on the passion of Christ (3 March), an engagement quickly followed by an extended Lenten Mass homily for 150 people in St Joseph's parish, Preston (5 March). Back in London I talked about 'praying the passion' of Christ to members of St James's parish, Spanish Place (12 March). The following day took me to Emmaus Centre, West Wickham, to give two lectures on Jesus as Redeemer to priests, deacons, and others of the Southwark Archdiocese. After Easter, the resurrection of Christ supplied the theme for a trail of three engagements: a study day with a group of Anglican clergy in a centre next to the Guildford cathedral (17 April); another study day (19 April), this time in a centre next to the Brentwood cathedral; and an evening lecture at the legendary Jesuit school in Yorkshire, Stonyhurst College (24 April).

Later in 2008, Scotland, Northern Ireland, and the United States provided major venues for lecturing on Jesus Christ. First, I headed up to Pluscarden (near Aberdeen) for eight sessions on Christology with the monks of an abbey, founded in the Middle Ages, partly destroyed at the Reformation, and re-founded in the mid-twentieth century (13–17 October). When the Benedictines returned, they put a roof back on the ruins and took up again monastic life there. Sheltered by the high, stone walls of the chapel, they celebrate Mass looking up at a vast, modern stained-glass window of Christ. It depicts him holding in one hand some bread and in the other hand a chalice. Below him are representations of the wheat and grapes from which the bread and wine are made for celebrating the Eucharist.

I was grateful for the chance of staying a few days at Pluscarden Abbey. The monks rise early to pray, sing the divine office six times during the day, eat very simple food, and altogether live a thoroughly austere life. They are also obviously united in a devout and happy community. When I joined them for the Eucharist, I lifted my eyes over the altar to the great window at the east end of the chapel and glimpsed the secret at the heart of those monks' existence. I saw, in gleaming red and gold, Christ holding bread and wine. He is the One who enables the monks to celebrate with strength and survive with joy.

One additional blessing at Pluscarden came with the chance of talking with Abbot Hugh Gilbert, now Bishop of Aberdeen. He alerted me to excellent insights about the priesthood of Christ coming from Tom Torrance (1913–2007), the Edinburgh professor who for many years had been the doyen of Presbyterian theology. I slotted insights from Torrance into the final text of *Jesus Our Priest*.

During those days at Pluscarden, autumn chill was slowly setting in. Pheasants swarmed everywhere in the surrounding fields and woods. The Thane of Cawdor's nearby home, better known as Macbeth's castle, was still attracting tourists from overseas. The charming and devout widow of the late Thane attended the Eucharist at Pluscarden. I could not help asking myself: 'what would Lady Macbeth think of these developments?'

I was hardly back in London before I took a flight to Belfast and was driven across the border to a conference centre near Letterkenny, Donegal. For the clergy and pastoral commission of the Raphoe Diocese, I gave four lectures on preaching Jesus and one on his beauty (20–21 October). During an afternoon break I strolled down to the stone wharf on a quiet inlet from the sea. Back in January 1974, Rose Dugdale, an English heiress and Oxford graduate who rebelled against her wealthy upbringing and joined the IRA, arrived there in a hijacked helicopter. Milk churns packed with high explosives were waiting on the wharf. Dugdale and her IRA lover flew over the border, circled a Royal Ulster Constabulary station in Strabane, and dropped the churns. But they failed to explode. Several months later Dugdale was arrested, convicted, and remained in gaol until 1980. The disturbing memory of a violent, recent past did not fit the peace of the tiny waves lapping the wharf in Donegal.

Early November took me on a swing through the USA, which began when I delivered the annual Newman Lecture, 'the beauty of Christ', at Yale University (5 November). That evening I found myself in competition with a visiting professor, Tony Blair. The ex-prime minister was over at Yale, teaching a mini-course for the Divinity School. Mike Jones welcomed me to his parish house in nearby Huntington, Connecticut. After speaking to the clergy of the Bridgeport Diocese on preaching Christ, I gave the annual Saint Augustine Lecture for the diocese: 'Christ at the Centre: Evangelizing with Words and Deeds' (6 November). In Cleveland, Ohio, I provided another annual event by delivering the Mullen Lecture to two hundred people: 'Christ at the Centre' (9 November). The following day I spoke to fifty clergy of Cleveland Diocese on preaching Christ in Advent, at Christmas, and in the New Year. The Cleveland visit brought me back to John Carroll University, which in May 2007 had flown me over from London to receive a doctorate *honoris causa*. On that occasion two other scholars and friends, John O'Malley and Jared Wicks, joined me to make it a Jesuit threesome being honoured in an academic way.

Home in England two engagements brought to a close, at least for the year of 2008, my speaking on Jesus to a wider public: a lecture on the infancy narrative in Matthew's Gospel to a small parish group in

Wimbledon Park (10 December), and a lecture in Catford to over one hundred people on 'knowing Jesus' (11 December).

The New Year continued to supply audiences anxious or at least willing to hear me hold forth on my favourite topic. One evening I spoke to seventy students at More House, Imperial College (London), on the theme: 'Who is Jesus? Why does it matter?'(25 January 2009). The following month I flew over to Ireland and gave seven lectures for the theology department at St Patrick's College, Maynooth, on 'Portraying Jesus' (9–13 February). That visit let me catch up with old friends and former students at Maynooth itself and then in Dublin, where I gave a lecture at the Milltown Institute on the priesthood of Christ (14 February).

Presenting Jesus Christ in the UK reached its peak with a lecture in London and a course in Edinburgh. The Archdiocese of Westminster's agency for evangelization, supported by the Mount Street Jesuit Centre, drew 250 people to the Westminster Cathedral Hall for an evening on 'Who is Jesus? Does it matter?' (25 March). For years the British Jesuits had run summer courses in theology for interested lay people. Before I left for Australia, they invited me to visit Edinburgh and lecture on Christology in their Living Theology programme (20–24 July). While the audience was lively, so too were aspects of the city's history.

Just a short distance from where I stayed, you come across an area of Edinburgh made infamous in 1828 by William Burke and William Hare. With the bodies of executed criminals and other legitimate sources of cadavers no longer meeting the demand at medical schools, body-snatchers, sometimes called 'resurrectionists', robbed graves and were well paid to make up the deficit. Burke and Hare went further: they smothered people and supplied at least sixteen victims for dissection at anatomy lectures before being arrested and put on trial for murder. A few yards from the Jesuit residence a pub named after Burke and Hare advertised in large letters the lap dancing available for clients. It seemed incongruous to exploit in that 'hot-blooded' way the memory of two cold-blooded murderers.

Frequently lecturing on Jesus helped fill my three years in England. Leading retreats and preaching created another, more direct avenue for promoting a deep relationship with the person of Jesus.

Leading Retreats and Preaching

England offered a variety of audiences and settings for leading 'retreats', or periods of quiet prayer and reflection built around the life, death, and resurrection of Jesus. The first such occasion came when I led the seminarians at Allen Hall, Chelsea, on a post-Easter retreat (22–29 April 2007). Occupying part of the grounds of the Great Hall, which St Thomas More built in 1524 and where he and his family lived until his arrest in 1534, the seminary boasts an ancient mulberry tree. The future martyr is supposed to have sat in its shade to talk with family and friends. In 1568 Cardinal William Allen founded a seminary in Douai, France, to train priests for the English mission. Between 1577 and 1680, 158 former members of the Douai seminary died as martyrs. After the penal laws against Catholics were relaxed, in 1793 the seminary came across the channel to the Old Hall Green in Ware (Hertfordshire). In 1975 it moved to the heart of London and its present location in Chelsea. At Allen Hall a sense of heroic history hangs in the air. It is only a short walk along the Thames to the church where Thomas More worshipped and where his first wife was buried. After he was beheaded, his body was interred near the Tower of London and not next to her in their parish church.

Shortly before I left for Australia in mid-September 2009, St John's Seminary, Wonersh (near Guildford), invited me to lead a retreat for twenty-five seminarians, plus some members of staff (20–25 June). Surrounded by the fields and woods of Surrey, the seminary blessed me with the sheer delight of a warm summer humming with life in the English countryside. One morning, however, windows had to be firmly shut when a mass of bees swarmed around the upper floors and kept searching for a new home until beekeepers arrived to take the swarm in hand.

Retreats for these two groups of seminarians bracketed my three years in England. Priests and lay people, however, provided the normal public for weekend or longer retreats that I was invited to lead. The Southwark Archdiocese came up with my first visit to Aylesford Priory, by asking me to lead the annual retreat for the clergy of the archdiocese (17–21 September 2007). Near Maidstone, Kent, this medieval monastery was founded in 1242 when a local crusader, Richard de Gray, brought a group of Carmelite hermits from the Holy Land. They prospered, and in the second half of the thirteenth centuries over thirty other Carmelite priories were opened in England and Wales. Dissolved in the sixteenth century by King Henry VIII, Aylesford Priory was restored in 1949 when the Carmelites were able to buy the property back from its impoverished owners. A place of peace and prayer, the priory gave me the chance not only of sleeping in a medieval cloister but also of dining in a medieval refectory where the windows looked out on the River Medway. Those days away from their parishes encouraged in the priests a fresh openness to Christ. In one-to-one meetings they shared with me the joys and sorrows that fashioned their pastoral experience and personal life.

With twenty clergy (including one auxiliary bishop) from the Westminster Archdiocese, I flew to Lyons in the autumn of 2008 and led a retreat for them (6–10 October) in nearby Ars, a small village made famous by its saintly parish priest, Jean-Baptiste Marie Vianney (1785–1859). A tasteful and expertly run modern centre housed us, and we breathed in the spirit of a very poor and most loving pastor. Famous for the help he offered people in confession, the Curé of Ars drew huge numbers of pilgrims from France and beyond; they confessed their sins to him and receive deeply spiritual encouragement.

In the church you still see the confessional where he sat for many hours every day, the pulpit from which he preached, and the pictures of saints that he hung on the walls. On our retreat a special blessing came when we concelebrated in his church and could use the chalice that he had constantly employed for the Eucharist.

At Easter 1974, thanks to John Todd, one of the founders of the publishing house Darton, Longman & Todd, I had begun leading retreats or giving lectures for Ammerdown Centre, a place steeped in the peace and beauty of Somerset. John strongly supported Lord Raymond Hylton, the owner of Ammerdown, when, with exquisite taste, he adapted buildings on his estate as a centre open to people of all faiths and none. With its memories of daffodils galore enriching the springtime, pheasants filling the woods, and, above all, the faces of hundreds of fascinating people who made Ammerdown an exceptional meeting place, the centre always tempts me to self-indulgent reminiscence.

House guests of the Hyltons included Quintin Hogg, Baron Hailsham of St Marylebone (1907–2001), who—among other achievements in his political career— had been Lord Chancellor for more than a decade. His beloved second wife had died in a horse-riding accident that took place before his eyes in Sydney. But he bore no grudges against Australia or Australians, and we chatted happily about many questions, including the frequent word for word correspondence between the first three Gospels. 'If Matthew, Mark, and Luke had appeared in court before me', he announced, 'I would have been certain of one thing: plagiarism had been going on'.[13] Lord Hailsham was remembered for having been fierce with judges and for having mistakenly appointed as Chief Justice Lord Widgery, the judge who presided over the whitewash of the 1972 shootings on Bloody Sunday in Derry. But I saw only the kindly, highly intelligent,

---

13 Most biblical scholars hold that, along with other sources, Matthew and Luke drew heavily on the Gospel of Mark.

and devout side of Lord Hailsham. As he used two sticks to walk with difficulty, he remained in his place at the veneration of the cross during a Good Friday service in the Ammerdown Centre's chapel. I can never forget the sense of love and personal fragility he showed when leaning forward to kiss the feet of the Crucified Christ.

Julian Earl of Asquith and Oxford (1916–2011) lived with his family in Mells, not far from Ammerdown, and was related to Raymond Hylton. In his last years Monsignor Ronald Knox stayed with the Asquiths and is buried in the exquisite country graveyard that surrounds the ancient church at Mells. When my years in Rome at the Gregorian University were coming to an end, I occasionally entertained the thought of offering myself as a chaplain to the Asquiths, but put the thought away as a dangerous temptation. Yet the link remained, and I had been able to send there for a short stay a young American priest who was writing a doctoral dissertation with me on Ronald Knox as an apologist. The Asquiths owned some unpublished papers of Knox, and generously made them available (see *On the Left Bank of the Tiber*, p. 78). The parents were always delightful company, and so too were their two sons and three daughters. Asquiths, Bonham-Carters, Horners, Sitwells, and other names on the tombs in the church and graveyard at Mells cast a spell over me. They summoned up a glorious and sometimes tragic past.

I had been coming to Ammerdown from Rome for over thirty years when I returned in late 2007 to conduct an individually directed retreat for eleven people (5–12 November). Ammerdown always brought its special surprises—this time two devout Anglican priests, women who gave their best in country parishes. A year later I was back at Ammerdown, once again to lead a retreat for eight people, who included a parish priest who flew over from Washington (17–21 November 2008). My Ammerdown experiences ended some months later when, at the height of a glorious spring, I guided six people on a retreat (4–11 May 2009).

Lord Hylton also used the Ammerdown Centre in the cause of political peace. On one notable occasion representatives from both sides flew over from Northern Ireland for a face-to-face encounter. Security police tried to make themselves inconspicuous behind trees or hidden in the woods on the Ammerdown estate. The Hyltons had a family stake in Northern Island. Their only daughter, Emily, spent years there working for peace, before returning to live in Somerset with her husband Ross, an Ulster man who had also done his best to be part of the solution rather than part of the problem.

Other centres invited me to lead retreats: a weekend retreat for 23 lay people at Loyola Hall, near Liverpool (27–29 March, 2009); and a day retreat to 35 lay people at the Tabor Retreat Centre, Preston (13 June, 2009). Both of those locales offer sacred space for coming closer to God and to oneself in prayer.

But the second retreat house (other than Ammerdown) that stays on vividly in my mind is Thornhill Centre high above the River Foyle in Donegal. Fifteen people signed up for a retreat with me at the height of spring (12–15 May, 2008). To the left the river runs into the large and picturesque Lough Foyle. In 1945 the surviving submarines of the German Atlantic Fleet assembled there, before being taken out into the ocean and scuttled in an act of wanton destruction. To the right the river heads upstream to Derry, which hit the world's headlines on 30 January 1972 when British troops shot dead thirteen marchers who were protesting against the government's policy of internment without trial. What offset for me a recent history of death and destruction was the memory of St Columba (d. 597). In 563 he sailed down the River Foyle as 'a pilgrim for Christ', crossed the sea, and founded a flourishing monastery on Iona, a small island of the Inner Hebrides. A centre of learning for centuries, the monastery sent missionaries to Scotland and England, and endured for centuries until abolished by the sixteenth-century reformation. From the late 1930s, the newly established Iona Community rebuilt the church and monastic buildings and became a popular place of pilgrimage and renewal. While stressing personal devotion and spiritual healing, the Community also reaches out through its commitment to social justice and stands tall for promoting peace in a world ravaged by the Great War, the Second World War, the civil strife of Northern Ireland, and ever so many other local wars.

The ministry of leading retreats blended easily with preaching engagements at universities and in parishes. The first such engagement took me back to my college in Cambridge, Pembroke College, to preach for the students at evensong on a Sunday (11 February 2007). Remembering advice from one of my aunts, 'tell them a story', I drew from *Stronger Than Hate*, the autobiography of a French gang leader and male prostitute. His life was transformed by the love he received from an elderly Dominican priest and a young woman, who became his wife and the mother of their four children. On such visits back to Cambridge I regularly stayed over the weekend at Fisher House, the Catholic chaplaincy built around a sixteenth-century pub, the Black Swan, and incorporating an early-seventeenth century building. The low, wood-beamed ceilings, narrow staircases, and creaking floors of such buildings have never gone out of fashion as far as I am concerned.

At least twice, the Catholic chaplain at the University of Durham invited me to come north and preach in his chaplaincy that also incorporated St Cuthbert's parish (25 November 2007, and 1 February 2009). The chaplaincy-parish nestles in the shadow of the magnificent Durham Cathedral, which houses the remains of the northern saints, Cuthbert and Bede.

I put much of myself into the homily that I preached during three Masses at Fisher House (24 May 2009). Walking down King's Parade and along the Cam triggered a bitter-sweet mood. I sensed that this would be my final visit to Cambridge, the gentle ending to all those experiences that stretched back to the autumn of 1965 when I arrived at Pembroke College to begin doctoral studies (see *A Midlife Journey*, pp. 275–351, 420).

But most of the invitations to preach took me to churches in or near London. Thus a summer mission at Our Lady and St George's Church, Walthamstow, involved preaching at five Masses, as well as giving a lecture on forgiveness to fifty people (7/8 June 2008). Fr Digby Samuels invited me to give three brief homilies at St Patrick's Wapping during an Advent service in St Patrick's Church, Wapping (6 Dec 2008). The most testing of all these engagements involved preaching at a service of healing and reconciliation for three hundred people at Holy Innocents, Orpington (19 March 2009). Not long before the parish priest had decamped with one of the parishioners.

Presiding and preaching at a requiem in Weybridge, shortly before I left for Australia, proved a real milestone at the end of my English interlude. Dying at the age of 98, Mary Stewart was easily the oldest of the de Bertodano family, who have been a constant blessing in my life. At school in London with the future, world-renowned actresses, Vivien Leigh and Maureen O'Sullivan, Mary had built up a fund of stories—about her parents and many other people who filled a long life marked but not destroyed by a broken marriage. Her father, the Marquis de Bertodano, had served in the Boer War and arrested 'Breaker' Morant, an expert horseman executed for shooting a civilian and either condemned as a criminal or honoured as a hero by the general public. Long before leaving Rome for Wimbledon in 2006, I used stopovers in London to visit Mary in Weybridge—first in her home and then in a series of retirement homes—to celebrate Mass in her room and then push her down the street in a wheel chair to have a bowl of pasta in Prezzo, a local Italian restaurant. I never told her how much I cherished her as a latter-day Mrs Miniver, a courageous English lady who never lapsed into self-pity and right to the end maintained a vital interest in the sayings and doings of relatives and friends. I am proud to have known her and been able to have celebrated her requiem.

Radio and Television

During my years in Rome and especially at the end, I did many broadcasts for the English section of Vatican Radio (*On the Left Bank of the Tiber*, pp. 198–200). They continued to contact me by phone to speak—about Benedict XVI's second encyclical, *Spe Salvi* (November 2007), about John Paul II on the third anniversary of his death (April 2008), and about other papal events. But various branches of BBC took over as my radio outlet.

Around 9 a.m. on 4 February 2007, I went for the first time to studios very close to the Houses of Parliament to do a Sunday morning interview with BBC Radio Northern Island. The topic or topics discussed with the presenter in Belfast have left no trail behind, apart from experiencing the infectious enthusiasm of someone the Italians would call 'simpatico'. A year later he asked me to discuss the issues that prompted Cardinal Ratzinger (now Benedict XVI) to lay charges ten years earlier against the theology of Jacques Dupuis (30 March 2008). I had a good deal to say about the case (see *On the Left Bank of the Tiber*, pp. 213–51).

A little earlier in March 2008, an official Vatican course for priests who hear confessions had aired the need to remember what has been traditionally classified under the 'seven deadly sins', to take into account 'new' sins of failure in matters of social justice, and to encourage Catholics to confess their sins more regularly. Talk of the seven deadly sins enjoys a regular appeal. The idea of 'few confessions and new sins' caught the instant fancy of various branches of the BBC. It seemed to them like old subject-matter overtaken by intriguing new spin. As well as speaking for Radio Ulster, I did interviews with Radio Four, World Service (radio), a BBC online article, and World Service (TV).

Two programmes made me rethink the challenge presented by radio journalism. One was a Mass, broadcast by Radio Four from Our Lady and the English Martyrs, OLEM as it is locally identified in Cambridge (6 May 2007). The night before, the presenter and his crew took us through the demanding dress rehearsal of a liturgy that went out live the following morning. The other programme concerned an annual event that has never gone out of fashion with the media: the annual liquefaction of the blood of St Januarius, the patron saint of Naples. 'Please don't be too hard on the Neapolitans', I pleaded in an interview with two BBC journalists before they headed down to Naples (21 April 2009). 'The Neapolitans suffer so much—from the camorra, unemployment, the drug trade, and much else besides. The liquefaction of the blood of Januarius may be one of the few things to cheer them up each year.'

In Rome, the BBC had featured me frequently on TV, and in London I had to accept doing much less for my favourite means of communication. Pope Benedict supplied some of the occasions. In April 2008 I did three interviews for programmes covering his trip to the USA and, in particular, his speech at the UN and visit to Ground Zero. A year later (18 March 2009) I commented on his visit to Africa (Chapter 2 above).

Two TV events have never left my memory, one frustrating and the other delightful. A Sunday-morning BBC programme 'The Big Questions' was scheduled to discuss the devil, but the presenter spent most of the time playing up to the Oxford professor and celebrated atheist, Richard Dawkins (6 April 2008). A spring fall of snow caused the car bringing Dawkins to slip into a ditch. But it was hauled out and he arrived in time to be seated on a throne and proceed to bang on about there being no evidence for the existence of God. My hand signal was not recognized and I could not put the question. 'Professor Dawkins, did you decide to marry your wife simply on evidence?' The morning was saved for me, however, by a young Muslim journalist sitting next to me. Dawkins was rudely dismissive of a devout, black lady from the Caribbean, and the journalist cut in: 'Freedom of speech, yes. Freedom to abuse, no.'

Shortly before that wasted Sunday morning, the BBC had interviewed me over what some office in the Vatican had prescribed for the feast of St Patrick. In 2008, Easter Sunday came extremely early—on 23 March. The Vatican officials wanted the feast of the best-loved Irish saint to be celebrated not on the usual date, 17 March, which fell that year on the Monday of Holy Week. They fixed a date in the week before. 'I don't think the Vatican officials should get too agitated about the right date for celebrating St Patrick. It will be another hundred years or so before Easter comes so early.' For good measure, I pointed out how most Americans were sticking to 17 March, and that the usual contingents of Irish of all persuasions were heading for the marches and parties in Boston, New York, Savannah, and Washington. I quoted a Protestant leader from Northern Ireland, 'St Patrick was a fine evangelical and Ulster man'. I added: 'We should put those Vatican officials on notice about the ecumenical power of St Patrick. Don't touch a saint who once a year brings Catholics and Protestants together, as he does.'

The Nuncio and the Bishops

The papal nuncio to the UK lived right across the Wimbledon Common, and now and then asked for advice. In April 2008, for example, I revised an address he was to make at the West London Synagogue. Around that time he had received complaints about a book, *Catholic Social Justice. Theological and Practical Explorations*—specifically about the chapter by Fr. Tissa Balasuriya, a Sri Lankan theologian, who commented inaccurately and peevishly on Pope Benedict's first encyclical, 'God is Love'. In a long report to the nuncio, I pointed out how Balasuriya lapsed into inaccurate and unreasonable remarks, argued, however, that they expressed nothing 'against faith and morals'—if one wants to use that language—regretted that the editors had done harm to their book by including Balasuriya's chapter, and concluded by saying that the nuncio could pass on my letter to anyone at all. I never kept a copy of my report, but I did seize the opportunity to write a short review of the book for the first issue of *The Pastoral Review* in 2008.

In June 2007, the Congregation for the Doctrine of the Faith sent the presidents of episcopal conferences (and of the synods of Eastern Catholic Churches) a document, accompanied by an official commentary, to 'explain' the 'authentic' meaning of some expressions they had used in previous documents—in particular, the meaning of the teaching drawn from Vatican II that the one Church of Christ 'subsists' in the Catholic Church. At the request of Cardinal Cormac Murphy-O'Connor, president of the Episcopal Conference of England and Wales, I wrote a report against the CDF's attempt to limit the scope of this teaching. We can and should hold that the one Church of Christ continues to exist *fully* in the Catholic Church. But, in the light of teaching from Vatican II and Pope John Paul II, it is incorrect to follow the CDF in holding that the one Church of Christ continues to exist *only* in the Catholic Church. 'Fully' is not equivalent to 'only'. Appendix Three below reprints my (blunter) report for the cardinal. Appendix Four reproduces a 'gentler' article I wrote for the *Tablet* apropos of the CDF's attempt to control the meaning of 'subsistit in'.

The following November the Episcopal Conference of England and Wales received a forthcoming CDF document on evangelisation and once again asked me for comments. After delivering a four-page report (now lost), I once again took the opportunity to write an article for *The Tablet* (15 December 2007). Once again the report was blunter about defects in the CDF document, whereas the article, 'Softly,

Softly', tried to highlight some more attractive features, which in fact it did display.

In May 2008 I worked on a text the bishops of England and Wales were preparing: 'Meeting God in Friend and Stranger'. This teaching document, which aimed at fostering mutual respect and dialogue between religions, eventually appeared in 2010.

Another truly worthwhile invitation came from the bishops, asking me to represent them at a meeting of Anglo-German Christian leaders. Held on a glorious spring day in the divinity school at the University of Cambridge (29 May 2008) and including lunch at King's College, this meeting recalled the efforts made a hundred years before by some English and German professors and church leaders to avoid the outbreak of war between their two countries. This group which included members of different churches had gathered in both London and Berlin to meet the political leaders and press the cause of peace. On that spring day in Cambridge we honoured the memory of this group's commitment to a truly Christian cause, but felt renewed sadness over the Great War and its dreadful legacy.

Shortly before Christmas 2007, I was sitting at my desk in Wimbledon when the phone rang. Sky Television was downstairs with the latest breaking news: the previous evening the former Prime Minister, Tony Blair, had been received by Cardinal Murphy-O'Connor into the Catholic Church at a private ceremony. A few minutes later I was standing in front of the Sacred Heart Church, Wimbledon, and facing the questions. 'Why did Tony Blair become a Catholic right now?' 'I can't answer for him', I replied. 'But it's certainly a happy Christmas present for his wife and children. As you know, they're all Catholics.' 'Did you see this coming?' 'Well', I answered, 'we all did. For some time now, Tony Blair has obviously been thinking of becoming a Catholic.' I paused and added: 'Last evening I was at a reception with the Cardinal. He put his glass down and excused himself. He had another appointment, but didn't say what it was. I couldn't help noticing the happy twinkle in his eyes as he slipped away.' A few minutes later, I was back at my desk when the phone rang. 'Cormac here. Thank you, and happy Christmas.' That interview for Sky had been gratefully received by the bishops' conference and their president.

All That and More as well

This chapter has set out to describe what I did when based in Wimbledon from December 2006 to September 2009. Far from pottering around in retirement from age 75 to 78, I was busier than ever with speaking and writing.

One engagement took me as far as Australia. On 30 March 2007, the Melbourne College of Divinity flew me out to Melbourne to speak at their annual graduation ceremony and to award me an honorary doctorate. The Wilson Hall of the University of Melbourne looked its shining best that evening, with hundreds of cheerful students in their academic robes and with my own family filling the front row.

Many people combined to energize me during those three years in England: former students from Rome, Jesuits and other friends, Christians and those of other faiths, and all the people who gave life in London such a buzz. Cardinal Murphy-O'Connor seemed a warm and encouraging 'bookend'. When I arrived in Rome to teach full-time at the Gregorian in 1974, he was the rector of the Venerable English College, and now, over thirty years later, he was here in London to share with me a large bowl of pasta in Archbishop's House.

I made some encouraging discoveries, like an Anglican-inspired group of 35 spiritual directors who met in Chelmsford and asked me to give them two lectures—on prayer and images of prayer (29 November 2008). Their leader, an Anglican canon, by bringing together for study and reflection Anglican, Catholic, and Free Church directors, aimed to improve the standard of their ministry and reduce the incidence of irresponsible gurus.

I met again some people who had disappeared from my life for many years, like Priscilla Chadwick, the daughter of an inspiring and now deceased friend, Henry Chadwick (see *On the Left Bank of the Tiber*, pp. 62, 288–89). In my final year of doctoral studies at the University of Cambridge, she came up to read theology and became 'rag queen' or Miss University in her first year at Girton College. After graduating, Priscilla was active for many years in educational and ecumenical affairs. At a formal dinner concerned with values in public life, our host sat us next to other. He knew that we had nearly forty years of personal history to share.

Contacts with the London *Tablet* gave me the same sense of recapturing my Cambridge past. In the spring of 1968, when I was in the desperate, last stages of polishing my dissertation, the editor, Tom Burns, refused to take no for an answer. He wanted an article for the Easter number, and so initiated years of contributing to that weekly journal. Once I arrived in London in December 2006, I could easily attend *Tablet* functions, including the *Tablet* table, which met regularly for Mass, drinks, and a discussion over a plate of food. For the meeting on 3 May 2007, the current editor, Catherine Pepinster, invited me to evaluate what the Congregation for the Doctrine of the Faith had recently stated about the writing by Jon Sobrino, SJ, on the person and work of Jesus Christ: 'not in conformity with the doctrine of the Church'. His books contain passages (not specified) that were 'either erroneous or dangerous and may cause harm to the faithful'. Ironically this CDF document espoused at least three misleading and unjustified positions, as I pointed out that evening and subsequently in an article published by *America* magazine (see Appendix 5 below). Back in the 1970s and so in the pre-Ratzinger days, the CDF had investigated the writing of Sobrino. He had been vigorously defended by one of their consultors, Juan Alfaro, SJ, and the matter had been dropped. But in 2006–2007 the CDF lacked any consultor of Alfaro's stature and integrity (*On the Left Bank of the Tiber*, pp. 11–12), and the critics of liberation theologians could have their way.

The opening pages of this chapter mentioned giving the annual *Tablet* lecture just before I left London, published as 'I have seven dreams' (19 September 2009). After the lecture Catherine hosted a most cheerful dinner for some close friends, and presented me with an amusing, framed cartoon entitled 'O'Collins goes home'. I did fly home to Melbourne a week later, but, as we shall see, I kept coming back to London until 2012.

Leaving London, September 2009

4

Australian Re-Entry

Not having lived in Australia since 1973, I wondered about coping with re-entry. But the Jesuits, my family, and friends, both old and new, were clear-eyed about arranging a smooth repatriation. Their humanity, empathy, and compassion dealt with any difficulties.

The JTC, the UFT, the CTC, and the ACU
I was assigned to the Jesuit Theological College (the JTC), an institution which bordered on the University of Melbourne, comprised ten nineteenth-century, two-storeyed terrace houses, and cared for the intellectual and spiritual training of younger members of the Society of Jesus. Since the student body came from East Timor, Indonesia, Korea, Singapore, and Vietnam, as well as from Australia, the college gave me a sense of living in a smaller version of Rome's International College of the Gesù. In any case, the JTC was home territory, since I lived there from 1969 to 1973 (see *A Midlife Journey*, pp. 363–64).

I was also familiar with the United Faculty of Theology (UFT), situated across Royal Parade and on the edge of Ormond College's property. Its new Dalton-McCaughey Library, one of the very best theological resources in Australia, supplied my needs for research and allowed me to get on with a new project: *Rethinking Fundamental Theology: Toward a New Fundamental Theology* (Oxford: Oxford University Press, 2011). Fr Bill Dalton, SJ, and Dr Davis McCaughey had led the way in crafting the UFT, a teaching institution within the Melbourne College of Divinity (MCD, and now called the University of Divinity) comprising Anglican, Jesuit, and Uniting Church in Australia (UCA) teachers and students.

When I returned in September 2009, both Dalton and McCaughey were dead, but some other old colleagues were still active. Up to 1973 I had taught fundamental theology and Christology (or doctrine of Christ) with Professor Norman Young. It gave me deep joy to give the keynote lecture, 'Easter Grace', at a three-day conference organized in his honour (November 2010). The proceedings were

With group at the Jesuit Theological College, late 2009

published in Sean Winter (ed.), *Immense, Unfathomed, Unconfined. The Grace of God in Creation, Church, and Community: Essays in Honour of Norman Young* (Melbourne: Uniting Academic Press, 2013). One of the most loved and competent teachers at the UFT, Norman embodied the best of Methodist holiness; it was a delight to reconnect with him. The new, younger generation of professors included Chris Mostert. He was quick off the mark in asking me to give two lectures on the resurrection of Jesus for his course on Christology (23 March 2010). This initiated our habit of lunching together regularly to share our theological insights and questions—not to mention indulging nostalgic reminiscences of the University of Cambridge and German professors, like Jürgen Moltmann and Wolfhart Pannenberg.

After directing to a successful completion over ninety doctoral dissertations at the Gregorian University, I did not intend to take on again the role of *Doktorvater*. But I was glad to make two exceptions: Fr Simon Wayte, MGL, and Fra' Richard Divall. At the Australian National University in Canberra, Simon defended a brilliant doctorate in astrophysics. He then joined the Missionaries of Divine Love, was ordained, and, with a view to teaching at Catholic Theological College, began doctoral studies at CTC (a recognized teaching institution of the University of Divinity) with myself as co-supervisor. Since his commitments in his religious institute allowed for only part-time research, Simon is still completing his dissertation, a fascinating application of insights from modern science to the question of Christ's universal presence in our world.

Richard, also enrolled at CTC, had been a very successful conductor for the Victoria State Opera and for other orchestras, as well as an editor of sacred and profane music. He had received at least two honorary doctorates, but had never earned a degree in his life. A mutual friend and former governor of the State of Victoria, Sir James Gobbo, encouraged Richard to engage himself with some formally academic research. I agreed to be the co-director of a doctoral thesis on the sacred music of an eighteenth-century, Maltese composer, Nicolò Isouard. A recently retired professor of music from the University of Melbourne took on the musical side of the project, while I attended to the biblical and theological side of Richard's work. Two overseas examiners, one in the United Kingdom and the other in Malta, acclaimed an outstanding thesis, and I stood proudly with Richard when he received the PhD from the University of Divinity in May 2014.

By enlisting me as a magistral chaplain, the Order of Malta brought me into frequent contact with Richard, the only professed member in Australia and, for that matter, in the Southern Hemisphere. Hence his religious title of 'Fra''. He was constantly available to drive me to the church or institution when I celebrated the Eucharist for the Knights and Dames of Malta, led them on an annual retreat, or offered a 'Lourdes Day' Mass for the sick and elderly at day care centres or retirement homes around Melbourne. 'If they can't make the long journey to Lourdes', the leaders of the Order of Malta announced, 'we will bring Lourdes to them'. They imported cans of water from the shrine of the Blessed Virgin Mary at Lourdes, in the south of France. The Lourdes Day Masses provided memorable moments as I offered the old folk the chance of receiving the sacrament of the anointing of the sick, celebrated the Eucharist, and walked around sprinkling them with water from Lourdes before sharing refreshments with those present. The sick and elderly felt cheered by the sight of Richard and other members of the Order of Malta who had dropped their regular work and come in their traditional robes to spend a morning with them. When driving to these religious events, Richard enthralled me with stories of Dame Joan Hammond,[14] Sir Charles Mackerras, Luciano Pavarotti, Katia Ricciarelli, and other 'greats' in the story of modern music, or else filled his car with recordings from

---

14 After the death of Dame Joan, her rosary beads were bequeathed to Richard.

eighteenth-century sacred music from Malta or Naples. While some men like to sing under the shower, I prefer to be bathed in glorious sounds in Richard's Peugeot.

At the risk of piling on too many details about Fra' Richard, let me add that he also provided me with unforgettable musical moments. He delighted me when he conducted an opera in the Athenaeum, a nineteenth-century London-style, period-piece theatre right in the heart of Melbourne. It was Georges Bizet's *The Pearl Fishers*; at the end I was glad to see the soprano escaping with her lover, leaving the baritone sprawled dead on the stage. Richard also conducted at the finals of the Herald-Sun Aria competition in the Hamer Hall, the principal concert hall in Melbourne. Three young men and three young women sang two arias each. Their parents, relatives, friends, and supporters gave those finals a cheerful and exciting buzz.

For some years, even though I was not yet living back in Australia, the Australian Catholic University had put me on their books as an adjunct professor. Now the ACU welcomed me home by awarding me an honorary doctorate at a graduation ceremony in the Melbourne Town Hall (7 June 2010). The executive dean of philosophy and theology and networker 'supreme', Anne Hunt, built up fruitful overseas links for her faculty by securing honorary doctorates for notable church leaders who visited Australia, and by inviting as guest lecturers such outstanding scholars as Francis Clooney, SJ, (Harvard University), Steve Evans (Baylor University), Kevin Hart (University of Virginia), Alberto Melloni (University of Bologna), and Eleonore Stump (St Louis University). As part of her commitment to promote vigorously the study and implementation of the teaching of the Second Vatican Council, Anne joined forces with the Yarra Theological Union (YTU) in staging a conference fifty years after the Council opened (19–21 September 2012). I delivered a paper on Vatican II and other religious faiths. That paper anticipated an international theological meeting on interfaith dialogue which Anne supported at ACU (26–29

May 2014) and at which I spoke on 'Intercessory Prayer for Others'. At such meetings she deployed her skills as a charming hostess, made everyone welcome, and spread the sense of theology being one of the most exciting activities in the world. Like Michael Hayes (Chapter 3 above), she knew the value of encouraging 'golden oldies', or retired but still active professors, to join the ACU as adjunct professors. She recognized the value of prompting her 'team' into publishing in the best journals. From 2009 to early 2014, *Theological Studies*, arguably the top Catholic quarterly in the world, carried fifteen articles contributed by teachers of theology in Australia; thirteen of the articles came from ACU.

These opening pages of Chapter 4 have featured a series of acronyms, and, specifically, three-letter words formed from the initial words in the full name of some institution. Ordinary speech in Melbourne seems to revel in such three-letter acronyms—starting from the Melbourne Cricket Club (the MCC), one of the legendary sporting clubs in the world. But one acronym I spotted when driving around the inner city startled me: 'CDF'. For a wild moment I read that as 'the Congregation for the Doctrine of the Faith', and concluded: 'Ratzinger and his mates have opened a branch office out here'. 'No, it means "Catholic Development Fund"', my companion assured me. 'That's the general fund for the Archdiocese of Melbourne.' He paused and added teasingly: 'just because you're paranoid, it doesn't mean that they're not after you.'

No clean break

At a farewell dinner in September 2009, the London *Tablet* presented me with a cheerful cartoon, 'O'Collins goes home'. Well, yes and no. Back in Australia I continued to write for the *Tablet*, and began to publish articles regularly in *The Irish Theological Quarterly*. Contacts with Oxford University Press did not slacken. Occasionally I read proposals OUP had received from other authors, but more often I was in contact over my own books. In 2013 OUP published *The Second Vatican Council on Other Religions*, and produced a revised, paperback edition the following year. At Christmas 2014 OUP put out a new, expanded edition of *Catholicism: The Story of Catholic Christianity*, a book I had written with Mario Farrugia, a colleague at the Gregorian University, and originally published in 2003. In 2011 OUP came up with an enticing invitation to contribute to a work in collaboration they were about to publish: Gabriel Flynn and Paul D. Murray (eds.), *Ressourcement: A Movement for Renewal in Twentieth-Century Catholic Theology*. At the last minute, OUP noticed that, although many of the authors discussed in the volume had retrieved, from the past, themes which guided them in drafting and revising the documents of Vatican II, no chapter presented their input at the Council. OUP sent me the other contributions, and, with some valuable suggestions from Jared Wicks, I worked at high speed to write a chapter ('*Ressourcement* and Vatican II') describing and evaluating the contribution made by such leaders in '*ressourcement*' as Yves Congar, Jean Daniélou, Henri de Lubac, Karl Rahner, and others.

Relocating to Australia did nothing to reduce contacts with OUP or with Darton, Longman & Todd (DLT, London). They suggested writing a rapid response to a book about Jesus that made a great splash. To much fanfare and on time for Easter 2010 and the Christian celebration of the resurrection, Philip Pullman, a master of fantasy fiction, published *The Good Man Jesus and the Scoundrel Christ*, an historical novel about Jesus (who died on the cross) and his (alleged) twin brother Christ, a spin doctor who fabricated the resurrection and embellished the story of Jesus to further the ambitions of church leaders. In his review for the *Financial Times*, Cole Moreton pointed out the deep irony here. Pullman embroidered the life of Jesus 'to reflect his conviction that there is no God'. Hence 'one could just as easily say the spin doctor is Pullman himself' (12 April 2010). By August the same year, DLT had published my *Philip Pullman's Jesus* and decked it out with a white cover embossed with gold—in imitation of Pullman's own book. But Pullman himself refused to be drawn into an argument. Very few reviewers took up my response, apart from Alison Flood writing in the *Guardian* (14 August 2010). The following month, on the occasion of Pope Benedict's visit to the UK, the *Guardian* ran an article by me, 'Living next door to the Pope', my memories of him from the long summer of 1968. I remain grateful to that paper for its interest. But no one else in the media joined forces with the *Guardian*, and, to the disappointment of DLT, *Philip Pullman's Jesus* went nowhere.

Relocating to Australia did nothing to diminish my publishing activity in the USA. Paulist Press produced a third edition of a widely used book that I had written with Edward G. Farrugia, SJ, *A Concise Dictionary of Theology* (2013), as well as a second edition of *The Tripersonal God: Understanding and Interpreting the Trinity* (2014). They maintained their long-standing support by publishing three new books of mine: *Believing in the Resurrection* (2011), *Pause for Thought: Making Time for Prayer, Jesus and God* (2011), and *The Spirituality of the Second Vatican Council* (2014). Liturgical Press (Collegeville, Minn.) became another American publishing house to take on what I have written, when they put out *The Second Vatican Council: Message and Meaning* (2014). They did a very generous amount of editorial work in preparing the manuscript for publication. I dedicated the book to 43 friends and colleagues 'who continue to contribute towards understanding and promoting the Council's teaching'. Baylor University Press (Waco, Texas), now headed by Carey Newman, a Baptist colleague who shared with me all four 'summit' conferences held in New York (*On the Left Bank of the Tiber*, pp 290–95), accepted for publication in 2015 a collection of essays, *Christology: Origins, Developments, Debates*. They too proved generous and painstaking in preparing the manuscript. I dedicated the book to all my Baptist friends in Australia, the United States, and elsewhere.

An invitation came to contribute to an ecumenical work in collaboration published in the US: James K. Beilby and Paul Rhodes Eddy (eds.), *Justification: Five Views* (Downers Grove, Il.; IVP Academic, 2011). Jim Beilby was also a co-editor (with Chad Meister) of *The Routledge Companion to Modern Christian Thought* (2013). In this case they asked me to contribute the entry on 'Christology'.

With 'Peter as Witness to Easter' (2012), I began once again publishing articles with *Theological Studies*. When Dan Kendall took over as the review editor of that quarterly, I started accepting even more books for review. I continued to contribute to *America* (April and October 2012 and August 2014), and was happily astonished by the magazine's extraordinarily positive review of *On the Left Bank of the Tiber* (24 November, 2014).

Overseas trips

The 'going home' theme of the *Tablet* cartoon did not signal reducing contacts with publishers in the British Isles or North America, let alone quietly breaking them off. Nor did it signal the end of overseas trips. Let me recall five of them.

In April 2010, I flew to London to chair a meeting at the Randolph Hotel in Oxford for the Templeton Foundation's Humble Approach Initiative. The goal of the initiative was to bring about the discovery of new spiritual knowledge by furthering high-quality scientific research. Just a year before this foundation had invited fourteen scientists and theologians to a symposium in Istanbul. The conversation drew together these scholars to share insights and research on a theme linked to core issues in both theology and science: light, and 'light from light'. Our follow-up in Oxford put the last touches on a volume, edited by Mary Ann Meyers and myself and published by Eerdmans as *Light from Light: Scientists and Theologians in Dialogue* (2012). The glories of ancient Constantinople and modern Istanbul gave some vigour and verve to our meeting on the Bosphorus. But an 'act of God' affected the meeting in Oxford. The ash from a volcanic eruption in Iceland cancelled flights across the Atlantic and Europe. Several participants could not arrive and share a debate, which was, nevertheless, encouraged and energized by the beauty of springtime in Oxford.

The cloud of ash eventually dissipated, and I was able to fly out of London in time to join my fellow author, Fr. Michael Keenan Jones, in his Connecticut parish to launch the book we had co-authored, *Jesus Our Priest* (see Chapter 3 above). Over two hundred copies were sold—making this the most successful book launch in my publishing life. A genial host, Mike's circle of friends and acquaintances extended everywhere. He was generosity personified, and always made his parish house a true home for me.

(2) The following October I returned to the USA, flying into San Francisco and staying briefly with Dan Kendall in the Jesuit residence at the University of San Francisco, a new, hill-top building featuring strong hints of Tuscan style and incorporating an exquisite garden that looked towards the Golden Gate bridge. Some time before, the Dalai Lama, when speaking in San Francisco, had stayed for a few days in the rooms I occupied. I hoped that sleeping in the same bed and using the same bathroom might stir in me some mystical contemplation. But I have remained solidly non-Buddhist.[15] The

---

15 A year or two before leaving Rome in 2006, I had been asked to co-direct a retreat in Florence with the Dalai Lama. To my intense regret, I had to decline. The retreat was scheduled for the first days of June, and would have meant missing the last day of lectures at the Gregorian University—a day when nervous students were anxious to have a final contact with the professor before the examinations and so hear possible hints about the questions that were to come up.

university church also served the parish of St Ignatius. I earned my keep by giving a lecture on 'Jesus Our Friend' to the people of the parish, a sympathetic group of lively Californians.

From San Francisco I flew on to New York and lectured on the priesthood of Jesus to priests of the archdiocese at St Joseph's Seminary, Dunwoodie, very familiar to me from the four 'summits'

With Michael Jones, chaplain on a visiting cruise ship, 2011

I co-chaired there (1996, 1998, 2000, and 2003). I sold my dream of Jesus' priesthood to an audience that included the former Archbishop of New York, Cardinal Edward Egan, and his successor, Archbishop Timothy Dolan, whom I knew very well from his years as rector of the North American College in Rome. At his classic residence in New York City, Tim now hosted a dinner, made a bitter-sweet occasion by the presence of a dear friend and benefactor, Dr Eugene McCarthy. Gaunt and desperately ill, Gene died some weeks later of cancer. He and his late wife Maureen had funded the four 'summit' meetings at St Joseph's—not to mention chairs for visiting professors in Rome (see *On the Left Bank of the Tiber*, pp 188–89, 288–91). That 'last supper' with Gene brought down the curtain on my many experiences of vibrant life in the Big Apple that had begun in late 1968. I was to pour my memories of Maureen and Gene into an article for the first number in 2011 of *The Pastoral Review*, 'Living the Sacrament of Matrimony', reproduced as Appendix Six below. I had already written about them in 'The Prayer of One Couple', *Reflections for Busy People: Making Time for Ourselves, Jesus, and God* (Mahwah, NJ: Paulist Press, 2009), pp. 10–12.

After the dinner at the Archbishop's residence, Mike Jones drove me up to his parish in Huntington, Connecticut. A couple of days later we moved north to the Viking Hotel in Newport, Rhode Island, and what paid for my final visit to the USA: a convocation for two hundred priests of the Bridgeport Diocese. My brief was to lecture on the priesthood, as well as preach a homily and share in a panel discussion on the same topic—my final speaking engagement for the 'Year of the Priest'. The scene of so many challenges for the America's Cup and of finals for the Davis Cup, Newport was bathed in delightful 'fall' weather and still thronged by tourists. The old hotels, the colonial buildings, and the sea evoked images of a glittering past centred on yachting and tennis.

The convocation offered me a rare chance of learning what works in the parish life of Catholics in New England. The experiences and ideals of the priests came alive over the three days.

'Being available for people in need is everything', Steve insisted. 'They are so grateful when their parish priest picks up the phone late at night and answers a sick call. That's what priests are for—to be ready to visit the sick and dying at any hour of day or night.' Steve ran a town-centre parish. His friend Paul, a country pastor, chipped in: 'In the winter those calls have the habit of coming at 2 a.m., when it's been snowing heavily.'

Steve told me of his young parochial vicar or curate: 'Recently he gave so much comfort to a woman, her husband and her family by being there day after day at her bedside before she died.' He explained how death had come to her: 'She went to a clinic for a routine colonoscopy, and the surgeon failed to notice that he had pierced the colon. After a week of agony, she died of peritonitis.'

Inevitably the Sacrament of Penance turned up on the agenda. 'You must schedule it at a convenient time', Mike assured me. 'That means making it available right before or right after the Saturday vigil Mass. Many people won't go to confession if it involves coming to church twice on Saturdays—once in the morning for the Sacrament of Reconciliation and once in the late afternoon for the Eucharist. On Sundays I hear confessions before the main Mass. That also works well for many parishioners.'

Mike talked too of what a difference it makes when the priest's house or rectory becomes a place of welcome. His predecessor had kept the blinds drawn and as many lights out as possible. Now the windows are open and the lights blaze into the night. The parish council meets there regularly, as well as members of the board of the primary school. At Christmas and on other occasions Mike also hosts receptions and meals for parishioners.

Other priests spelled out what they did for the religious and biblical education of their people. Marty tackled the religious education of his parish's children in three ways. 'For some who attend public or state schools, there are classes two or three times a week in the afternoon. For others, I arranged intensive courses at the beginning or the end of the summer holidays. We call them Emmaus programmes.' 'What', I asked him, 'about children with special needs? ' 'We work with the parents', he told me. 'They are the best educators of their children, and particularly in these cases.'

John astonished me with the success of his Bible study groups. 'There are six of these groups, including one for youth and one on Saturday morning just for men.' 'How did you manage all that?' I enquired. 'I got hold of a great facilitator, a man whose business is advertising. He was surprised when I asked him. But he had the expertise to make the groups take off and continue to work well. The people find how the Scriptures are a great path to God. Those Bible study groups have practical results. I never lack readers and altar servers for Mass.' Part of the secret for John's success came out when he admitted: 'The parishioners know that every night I read a page of the gospels slowly before I go to bed.'

Tensions in the church naturally came up for discussion. '"Liberals" and "conservatives" are two containers in which we put our anxieties', Ron told me. 'We have to stop talking *about* each other and start talking *to* each other. You have to give those who differ from you the credit of loving Jesus and the Church as much as you do.'

Ron pressed the need for better-prepared homilies: 'We have a *pulpit* problem, not an *altar* problem. People don't understand what happens in the Eucharist when they don't learn what they should from the pulpit.'

Other priests shared with me the painful challenge that may come from parents whose children lead an 'alternate and even dysfunctional existence'. 'Because their children live in ways that don't match their own family's expectations and the Church teaching, parents can get very upset. Some parents take it out on the parish by disowning Catholicism', said one of them.

Many priests spoke of the moving, grace-filled occasions they experienced on parish pilgrimages to Lourdes and elsewhere. The most poignant stories came from one priest who had recently taken a group to El Salvador, where they visited Tierra Bianca, a country village ravaged by twelve years of civil war.

Wilbur, one of those who lived in the village, showed the visiting party a tree trunk where government soldiers stood when they killed a ten-year-old boy and ripped his body apart with machine-gun fire. Then Wilbur pointed to a small cross: 'That's where one of our saints is buried'. When the soldiers identified the mother of two teenage boys who had joined the resistance, they took her out into a field and skinned her alive, and chopped off her arms and feet. Wilbur added: 'We heard them laughing as she was screaming'.

The visiting priest asked him: 'Since you know where those soldiers now live, why don't you want to kill them?' Wilbur was taken aback and replied: 'No, we help one another to forgive because we follow Jesus. If we were to kill them, we would be like what they once were.' The visitors burst into tears and stood trying to grasp the amazing gift of forgiveness that following Jesus can bring.

The three days at the Newport convention let me hear ideals that parish priests embrace about availability, schedules that suit the parishioners, hospitality, and homilies. I learned of programmes in religious and biblical education that work well, and of the powerful impact that pilgrimages can have on parishioners.

Over the years, many people have asked me: where will new life for parishes come from? Some inspiring answers to that question came from the experiences and hopes which priests shared with me during three lovely autumn days in Newport, Rhode Island.

When the convocation ended, a priest whom I had taught at the Gregorian University drove me up to Logan Airport, Boston. He apologized for dropping me off well before my flight departed. But those hours enabled me to share on TV with a billion other viewers around the world the rescue of thirty-three miners in Northern Chile. They had been trapped seven hundred metres underground for sixty-nine days. Seventeen days after a copper-gold mine collapsed, a bore hole contacted the miners and established that they were all still alive. But then it took more than seven weeks to create a tunnel for the escape capsule. Tears streamed down my face, when on 13 October 2010 I watched some of them being winched to safety one after another, in an operation that took nearly twenty-two hours. I was seeing the best human technology at work in the service of saving, not destroying, human lives.

(3) Another Templeton Foundation conference—this time on the incarnation of the Son of God— took me in August 2011 to Denmark and a meeting with theologians and philosophers in Helsingør, known to the world as Elsinore through Shakespeare's masterpiece. From the hotel where we met, we looked along the shore towards Hamlet's castle, which was struck by lightning on the last night of our conference. For a mad moment I wondered whether God was 'fulminating' against our proceedings. The storm was an unforeseen, spectacular backdrop to the discussion of how the coming of Christ changed our world.

(4) The British Province of the Society of Jesus extended the range of my experience by inviting me to lecture in the Republic of South Africa (16 July–15 August 2010), under the auspices of the Jesuit Institute of South Africa and the South African Bishops' Conference. The organizers packed as much as possible into the month: twelve lectures on Jesus Christ's identity and redemptive work delivered, successively, as mini-courses for priests, religious, and lay people in Johannesburg, Bloemfontein, Cape Town, and Durban. In

Bloemfontein, I gave a stand-alone lecture ('Trends in Christology') to the theology students at the Free State University. The month slid past quickly and happily, thanks to the hospitality of local Catholics and to the population's general sense of cheerful success. South Africa had just hosted efficiently the World Cup in soccer.

I had flown into Johannesburg and went back there (by road from Durban) for the return flight to Australia. In many ways the visit to South Africa took me well and truly out of my comfort zone. Yes, there were former students from Rome and others whose welcome provided a happy bridge with the past. The main challenge came through engaging and communicating with audiences shaped by the events of the Apartheid and post-Apartheid situations. An immensely satisfying Sunday rounded off the whole month.

A friend drove me out from Johannesburg to Soweto to visit the homes of Nelson Mandela and Bishop Desmond Tutu and spend time in a museum commemorating the struggle for freedom. Since Mandela and Tutu lived on the same street, it was, and probably still is, the only street in the world boasting two Nobel laureates. The museum featured a film on Steve Biko, the activist murdered by the security forces in 1977, to whose memory I dedicated my first book in Christology, *Interpreting Jesus* (London: Geoffrey Chapman, 1983). My friend took me to concelebrate the Eucharist in the Church of St Martin de Porres. Alive with energy, the packed congregation enjoyed two choirs: an adult choir and a youth choir. Throughout the whole service, their liturgy combined the devotion, exuberance, and vivid unity of the congregation. The offering of gifts put in the shade what I have often sat through in Australia, the UK, the USA, and elsewhere, when quiet organ music is played while the collection 'plates' move silently around to collect donations of money. In St Martin de Porres, lively music accompanied the parishioners as they danced up to the altar with various gifts: not only money and bottles of wine (to be used for 'communion under both kinds'), but also food for the poor and some thoroughly practical gifts like rolls of toilet paper. From being a mere interlude in the service, they charged the offering of the gifts with life and a deep sense of reality.

(5) In October 2012, on the occasion of fifty years since the opening of the Second Vatican Council (1962–65), the Diocese of Portsmouth invited me to stay in Winchester, and deliver lectures on the Council's teaching in different centres across the diocese: to lay people, religious, priests, and the incoming bishop, Philip Egan, a former student from Rome. At the parish in Basingstoke, George and Eileen Carey joined me for lunch and stayed on for the afternoon session. It was a delight to catch up with them, and I was particularly grateful to George for leading the first session after lunch. He reflected on the value of Vatican II's teaching, and shared his affection for Pope John Paul II. Some weeks earlier George had received an ugly, threatening letter from one of the parishioners who warned him not to come. George laughed it off, and in the event the Catholic parishioners showed their deep pleasure at having the former Archbishop of Canterbury and his wife come to visit them.

From Basingstoke I slipped down to Gloucestershire to spend the weekend with two dear friends, Martin and Tessa de Bertodano. Their tall and beautiful daughter Sylvia, now a judge, and wonderful husband Stuart, soon to become a QC, drove over from Oxfordshire with their four small children. Years before in the private chapel of Hendred House, a late medieval home in the Vale of the White Horse, I had celebrated the wedding of Sylvia and Stuart, and later, in London and elsewhere, christened Maymie, Corin, Roualeyn, and Tallis. When my judgement day arrives, I will be proud to say to our loving God: 'I did the wedding for Sylvia and Stuart and baptized their two girls and two boys'.

The glorious October weather seemed designed specifically to enhance my two-week stay in England, which closed with a stopover in London. Heythrop College gathered 150 people for an evening lecture on the changes brought by the Second Vatican Council—a preview of an article about to appear in *Theological Studies*, 'Does the Second Vatican Council Represent Continuity or Discontinuity?'

With George and Eileen Carey, and, below, with George Carey, 2012

The Second Vatican Council

That article in *Theological Studies* signalled my renewed interest in re-reading, interpreting, and applying the documents of Vatican II. Shortly before the October 2012 visit to the UK, I had already been speaking on the Council to audiences in Canberra, Melbourne, and Sydney. The following year quickly brought fresh invitations to present and rethink Vatican II—from mid-January to late October 2013, and for diverse groups of Catholics and other Christians in Bendigo, Melbourne (repeatedly), Perth, and Sydney. Many Catholics recognized that the reforms mandated by the Council had been largely followed through 'ad extra', or beyond the Church: in relations with other Christians, with those of other living faiths, and with those of no religious faith at all. But 'ad intra', in the inner life of the Catholic Church, they felt that the teaching of the Council on such matters as the reform of the liturgy and the practice of 'collegiality' (or shared decision making) had been stolen from them by some leaders in the Church and groups who walked the corridors of power.

As well as lecturing on Vatican II right through 2013, I published articles on the Council's teaching in *Asian Horizons* (an Indian journal), *Pacifica* (an Australian journal), and *The Pastoral Review* (Twickenham, UK). One article, 'Was the Teaching of the Second Vatican Council Nourished and Guided by the Word of God', appeared in German in the *Theologische Quartalschrift Tübingen* 193 (2013), pp. 116–40. For the sake of those who do not read German, I reprinted an English version of that article in *The Second Vatican Council: Message and Meaning* (Collegeville, Minn.: Liturgical Press, 2014). That book also contained a chapter on '*Sacrosanctum Concilium* as a Hermeneutical Key for Vatican II', the result of discussions about the view of Massimo Faggioli, an Italian scholar now living and lecturing in the USA. He had suggested that the very first document of Vatican II, the Constitution on the Sacred Liturgy of 4 December 1963, prepared the way for the teaching that was to come in subsequent conciliar documents. The

Council's 'law of praying (*lex orandi*)' was a key for those who interpret its 'law of believing (*lex credendi*)—in seven themes where he found this dynamic operating. I added five more themes, and also included something that needed attention: rules for interpreting the texts of Vatican II.

In June 2013 the national assembly of the Order of Malta took place in Melbourne, and I spoke to the Knights and Dames, plus some of their relatives and friends, on the spiritual 'invitations' to be found in the teaching of the Council. The positive reaction to this presentation prompted me to write *The Spirituality of the Second Vatican Council* (Mahwah, NJ: Paulist Press, 2014), a book that the publishers decked out with a delicately beautiful cover that shows windows opening onto an enchanting garden.

Thinking and publishing on Vatican II also brought into play its teaching on other living faiths. Above I mentioned my 2013 book, *The Second Vatican Council on Other Religions*, which went beyond the ground-breaking Declaration on the Relation of the Church to Non-Christian Religions (*Nostra Aetate* of 28 October 1965) to include much relevant teaching from other conciliar documents. It is at our peril that we dodge what those other texts say, right through to the Pastoral Constitution on the Church in the Modern World (*Gaudium et Spes* of 7 December 1965). What Vatican II taught on 'the others' has already had a game-changing impact on the life of the Catholic Church and her relationship with those of other faiths or none at all. Yet many commentators still need to take on board the full scope of that teaching.

The Second Vatican Council on Other Religions, after examining the Council's documents, added two further chapters, respectively, on the teaching of John Paul II about other religions and the theology of Jacques Dupuis (and what he came eventually to call 'inclusive pluralism'). The Pope's vision of the universal presence and activity of the Holy Spirit found a certain counterpart in Dupuis's views on the Trinitarian face of the divine grace being mediated to all people. Inevitably, I found myself in debate, both about the teaching of Vatican II and the theology of Dupuis, with Gavin D'Costa, a professor of Catholic theology at the University of Bristol.

D'Costa bulked large in the authors considered in 'Jacques Dupuis: The Ongoing Debate', *Theological Studies* 74 (2013), pp. 632–54, my article that reported and critiqued some of what had been written about Dupuis's theology of the religions since his death in December 2004. Along with the article in *Theological Studies*, I also published an article disputing D'Costa's attempt to label (and dismiss?) Dupuis as a neo-Rahnerian, someone who (merely?) took up reflection on other religions where Karl Rahner (1904–1984) had left off: 'Was Jacques Dupuis a Neo-Rahnerian', *Asian Horizons* 7 (2013), pp. 568–81. In elaborate detail I rejected this thesis and expressed my agreement with Frank Clooney: Rahner and Dupuis are two outstanding theologians, who stand alongside each other and 'balance claims to Christian uniqueness with a necessary openness to learning from other religions' (Clooney).

In *The Tablet* for 22 June 2013, D'Costa reviewed William Burrows (ed.), *Jacques Dupuis Faces the Inquisition* (Eugene, OR: Pickwick Publications, 2013), which contained two hitherto unpublished essays that Dupuis wrote in reaction to the CDF's painful investigation of his theology of religions and to their declaration on Christ's unique and universal work as Saviour, *Dominus Iesus* (see *On the Left Bank of the Tiber*, pp. 213–51). In his review D'Costa claimed that Dupuis 'failed convincingly to address four of the eight questions he had received from the CDF' and that 'ambiguities persist in Dupuis' corpus'. In a letter to *The Tablet* (6 July 2013), I rejected these judgments, referred readers to my fully deployed rebuttal, argued that 'the ambiguities and plain mistakes persist in what D'Costa himself has written about Dupuis', and added:

At the end of his review D'Costa correctly points out that all the evidence about the Dupuis case is not yet available. This leads him to suggest that 'some of the speculation in this [Burrows's] book might verge on slander.' Having been from the outset Dupuis's official consultor, I read the two sets of accusations he received from the CDF, helped him prepare his (written) responses, spoke for him when we finally met Cardinal Ratzinger on 4 September 2000 (a meeting at which, incidentally, no transcripts were recorded), and in other ways shared as an insider in the whole affair. Far from verging on 'slander', what Burrows has written in introducing and commenting on the two essays by Dupuis is thoroughly accurate. He tends, in fact, to assess the actions of the protagonists in the Dupuis affair in a kindlier fashion than some of them deserve.

A forthcoming issue of *Theological Studies* will introduce a footnote in the debate with D'Costa—my review of his *Vatican II: Catholic Doctrines on Jews & Muslims* (Oxford: Oxford University Press, 2014). A radical problem with the book is his refusal to accept doctrinal discontinuity in official teaching about those of other living faiths. This refusal sits uneasily with his willingness to recognize different grades of authority in Church teaching. Discontinuity does not affect the most authoritative teaching expressed in the Nicene and Apostles' Creed. In less authoritative areas, including official teaching about those of other faiths, historical evidence establishes a range of (thoroughly justified rather than embarrassing) discontinuities.

By the time I wrote that review, however, further research and reflection had taken me to three conclusions that go beyond Dupuis, D'Costa, and other writers on the theology of religions. First, no matter what their particular conclusions, their mode of interpreting the Vatican II documents has unilaterally privileged the authors who framed those texts. This has been a mistake. The interpretation (and implementation) of the Council's texts should respect but press beyond the authorial intentions of the original drafters to unfold the meaning of these texts *as such*, and the meaning they have *also* received from successive generations of readers in successively new contexts. Thus those who interpret the Vatican II documents should honour the priority of the *texts* themselves, as well as paying attention to the *readers* of those texts, the *contexts* in which they have been read (and implemented), and the *authors* who crafted the texts at the Council. To do all this would be to fall into line with literary critics, philosophers, biblical scholars, and canon lawyers; they emphatically do not limit their interpretation to what they can establish about the intentions of the original authors. Readers interested in this issue could consult Appendix Seven below.

The second, new insight that enriched my thinking about those who follow 'other' religions faiths or none at all focused on something widely neglected in Christian theology, *the priesthood of Christ*. The Letter to the Hebrews must encourage us to confess not only 'of his kingship there is no end' but also 'of his priesthood there is no end'. His never-ending priestly intercession for all human beings should have a key role to play when Christians ponder the situation of those who follow 'other' paths. The theology of religions would move beyond the dull discussions in which it currently seems stuck if it came to honour Christ's priestly activity for the good of all human beings. It is supremely at the Eucharist that the faithful can actively participate in this loving activity of Christ.

That brings me to a third insight about something consistently ignored in the theology of religions: *the power of love*, inspiring not merely doing things for others but also *praying for others*. The Christian tradition provides huge resources for thinking about the efficacious power of love and the nature of the prayer of intercession that love inspires. Theologians who write about 'other' religions would benefit enormously if they were to tap into these resources.

I have made out a case for bringing into the theology of religions the priesthood of Christ and the efficacious love deployed in intercessory prayer: 'The Church and the Power of Prayer for "the Others"', *Horizons* 41 (2014), pp. 211–29.[16] But it will be a hard sell. Many theologians, in whatever field of theology, are reluctant to modify their views; like old friends, these views have long become familiar to them and even part of them.

Lecturing to New Audiences

The invitations that followed my return to Melbourne in September 2009 made my work in Australia an extension of the three years in the UK. The new audiences looked for reflection on three topics: Jesus, his priesthood, and the Second Vatican Council. Sometimes they gave a mind-expanding setting or twist to these familiar themes.

One evening a large pub in a Melbourne suburb, Yarraville, hosted over a hundred people to hear me speak on 'Who is Jesus? Does it matter?' (16 March 2010). The following day thirty priests came to an afternoon session in Corpus Christi Seminary on 'preaching the death and resurrection of Jesus'. The Irish priest responsible for clergy in service training thought that an appropriate way to spend the afternoon of St Patrick's Day.

At a centre next to St Patrick's Cathedral, around 230 people heard me speak on 'Jesus Our Priest' (19 May). This Cardinal Knox Lecture for 2010, which commemorated annually the founder of Catholic Theological College, seemed more than a merely straightforward occasion. Theology had been the occupation of my lifetime, spent largely overseas. Here was a chance for the home public to decide whether my later work was proving a development or a decline.

This sense of being assessed returned the following month when

---

16 See also 'The Priesthood of Christ and the Followers of Other Faiths', *Irish Theological Quarterly* 78 (2013), pp. 262–78.

I spoke on the ordained priesthood to a convocation of 120 priests of the Melbourne Archdiocese held at the Mercure Hotel in Geelong. Many of the older ones had taken my courses years before when they were studying at Corpus Christi Seminary; some of the younger ones had attended my lectures at the Gregorian University in Rome. The lecture put on display for them my current view of theology and church life—but only indirectly. I spoke about priests, like someone I identified simply as 'Fr Luke', whom I had come to know and admire in Rome and around the world.

Luke worked for thirty years as a prison chaplain in a country that enforced capital punishment. He attended hangings, standing on the gallows next to the condemned men and holding their hands before they were dropped with a rope around their necks. He remembered vividly the precise number of executions he witnessed—fifty-eight— as well as many details of what led up to each hanging. He knew how barbaric and useless the hangings were. Somehow, before the men died, he managed to reconcile to God every one of the condemned. I think it was the unaffected goodness and simplicity which shone from his rough-hewn face that touched all those hearts. No one has ever taught me more about human compassion.

A day-long e-conference on 'Jesus the Christ', broadcast on 16 September 2010 for the Australian Catholic Bishops from the Broken Bay Institute (Pennant Hills, Sydney), linked me and the others on the panel with audiences around Australia and beyond. The organizers showed a great feel for the practical. The day became a two-way process, as many groups and individuals rapidly e-mailed their questions and comments and the organizers skilfully classified them. These responses persistently set aside superficial matters and penetrated into the deep issues that the person and work of Christ raise. After engaging with as many concerns as possible, I finished by professing my own faith: 'Jesus is Lord. Jesus is King. Jesus is our everything.'

A year of lecturing about Jesus ended with a long day, 10 November. The day began with a breakfast attended by 70 parishioners of Hawthorn (Melbourne) at the Kooyong Tennis Club. My brief was to address the theme, 'Following Jesus in Post-Modern Australia'. The day ended 150 kilometres away, north-west of Melbourne, when I spoke on 'Jesus and the Homeless' for the St Vincent de Paul Society in Bendigo. Again around 70 people attended. In the event, the lecture went out to a much larger audience when some British Jesuits and their lay collaborators picked up the text and put it on their website for 'Thinking Faith' (3 February 2011). In the middle of the Northern Hemisphere winter, they were keen to promote reflection on the homeless and action on their behalf. The picture of Jesus 'sleeping rough' and dying in total destitution could help that cause.

Destitution and the further challenge of distance confronted me in May 2011, when 20 priests from the Diocese of Port Pirie attended a two-day course on the life, death and resurrection of Jesus that I offered at Sevenhill. This Jesuit centre of spirituality is around 130 kilometres north of Adelaide, where the boundary of the Adelaide Archdiocese touches the Diocese of Port Pirie.

Three times the size of Italy, the Diocese of Port Pirie runs up into the centre of Australia. It takes in Uluru (or Ayers Rock), and Woomera where the population has fallen to around 400 after peaking at 7,000 during its days as a rocket test site and then as a notorious detention centre for asylum seekers. The parish of Woomera runs east to Andamooka, where open cut opal mines support a population of around 600. Copper, gold, and uranium deposits have put Roxby Downs on the map. Taking on long shifts at the mines, the workers fly in and out of town. They are well paid, but their lifestyle can put a disastrous strain on their marriages and families. There is a cemetery, but it lacks graves because Roxby Downs is a town no one calls home.

Artificial opals now threaten the opal mining that created Coober

Pedy, a town halfway between Adelaide and Alice Springs, which is famous for its below-ground residences built to cope with the fierce summer temperatures. Like many others, Paul lived in a dugout. His parish church was also underground. 30 years ago, Paul served as the parish priest of Coober Pedy. When he returned around Christmas 2010, he found how little had changed. Fringe dwellers were still sitting under peppercorn trees right outside his dugout. He was greeted with a 'G'day, Paul' by someone he had last met away to the south, in a large gaol at Port Augusta.

For Paul, being there for the fringe dwellers and others made some sense and some difference. Like Jesus, he said, the least we can do is to offer people our presence.

The southern part of the Diocese of Port Pirie includes much fertile country, but parish life there also has its problems. One priest told me he is sometimes asked by the farmers to pray for rain, at a time when the 'blockies' who run vineyards don't want rain. His answer is to pray that water will be supplied and properly used.

Led by the only Jesuit bishop in Australia, Greg O'Kelly, the priests were proud of their strong links with Mother Mary MacKillop (1842–1909). She opened 22 primary schools in the immense northern stretches of South Australia. The diocese celebrated her canonization in October 2010, and on 19 March 2011 declared her to be, along with the Blessed Virgin Mary, their co-patron. Pilgrimages bring visitors to the scenes of her ministry, and regularly to Sevenhill, the bush parish where she founded a school and came to visit her younger brother, Donald MacKillop.

He was one of the earliest Australian-born Jesuits, studying at the Sevenhill College, the first Catholic boarding school for boys outside Sydney. It opened in 1856 and closed in 1886 after other Catholic high schools were established in Adelaide, Melbourne, and elsewhere. From 1863 to 1885, it also operated as a Jesuit novitiate, student house, and seminary that produced 16 diocesan priests. The first student to be ordained was Julian Tenison Woods. This learned and impulsive priest played a key role in helping Mother Mary found a religious institute, the Sisters of St Joseph, but then proved a thorn in her side.

The Jesuit presence in Australia and at Sevenhill began in December 1848, when a German sailing ship landed two Austrian priests in Adelaide. Fr Aloysius Kranewitter left Fr Maximilian Klinkostroem to work with new settlers in Adelaide and pushed north to the Clare Valley. He wanted to establish another 'little Rome'—a Catholic centre on a country site with seven hills. He followed German spelling by calling it Sevenhill (*Siebenhügel*), and gave the name of the Tiber to a stream that ran though the property. The bush mission was supported by other Jesuits, who anglicised their first names and learned English fast.

A vineyard was planted in 1851, the first winery in the Clare Valley, which now has around 40 wineries. They include Good Catholic Girl Wines, which boasts that it harvests its grapes on St Patrick's Day to secure an extra blessing from on high. Sevenhill Cellars, the only ecclesiastical winery in Australia, sells altar wines to Christian Churches across Australia, New Zealand, and Asia. After more than 50 years at the winery, Brother John May still leads tours of Sevenhill but is now winemaker emeritus. When Pope John Paul II celebrated Mass in Adelaide in 1986, it was Br May as a national treasure who joined the procession at the offering of the gifts and carried a carafe of wine up to the altar.

Before the Diocese of Port Pirie was established in 1887, the Jesuit mission at Sevenhill ran right up to Palmerston North, long ago renamed Darwin. For 29 years, 19 Jesuits worked on the Daly River aboriginal mission. The Austrian fathers and brothers built 24 churches in what is now the territory of the Port Pirie Diocese. Four or five times a year, Fr Pallhuber made a 1,000-mile round trip deep into the north and right up to the centre of Australia. He rode on horse into that vast outback country to bring the Eucharist and the other sacraments to scattered groups of Catholics.

Sevenhill sits near the top of tourist and pilgrimage rankings in South Australia. It showcases the work of Mother Mary, the pioneer priests, and the Jesuit brothers. The old college, the great stone church, and the acres of vineyards embody their memory. When you go there, you journey into the past but also into the future. I returned to my home in Melbourne, heartened by the way Mother Mary continues to galvanise the Diocese of Port Pirie. She remains vividly present, leading and inspiring the bishop, the priests, the religious, and the many laymen and laywomen in the Diocese of Port Pirie. They work for Jesus Christ in a diocese that is the size of France and Germany combined.

More than 35 years of living in Rome and Wimbledon had meant my losing touch with much that was happening in my own country. But numerous invitations and experiences planted my feet back on firm, Australian ground. The next chapter will continue the story of how that took place.

5

Lights and Shadows

For many people, theology can seem an odd way to make a living. Does the theory and practice of faith need any input from professionals? Surely all Christian believers, followers of other living faiths, and those who profess no faith have the right to be heard when they speak about what they have or have not experienced religiously? Would it be preferable to conduct our religious discussion with the gifted or not so gifted amateurs and leave professionals out in the cold? Why not let theology happen without too much sweat? Why not be satisfied with ready-made, cheap theology? Professionalism in religious studies can be the last thing many people want to hear about. They seem all too ready to take a show of scholarship for the real thing.

Last December a business journal published in Australia provided a spectacular example of how 'amateurs' can lead us astray if we take as gospel what they say and write. This journal published an article on the feast of Christmas by a Chinese herbalist. He had done a few minutes' googling and then felt authorized to inform readers about the historical origins of this feast. He began by confusing the immaculate conception of Mary with the virginal conception of Christ. The first belief holds that, in view of her Son's merits and divine identity, Mary was preserved, right from her conception, free from all sin, including original sin. The second belief holds that, through a special action of God, Mary was enabled to conceive and bring to birth her Son, without a biological father being involved. One may dismiss these beliefs as mere 'fables', as the herbalist did, but only the ignorant will identify them. After this initial confusion, the article went from bad to worse.

In a letter to the editor I asked: 'would you run an article in politics and economics by using, let's say, a water diviner who does a bit of googling and then tells readers about opportunities of trade with China and the direction of Chinese politics?' 'The ill-informed level' of your article on Christmas, I added, 'makes me wonder whether I can give credence to other articles in your journal.'

Australia has a small theological market. The media can deceive itself into thinking that they are doing their bit by a little seasonal journalism, often of questionable quality, at Christmas and Easter. But many factors, not least the huge commitment to education on the part of Christians and others, continue to generate a hunger for professional presentation of basic beliefs and what they contribute to life. A sense of that hunger encouraged the doyen of Australian historians, Geoffrey Blainey, into writing *A Short History of Christianity* (Camberwell, Victoria: Viking, 2011), and prompted me in revising and updating a book I originally wrote with Mario Farrugia in 2003: *Catholicism: The Story of Catholic Christianity* (Oxford: Oxford University Press, 2014).

Teaching teachers

My contacts with Australian educators resumed with a bang. In January 2011, 400 principals, teachers, and others working for education in the Parramatta Diocese (to the west of Sydney) packed the hall at a local racecourse to hear me speak about *Jesus: A Portrait*. Like their counterparts I had met in English dioceses, they wanted to hear about the Founder of Christianity—who he was/is and what he has done for us and for our world. They too were attracted by the central theme of the book: the unique beauty of Jesus which can spark our love and a lifetime of discipleship.

The following month the coordinators of religious education in the Sandhurst (Bendigo) Diocese also put Jesus at the centre.

They brought me up from Melbourne for a day-long conference on 'Knowing Jesus', 'Believing in the Risen Christ', and 'Jesus and Social Justice'. The gifted and effective Director of the Catholic Education Office in Bendigo, Philomena Billington, had heard me speak the previous year for the St Vincent de Paul Society— on 'Jesus and the Homeless'. She now pressed me into service for the diocese.

Some snow was still visible on the Australian Alps when she gathered 55 staff members at Feathertop Chalet in Harrietville for a day-long conference built around two lectures: 'God in Our Lives' and 'The Presence of Christ in the Liturgy' (3 October 2011). The clean, rushing waters of the Ovens River and the spring flowers everywhere conveyed the mood of new life and growth that Phil wanted to promote.

By that time another Australian diocese had co-opted me as it continued to rethink the challenges of religious education. At a two-day conference for 90 principals and teachers in Lismore (northern New South Wales) (27–28 June 2011), I lectured on 'The Church in Post-modern Australia' and 'Jesus in Post-Modern Australia'. They revealed the personal and vital experiences of their communities. Faced now with government plans for a national curriculum, they went to the heart of the matter: what was an integrated Catholic world-view which could allow the deep implications of faith in Christ to emerge and inspire the entire life of their schools? Rather than let themselves be absorbed simply with the specific strengths and weaknesses of the proposed curriculum, they twice invited me back to lecture on 'the Catholic world-view' (14–15 November 2013, and 6 March 2014). Those who lead education for the Lismore Diocese have found this world-view happily expressed in the long apostolic exhortation published by Pope Francis at the end of 2013, *Evangelii Gaudium* (the Joy of the Gospel). They had me return again and spend a week (February 2015) in the diocese helping different groups of teachers appropriate the exhortation, not only intellectually but also spiritually.

In grasping what happens in Catholic and other schools across Australia, I relied mainly on what teachers told me. Some contacts with teenagers also helped shape my vision. My old school, Xavier College (Kew, Victoria), invited me to share with 25 year-twelve boys my experience of writing and publishing books (20 May 2010). Some staff member judged that, having by then authored or co-authored nearly sixty books, I must be the most published old-boy in the college's history and might prompt one or more of the young into aiming at becoming writers. I warned the boys that writing books involves more than crafting a nice sentence and spinning a good yarn.

Xavier was one of the original six institutions in Victoria that made up the Associated Public Schools. They included two Anglican schools, Melbourne Grammar School (which follows the dark blue colours of the University of Oxford and is situated in central Melbourne) and Geelong Grammar School (which follows the light blue of the University of Cambridge and borders on Port Phillip, a few miles north of the city of Geelong). A few years ago some benefactors of Geelong Grammar endowed a visiting fellowship that brings artists, historians, philosophers, retired generals and judges, theologians, writers, and other notable achievers to meet and speak with the boys and girls, the staff, and local people who attend functions on the campus of what is Australia's largest co-educational boarding school. Through the visiting fellows, the students get to know the state of the art in a range of professions.

In March 2011, Geelong Grammar declined my offer to take the train from Melbourne, and sent a car to bring me down to the campus. Their invitation focussed squarely on Jesus: a lecture to the general public on his resurrection; a lecture to Year 11 on what we know about Jesus from an historical point of view; a homily at a chapel service for Year 11 on 'Jesus Our Friend'; and a lecture to Year 10 students on 'Why did Jesus die?' I enjoyed the hospitality of an acclaimed school that seemed like Eton College in the Southern Hemisphere and lived up to its ideal of 'exceptional education'. I knew that its old-boys included Prince Charles, at least one Australian prime minister, some leading writers, and other high performers, but had no idea that the list also included Rupert Murdoch. As a boy he edited the school newspaper, anticipating the shape of things to come.

Two years later Geelong Grammar wanted me back in the early, 'honeymoon' months of the pontificate of Pope Francis. Once again they sent a car to bring me to their campus. This time I did not suggest taking the train, as I knew the answer would be a firm 'no'. As well as lecturing on the new Pope and the prospects for his papacy, I preached at two services during 'the Geelong Grammar Holy Week'. Since the students (predominantly boarders) return home before Easter for a mid-term break, the school has for years anticipated by a week or two the liturgy of Holy Thursday and Good Friday. Executed with Anglican precision and decorum, this practice brings into focus for the boys and girls what sustains Christianity: a faith in the crucified and risen Jesus embodied in life and worship.

Ecumenical relations

Invitations from Anglicans and others quickly ensured that my ecumenical contacts were to endure and prosper in Australia. The Institute for Spiritual Studies located at St Peter's, Eastern Hill (Melbourne), brought me together with Dr Peter Carnley for a day on Anglican-Roman Catholic relations (15 May 2010). A dear friend from our years at the University of Cambridge, Peter was now retired Anglican Archbishop of Perth. In August I was back at St Peter's to lead a day of prayer for an ecumenical group, the Australian Christian Meditation Community. The following year the same group took me into the mountains outside Melbourne to lead a weekend retreat for 35 of their members at Pallotti College, Millgrove (8–10 April 2011). Their disciplined adherence to meditative prayer drew inspiration from the lively birds and spring flowers that filled the surrounding forest. A hermit whose house you could glimpse among the trees on the college property summoned up further possibilities for prayer.

Groups who meet near where I live at the Jesuit Theological College (JTC) in Parkville have fostered contacts with other Christians and with contemporary theology. For a meeting at (the Baptist) Whitley College, the Mission Studies Network invited me to present my *Salvation for All: God's Other Peoples* (13 May 2011). One professor of Whitley College, Mark Brett, enhanced the discussion by firmly placing within the divine plan for salvation various peoples mentioned in the Old Testament. His creative interpretation and application of the Scriptures make me regret not having engaged in more contact with Mark.

Where Whitley College is a short distance up Royal Parade to the north of the JTC, Trinity College looms large also on Royal Parade, but this time to the south. The (Anglican) Society of Priests invited me to join them at Trinity for a conference on 'Atonement' (8 November 2011). The 40 participants heard Dorothy Lee and me present reflections on the nature of the reconciliation with God effected by the life, death, and resurrection of Christ. An outstanding commentator on the Gospel of John, Dorothy had contributed to the volume which Dan Kendall and I edited in honour of Jacques Dupuis on the occasion of his eightieth birthday, *In Many and Diverse Ways* (Maryknoll, NY: Orbis, 2003). The incarnation of vivacious cheerfulness, red-haired Dorothy rubs shoulders with the Christian establishment in Melbourne, and as a teacher has blessed generations of seminarians and other students with her scholarship and friendship.

Later in the same November I addressed the Prayer Book Society on what the Second Vatican Council taught about the different presences of Christ in its Constitution on the Sacred Liturgy of 1963 (*Sacrosanctum Concilium*). Since both philosophers and theologians widely neglect reflection on the concept of 'presence', I have continued to evangelize audiences on the 'possibilities of presence'. Whenever respect is paid to the wide varieties and intensities of divine presence, opportunities open up for appreciating the activity of the Holy Spirit and the risen Christ not only in Christian worship but also in the lives of those who follow faiths other than Christianity. The language of 'outside' and 'inside' the Church has sadly masked the richness of the divine presence. God is absent to no one, but—through indefinitely many ways— actively present to everyone.

The launch in Adelaide of the latest document from the Australian Lutheran-Roman Catholic Dialogue, 'Living Word, Living Tradition' (1 December 2011) rounded off an ecumenical year. More than 100 people attended the ceremony in St Francis Xavier Cathedral at which I congratulated the joint commission and made several comments on their text, including the possibility of interpreting tradition as the collective memory of the Church.[17] Here recent developments in memory studies coming from historiography, neuroscience, philosophy, psychology, sociology, and other disciplines offered possible ways towards understanding the life and function of Christian tradition. But so far theologians had hardly explored the theme of tradition as collective memory. I was not suggesting that modern memory studies should simply dictate what was to be said about the tradition of faith and life that derives from Jesus and the first Christians. But helpful developments in those studies could help organize what theologians and official teachers might say about tradition as the collective memory of the Church.

At the reception which followed the official ceremony, there were many Lutheran pastors and laypersons among the cast of characters I met. Inevitably I exploited a feature of my family background. For nearly 20 years, a maternal grandfather, Patrick McMahon Glynn

---

17 My lecture is reproduced in Appendix Nine below. To encourage attention to tradition as collective memory, David Braithwaite and I published an article on that theme in *Theological Studies* for March 2015.

(d. 1931) represented in the federal parliament a South Australian electorate that was heavily and devoutly Lutheran.

Friendship with other Christians luminously accompanied the launch of my memoirs: *A Midlife Journey* (July 2012), and *On the Left Bank of the Tiber* (August 2013). At the Celtic Club in downtown Melbourne, two Anglicans did the honours, Dorothy Lee for the first volume and David Richardson a year later for the second. Dorothy was breathtakingly direct in exploring *A Midlife Journey* as a story to be read in a spiritual key. A few days later in North Sydney, an acclaimed TV and radio presenter, Geraldine Doogue, did the same when she launched the volume. She raised pressing questions about the 'self' the book put on display, and explored the connection between autobiography and the mystery of divine guidance.

After serving as a much-loved dean of St Peter's Cathedral in Adelaide and St Paul's Cathedral in Melbourne, David moved with his wife Margie to Rome and some halcyon years as director of the Anglican Centre. He returned to Melbourne just in time to launch a memoir of my life in Rome from 1974 to 2006, *On the Left Bank of the Tiber*. He held the audience spellbound by mixing comments on my text with his own personal reminiscences of the eternal city. A couple of weeks later, at a second launch, this time held at Catholic Theological College in East Melbourne, Tim Fischer, a former Deputy Prime Minister of Australia and former Australian Ambassador to the Holy See (2009–2012), did something similar. His own memoir, *Holy See, Unholy Me—1000 Days in Rome*, had appeared a few days earlier. It was through the lens of his own experience that Tim could happily interpret my personal narrative.

Unquestionably, my most treasured ecumenical contact remained a friendship with John Batt, a fellow student of the classics at Melbourne University in the 1950s and now a retired judge of the Court of Appeal of Victoria. John is a devoted Anglican who has served his Church and the wider community with quiet and informed generosity. He had been the organizer behind the scenes when in 2006 the Australian government created me a Companion of the General Division of the Order of Australia (AC) (*On the Left Bank of the Tiber*, p. 297). When he learned that I would be returning to Melbourne in late 2009, he was again a prime mover in putting me up for election to the Melbourne Club. When he wrote to check this proposal with me, I said to myself: 'If John thinks this is a good idea, it must be a good idea.'

The Melbourne Club continues to provide endless opportunities for exchanging ideas and experiences with remarkable members and their guests. Their activities and interests know no boundaries. Over lunch a genial retired philosopher, Denis White, constantly enlightens and entertains me with reminiscences of his studies in London, teaching at Monash University, and work as a speechwriter for Malcolm Fraser and then as director of the PM's private office. His job was to help Fraser reach clear lines on what to think and do about complex issues and how to explain things. Later Denis turned around the Trinity Foundation and made it a vibrantly successful centre for preparing students (predominantly Asian) through a year of foundational studies for enrolment at the University of Melbourne. For twenty years Denis and his wife Carnie made their home available for players allocated by Tennis Australia. Denis has amusing and affectionate stories to tell of his guests, who included Jennifer Capriati and Petr Korda, who were both to enjoy, respectively, the No. 1 and No 2 ranking in the tennis world. Though his consultancy practice, Denis continues to gather relevant data and offer inventive advice for clients who range from Australian vegetable growers to local councils wanting to improve tertiary education in their cities. For good measure, Denis produces superb olive oil, which he extracts at his own small press. He took a highly technical course to learn the necessary know-how. He regularly gives me one or two bottles of 'Your Olive Oil', and takes pleasure at the way I constantly use his oil on toast at breakfast.

I have singled out Denis White, but could name numerous other members who are equally many-sided, show the same enquiring cast of mind, and also prove delightful company—not least those from the Western District of Victoria. They sometimes belong to families who settled there before 1850, that is to say, before the separate Colony of Victoria was created in July 1851and the Commonwealth of Australia formed in 1901.

A portrait of the ill-fated explorer, Robert O'Hara Burke, presides over the Club's dining room in Melbourne. In 1861 he led an expedition that travelled from Melbourne in the south to the Gulf of Carpenteria in the north, a distance of 3,250 kilometres. He and his colleague William John Wills perished on the return journey. I cannot escape from Burke and Wills. They took their last lunch in Melbourne at the Royal Artillery Hotel, just down the road towards what is now the Central Business District. Right behind where I live in the Jesuit Theological College, a cairn commemorates the place where the expedition camped on its first night. From my office I look across Princes Park to the Melbourne General Cemetery, where the remains of Buke and Wills were brought for final burial.

John Batt and others have encouraged me to step forward and contribute to the life of the Club. At a dinner in the library on 30 April 2014 I spoke about the challenges and pitfalls involved in writing the two volumes of my autobiography. What could prompt me or anyone else into putting ourselves on display by writing 750 pages of memoirs? We all have an instinct to map our lives, I explained. We want to look back at the journey and inspect at a distance our dreams and griefs, our successes and failures. How has the world impacted on us, and how have our lives impacted on the world around us? What do we make of it all now?

Membership of the Melbourne Club got me into my stride about two projects: one financial and the other literary. Through lunches and lectures to promote 'classics in the city', Michael Bartlett has led the cause of endowing a new Chair of Classics at the University of Melbourne. Sheer gratitude for what the Department of Classics did for me and other Jesuits over many years made me agree at once to join Michael's committee. So far I have proved unsuccessful in directly raising funds; I have brought in only $2,000. But I managed to produce something useful for Michael by collecting statements of support from the Most Rev. Rowan Williams, the former Archbishop of Canterbury, and other notable people around the world, including Boris Johnson, the Mayor of London. During my three years in Wimbledon, the post came up for election and I voted for Johnson rather than the incumbent mayor, Ken Livingstone.

For a writers' festival in 2013, Johnson came to Melbourne and concluded his round of engagements by speaking to several hundred people in Sofitel, a hotel at the top of Collins Street. When question time came, I managed to secure the roving mike and said: 'Mr Johnson, I must be the only person here who voted for you as Mayor of London'. I looked around the hall, but no one challenged my claim, and so I could continue: 'I did something for you. Would you consider doing something for me and my friends by speaking in favour of the classics and a new Chair of Classics to be endowed at the University of Melbourne?' Johnson replied: 'I urge everyone who can to study classics at Melbourne. You will not only receive the keys to two thousand years of Western culture and civilization. You will also be deeply and permanently acquainted with the best literature, poetry, and philosophy that humanity has ever produced.' He paused, remembered visiting Northern Australia years before, and swept on: 'If you are up a tree in Kakadu National Park with a crocodile waiting for you below, you could take your mind off the situation by recalling some verses from Horace.' Then Johnson sprang to his feet and delighted the crowd by reciting in ancient Greek the opening lines of Homer's *Iliad* and expressing their meaning by dancing around the stage.

Another member of the Melbourne Club enlisted my cooperation—not in fund-raising but in writing a scholarly article for the December 2014 number of the *Victorian Historical Journal*. When I returned to Melbourne in late 2009, I underwent a TURP operation at the hands of David Webb; that is to say, he removed half my prostate. His disciplined adherence to scientific evidence, joined to his love for history and cricket, had led him to question the commonly cited foundation date for one of the greatest sporting clubs in the world, the Melbourne Cricket Club. Primary evidence from contemporary newspapers and other sources fails to support a foundation in November 1838. Cricket was played in Melbourne from that date, and the names of some of the earliest teams and players have been preserved. But the highly successful Melbourne Cricket Club itself was founded only in late 1841.

David and I, both long-standing and grateful members of the MCC, felt we had to challenge its 'historians'. The front cover of the November 2013 issue of the *MCC News* had proudly announced 'a milestone to remember: Australia's oldest sporting club turns 175'. Around 1,500 members and guests attended the highpoint of the '175th anniversary', a 'gala night' on 15 November. It featured a light show re-enacting 'the beginnings' of the club in 1838 when six of the first British settlers in Melbourne allegedly acquired equipment, formed the MCC, and played in its first match two days later. But is this foundation myth, so often conveyed to the Australian public, true? The conclusion from the historical research that David made and I completed was clear, even dazzlingly clear: the MCC was founded three years later, in November 1841.

Disappointments

After I came home to Australia in late 2009, many events and moments caught my attention. If I join them up, plenty of lights break through but also a few shadows.

Philip Freier and Graham Smith at launch of *A Midlife Journey* and, below, with Moira Peters and Tim Fischer at launch of *On the Left Bank of the Tiber*

With Geoffrey Blainey at launch of *On the Left Bank of the Tiber* and, below, with John Batt and Evarist Shigi at launch of *Ten African Cardinals*

The heartless, unjust, and even barbaric treatment of refugees and asylum seekers, practised by different national governments and apparently supported by a majority of voters, continues to grieve me deeply. This is a high price to pay to preserve the privileged life of Australians.[18]

A new national development has also saddened me: the decision by the Australian Broadcasting Commission to cut back religious programmes for both radio and television. On 14 December 2014, I wrote to the ABC pointing out that 'Australia and the whole world need, more than ever, an intelligent and informed presentation of religious affairs. For the ABC to reduce radically production and staffing in the area of religious affairs seems quite dangerous.' It makes room for 'uninformed commentators and fundamentalists to take over'. The ABC should 'maintain and even enlarge its professional leadership in religious broadcasting'. A two-page official answer arrived. But it stressed the need to make budget cuts, and refused to discuss whether the common good requires more and not less public debate about issues and events that concern faith and values.

Before I returned to Melbourne in 2009, Sally Ninham, the busy wife of my nephew James Peters (see *On the Left Bank of the Tiber*, pp. 37–38, 231–32), had managed to complete her PhD. In the area of oral history, the dissertation emerged from interviews with nearly one hundred Australians who, between 1949 and 1964, decided against applying to Oxford and Cambridge, did further studies in the United States (often supported by Fulbright scholarships), returned to Australia, and played leading roles in academia, law, and the world of business. Sally's thesis threw light on what these postgraduates had drawn from their American experience and how they made a far-reaching impact on teaching and research at Australian universities. Tall and slim, Sally looked lovely and elegant when she received her

---

18 See Jane McAdam and Fiona Chong, *Refugees: Why Seeking Asylum is Legal and Australia's Policies are Not* (Sydney: University of New South Wales Press, 2014).

degree at Latrobe University (Melbourne). In 2011, Connor Court (now Ballarat, Victoria) published the thesis as *A Cohort of Pioneers: Australian postgraduate students and American postgraduate degrees (1949–1964)*.

After skilfully organizing her time with a barrister husband and five small children to achieve this outstanding success, Sally now wondered what new project she might put her mind to. I suggested interviewing Cardinal Wilfrid Napier, the Catholic Archbishop of Durban, who was visiting Melbourne to deliver some lectures. This meeting sowed the idea of conducting interviews in Africa and elsewhere with as many African cardinals as possible. For months this venture kept her at full stretch, when she courageously travelled to Mozambique, the Ivory Coast, Cameroon, Uganda, Ghana, and elsewhere in Africa, as well as visiting Rome to conduct interviews with several of her cardinals. Friends in Rome and Africans whom I had taught years before at the Gregorian University outdid themselves in welcoming and helping Sally. They were startled at her outstanding feat of courage in going up and down Africa to meet their church leaders.

Many of the cardinals and other leaders Sally interviewed had played a crucial part in leading countries, racked by war, poverty, disease, corruption, and endemic political turmoil. She was captivated by the way they had stepped forward and stood tall in the cause of freedom, justice, education, and health services. Sally worked hard at the process of absorbing and assessing the material, finished the book, and attracted some powerful endorsements for the back cover.

A big crowd came to the two Melbourne launches of *Ten African Cardinals* in late 2013. I did the honours at one, while Archbishop Paul Gallagher, the Vatican's apostolic nuncio (and now back in Rome as the Pope's Secretary for Relations with States), flew down from Canberra to speak at the other. Paul, a former student of mine from the Gregorian and a long-time papal diplomat, had been posted twice to Africa: first in Tanzania and later in Burundi. Sally did some radio interviews in Sydney and wrote an article on her book for *The Catholic Herald* (London). Another UK-based journal, *New Directions*, reviewed it, and so too did the New York-based *America* magazine and an Australian journal, *Quadrant*. Otherwise not only the media but also popular papers and professional journals stayed away from *Ten African Cardinals*. Did she suffer this neglect because she does not hold a university post? I felt outraged when an editor of a quarterly apologized to me for not running a review of the book; the journalist to whom he sent a copy turned it down, 'explaining', among other things, that Sally had failed to put to the Africans questions that he would have asked. Sally asked gentle, friendly questions, which obviously encouraged the cardinals and others to share their experiences and feelings. The journalist wished that she had put 'challenging'—that is to say, aggressive— questions.

But *Ten African Cardinals* did not vanish into oblivion everywhere. Pope Francis had one of his secretaries write to thank Sally for the book: 'The Holy Father has asked me to thank you for your greetings for Christmas and the New Year, and for the gift of your book on the ten African cardinals. He very much appreciates the sentiments which prompted this kind gesture. In commending your efforts to support the shepherds of the Church in Africa, His Holiness gladly imparts his apostolic blessing' (5 February 2014) Is the moral of the whole story that it is better to have one papal reader than one hundred reviews and ten thousand readers?

A further disappointment I faced on returning to Melbourne was the decline of *The Age*, the local daily founded in 1854 and for many years one of the world's most successful newspapers. It regularly provided my grandmother with her views and with reasons for holding them, but now seems to have partly lost the plot. While its circulation continues to slip, it advertises itself by claiming to be 'possibly the best news organization in the free world', and by assuring readers: 'our passion for the truth means you always know what's going on'.

Their prime aim is to pursue and expose 'evil' wherever they find it or suspect that they find it. As their self-advertisement put matters, 'there will always be evil, and it's our job not to turn away'. This is a far cry from the *New York Times*'s balanced policy of publishing 'all the news that's fit to print'—good news as well as bad news.

After police shot dead a demented young terrorist who attacked them in 2014, *The Age* managed to put on its front page the photo of another young man who was still very much alive and who had nothing whatsoever to do with the attack. *The Age* paid out hundreds of thousands of dollars in damages. The paper's ideological bent shows up in tendentious, if not blatantly unfair, headlines, and in a persistent refusal to publish letters and articles that dissent from its policies or reporting. It would not, for example, run an article on palliative care written by world expert, an Australian who had returned from holding a professorship at a leading American university to take up a similar post at a university in Melbourne. His informed views on making the dying comfortable by reducing their pain would have threatened *The Age's* campaign for 'doctor-assisted suicide'. The paper continues to be characterized by unfair reporting, occasional fabrications, and a constant prejudice against private ('faith') schools, the Catholic Church, and some other institutions and groups. Let me provide the details of one flagrant example.

Italians have migrated to Australia since the mid-nineteenth century. Thousands of Italian prisoners-of-war spent part of the Second World War working on Australian farms. From the early 1950s, Italian families and individuals arrived in large numbers and contributed to the economic, cultural, and religious growth of Australia. In 1967 prominent Italians founded Comitato Assistenza Italiani (Co.As.It.) or Italian Assistance Association to provide a range of social services for the aged and disabled, resource programmes for studying the Italian language, culture, and history, and other key services. Funding came and comes from the Italian government, the federal government of

Australia, the state government of Victoria, some Italian universities, and other sources. The Governor of Victoria has regularly been the patron-in-chief. The list of other patrons and members of several committees reads like a roll call of Italians who have 'made it' in Australia as lawyers, judges, business people, right up to a former Governor of Victoria, Sir James Gobbo.

During 2012 an ex-member of the Victorian Parliament and a part-time employee of Co.As.It. began making false and mischievous allegations against the organization. He engaged with *The Age* to damage Co.As.It.'s excellent reputation in the Italian and wider community. His misinformation, innuendos, and outright fabrications appealed to old prejudices and suspicions that *The Age* has entertained and fostered against persons of Italian descent.

The Victorian Police and the Australian Charities and Not-for-profits Commission (ACNC) began separate and comprehensive investigations of Co.As.It. Doubtless, if they had declined to do so, *The Age* would have blasted them for committing a cover-up. The paper

With James Gobbo, December 2012

opened its defamatory campaign against Co.As.It. with an article on 20 December 2012, and suggested 'guilt by association' by featuring it on the front page along with an article on organized crime moving drugs through Sydney airport. A few months later it repeated the allegations against those running Co.As.It. in a four-page article for the *Saturday Age* on 27 April 2013, followed up by a shorter article in *The Age* two days later. This attack struck me as quite unfair and unreasonable. By then *The Age* knew that the police were investigating Co.As.It., and that the ACNC were conducting their enquiry. Why then present a mega-article, decked out with sinister innuendos, instead of waiting for the results of the investigations by the police and the ACNC? On 26 January 2014, *The Age* once again repeated these accusations about funds being misused and fraud committed. This final attack struck me as an ugly way to smear the Italian community and its leading members on the occasion of Australia Day, a holiday weekend when newspapers and others should have been celebrating what different ethnic groups have contributed to the life and wellbeing of Australia.

A few weeks later the police investigation was completed, with the Fraud and Extortion Squad identifying no criminal offences. The detective in charge wrote on 6 March 2014 to thank the officials of Co.As.It. for the thorough assistance they gave during the investigation and to assure them that 'there will be no further police involvement in the matter'. On 30 April 2014 the compliance director of ACNC informed Co.As.It. that their separate investigation was also finalised. They had found 'no evidence of mismanagement or misappropriation', and the director ended by saying: 'I wish you well in your future charitable endeavours'. As far as I know, *The Age* never reported the positive results from the two investigations. So much again for the paper's 'passion for the truth'!

The whole ugly campaign proved a classic example of a newspaper (because of its ideology) believing a disgruntled individual, taking the opportunity to smear an ethnic group, and encouraging a million dollars or more of public money to be spent on two separate investigations that informed and honest members of the community already knew were unnecessary and that resulted in the total exoneration of the organization that had been defamed.

Having explained why *The Age* has disenchanted me, I should, however, end by qualifying this bleak picture by expressing thanks to the paper for printing a number of obituaries that I wrote. Before returning to Australia, I had published three obituaries in the London *Tablet*: of Prince Frank and Princess Orietta Doria Pamphilj and Cardinal Avery Dulles. Back home in Melbourne, I kept up this habit by writing for *The Age* obituaries of the surgeon James Peters (my brother-in-law), the priest and poet Peter Steele, SJ, Cardinal Carlo Maria Martini, and other high achievers. Six of these obituaries are reproduced in Appendix Eight.

6

Torturing the Language and Welcoming the New Pope

On 9 August 2014, the London *Tablet* published my letter, 'A flawed peace'. I had learned that the Congregation for Divine Worship and the Discipline of the Sacraments had just instructed priests around the world that, even at funerals and weddings, they were not to leave their place at the altar to exchange a greeting of peace with the faithful, not even with those mourning a death in the family or happily joining themselves in matrimony. I asked: 'Is this act of micro-management compatible with what St John Paul II wrote in [his encyclical] *Veritatis Splendor* (no. 2): "Jesus' way of acting, his words, his deeds, and his precepts constitute the moral rule of Christian life"?'

I drove home the point: 'At the Last Supper, Jesus stood up, removed his outer garments, and stepped down to wash the feet of his disciples. What would Jesus do today at the celebration of the Eucharist? Are we to imagine that he would remain rigidly behind the altar and not "step down" to share the sorrows and joys of people, especially those mourning a death or celebrating their marriage? The example of Jesus trumps the latest instruction from the Congregation for Divine Worship.'

In the English-speaking world this instruction has been widely ignored—not least because this same Congregation for Divine Worship did much harm through the unfortunate translation of the *Roman Missal* with which it saddled English-speaking Catholics in late

2011. Let me tell the story of how this came to pass and what it involved, before moving to the blessing Pope Francis has brought the Church and the world.

An unfortunate translation

In the first document it promulgated, the Constitution on the Sacred Liturgy of 1963 (*Sacrosanctum Concilium*), the Second Vatican Council (1962–65) proposed that the primary responsibility in the work of revising and adapting the liturgy for those of the western or Roman rite belonged to the Holy See (that is to say, to the pope and those who work for him in the Vatican) and to the bishops of different regions (nos. 22, 37–40). The same document allowed for the use of vernacular translations, and expected the bishops of different regions to 'approve' the 'translations from the Latin for use in the liturgy' (no. 36.4). Here the Council made no explicit mention of any obligation to have these translations (into Chinese, English, French, German, Hindi, Spanish, and so forth) 'confirmed' or 'recognized' by the Holy See. However, such an express obligation appeared soon enough.

When the revised *Missale Romanum*, sometimes called 'the Paul VI Missal', appeared in 1970, conferences of bishops around the world were asked to prepare editions in the vernacular, but these editions would come into force only 'after being confirmed by the Holy See'. These editions were prepared everywhere, and the confirmation was forthcoming. Then minor revisions were introduced into the *Missale Romanum* in a second edition of 1975 and in a third edition of 2000. On the occasion of the publication of the third edition, the new Prefect of the Congregation for Divine Worship, Cardinal Jorge Medina Estévez of Chile, a council *peritus* who was an esteemed colleague of Yves Congar at Vatican II but who subsequently took a decisive 'turn to the right', required that new vernacular versions were to be prepared. 'The preceding versions in use until now' were to be 'emended accurately in fidelity to the original Latin text' (letter of 20 April 2000). Notice the emphasis on translations being 'faithful' and 'accurate', without a word being said about their being intelligible and clear in a way that would enable and encourage something central to Vatican II's Constitution on the Sacred Liturgy: the full and active participation in worship by all those present.

A year later the cardinal published in 2001 *Liturgiam Authenticam* (LA), a document governing liturgical translations which was widely criticized by experts in the art of translation for inculcating a one-sided 'transliteralization' from the Latin into the various vernaculars. LA required translators to practise verbal equality with the original Latin, and to follow it in its grammar and syntax. Such strict adherence to the Latin original ignored the fact that English—to cite the vernacular that we are concerned with—does not have a Latin structure in its sentences. Contemporary English does not indulge, for instance, the long periods of Ciceronian and classical liturgical Latin. The guidelines from LA did not aim at producing a recognizably English vernacular but at Latin texts transposed into English words, texts that regularly sound more like Latin than English.[19]

LA forgot a principle spelled out in an Oxford University lecture by a notable English writer and translator, Ronald Knox (d. 1957): a translation should 'read like a first-rate native thing'. One could quote endless other authoritative voices from the past and the present who agree with Knox. Sacrificing everything to alleged 'fidelity' will lead to texts that do not pass from one language into a recognizable and intelligible version of the other language. Translations must sound like original compositions in the receiver language. George Steiner wrote of a 'faithful but autonomous restatement'. He explained: 'The

---

19 Peter Jeffrey, professor of music at Princeton University, described LA as 'the most ignorant statement on liturgy ever issued by a modern Vatican congregation', and wrote four articles criticizing it: *Worship* 78 (2004), pp. 2–24, 139–64, 236–65, 309–41.

translator closely reproduces the original but composes a text that is natural to his own tongue, which can stand on its own'.[20]

Long before LA appeared in 2001, the International Commission on English in the Liturgy (ICEL) had been working painstakingly for seventeen years to revise the original English translation of the Paul VI Missal. ICEL submitted their new text (dated 1998) to the eleven English-speaking bishops' conferences around the world.[21] They all approved it and authorized it being sent to Rome for confirmation. But, without any dialogue or discussion with the bishops and with ICEL, Cardinal Medina Estévez and his colleagues simply consigned to oblivion the 1998 *Missal*, the 'missal that never was'. They issued LA, changed the membership of ICEL, demanded that its statutes be revised, and added a committee, called 'Vox Clara' (clear voice), who endorsed the principles of LA and were largely responsible for the 'revised' translation of the third edition of the *Missale Romanum*. Ironically, the results produced by 'Vox Clara' were all too often unclear and even verging on the unintelligible.

The former chairman of ICEL, Bishop Maurice Taylor of the Diocese of Galloway, and others were swept aside, and new membership installed, with a key role being played by Monsignor Bruce Harbert, who from 2002 to 2009 was the Executive Director of the Secretariat of the new ICEL. The 'revised' translation was sent to the English-speaking bishops' conferences for approval. Unlike their counterparts in, for example, the German-speaking world (who held the line against translations guided by the flawed norms of LA), they caved in to pressure from Rome. Cardinal Thomas Winning of Glasgow (d. 2001) was one of the few English-speaking bishops to oppose publicly the scandalously highhanded tactics of Cardinal

---

20 G. Steiner, *After Babel: Aspects of Language and Translation* (Oxford: Oxford University Press, 1977), p. 253.
21 In 1995, Canterbury Press (Norwich) had published ICEL's proposed, new collects as *Opening Prayers*.

Medina Estévez. Astonishingly, even *after* securing the reluctant agreement of English-speaking bishops to their new translation, the Congregation for Divine Worship, through 'Vox Clara', unilaterally introduced thousands of changes, some of a minor nature (e.g. matters of punctuation) but some of a substantial nature. It was this text that was imposed on English-speaking Catholics from the First Sunday of Advent 27 November 2011.[22]

Under the auspices of the Catholic Academy of Liturgy and with a supporting foreword by the emeritus Archbishop of Los Angeles, Cardinal Roger Mahony, Edward Foley edited a critical and scholarly *Commentary on the Order of Mass of the Roman Missal* (Collegeville, Minn.: Liturgical Press, 2011), Monsignor Harbert was also quick off the mark and produced in defence of the new missal a Catholic Truth Society pamphlet of 2011, *Companion to the Order of Mass: The New Translation*.

In other places, for instance, in a review for *New Blackfriars* 95 (2014), pp. 625–26, Harbert has set out principles that he endorses when translating the Latin liturgy into English. One principle proposes that 'the *effect* of a text on its original audience should be reproduced' (emphasis original). This is to ignore that with so much of the Latin liturgy (e.g. the Roman canon apparently used since the end of the fifth century), not to mention most classical literature, we have simply no idea whatsoever who constituted 'its original audience', let alone the effect on them of the text that they were hearing or using for the first time. We could label this theory as the 'original-audience fallacy'. This fallacy resembles the 'intentional fallacy', classically expounded by E. D. Hirsch (see Appendix 7 below).

A central principle behind the 2010 English translation of the

---

22 On the destruction of ICEL as it had been, see John Wilkins, 'Lost in Translation', *Commonweal* (November 2005), pp. 12–20. On some problems with the translation imposed in 2011 Jean Riordan, 'Let us pray in good English', *The Pastoral Review* 11/1 (January/February, 2015), pp. 48–53.

Missal, Harbert tells us, was 'a sacral style that will inspire its users'.[23] But such a 'sacral style' seems alien to the model of all Christian prayer, the 'Our Father', and simply does not characterize such petitions as 'thy will be done', 'give us this day our daily bread', and 'deliver us from evil'. Jesus never suggested that we would honour God more and find ourselves more 'inspired' by adopting a 'sacral style' in our prayers, as if we should say: 'may thy will, we pray, be graciously done'; 'graciously grant us today our daily bread'; 'grant, we pray, that we may be delivered from evil'. Furthermore, it is the straightforward, and not particularly 'sacral', style of the Psalms that fed Jesus' own prayer, and has made them enduringly effective as prayers for Jews and Christians alike. The language is simple and powerfully direct, and does not keep intelligibility at bay: 'Have mercy on me, Lord, I have no strength'; 'I will praise you, Lord, with all my heart'; 'Lord God, I take refuge in you'. A sacral style was not a principle that inspired either Jesus or the psalmists. Have Harbert and his associates set up a human 'tradition' and not followed the example and teaching of Jesus himself?

Some remarks of St Cyprian in his treatise *On the Lord's Prayer* seem apropos: 'To pray otherwise than as he [Jesus] taught us is more than a mistake, it is a fault, for he laid down: "You reject the commandment of God in order to set up your own tradition." Let us pray as our Master himself taught us. Our prayer is friendly and intimate when we petition God with his own prayer' (Chs. 2–3). Surely the teaching and example of Jesus should be the rule not only of Christian life but also of Christian liturgy?

Finally, Monsignor Harbert also insists that 'it is a mistake to entrust the liturgy to a few powerful hands'. One might ask: was it a mistake to seize control of the translation of the liturgy into English and put it into the hands of the few powerful people who made up 'Vox Clara'?

---

23 Harbert introduces an old-fashioned adjective by speaking of 'a *sacral* style' rather than of 'a *sacred* style'. An excellent, online prayer service calls itself 'Sacred Space' and not 'Sacral Space'.

Some supporters of the 2010 translation have appealed to the fact that around the world those who were to produce translations into other languages knew English but had at best a limited knowledge of the Latin original. They would turn to the English translation for guidance. This strange view pictured the English translation as a kind of 'crib' for other translations, and failed to acknowledge that an odd, Latinized translation fails to meet the liturgical needs of the native English-speakers and inhibits their sharing in worship. If translators for other language groups needed a 'crib' or an 'interlinear' trans-literalization as they grappled with the original Latin, by all means let someone supply them with such an aid. But why foist on English-speakers what is hardly more than a 'crib' of the original Latin text?

Surveys in the USA, the British Isles, and New Zealand have shown how seriously dissatisfied the majority of lay people and clergy are with the 2010 *Missal*. Too often its new renderings are hard to speak, unpleasant to listen to, and difficult to understand. The translators forgot how Vatican II's Constitution on the Sacred Liturgy insisted on a lucid clarity that would facilitate active sharing in public worship. As Michael G. Ryan has commented, 'such slavish attention to the Latin' has resulted in 'translations that are museum pieces—about as fresh as a fossil preserved in amber' (*The Tablet*, 29 November 2014). When I complained about the new translation to a bishop, I was told: 'Give it time. You will get used to it.' 'Yes', I said, 'it will be like getting used to a colleague in the office who speaks poor English. I may be obediently resigned to this translation, but I could never approve of it or welcome it.' Perhaps I should have quoted a friend who said: 'This new translation sounds like something written by people for whom English was a second language'.

Thus far we have been looking more at the headlines rather than the small print. Let me now move to six areas in which the deficiencies of the new translation show up: the choice of odd, 'stately' words; obsequious ways of addressing God; the failure to use inclusive language; inaccurate rendering of the Nicene Creed, which is in fact the Nicene-Constantinopolitan Creed of 381; a total lack of ecumenical sensibility; and misleading or even mistaken translations.

Six areas of failure

First, a desire for 'sacral' and more formal language dictated the repeated preference in the 2010 translation of the *Missal* for 'charity' over 'love', 'compunction' over 'repentance', 'conciliation' over 'reconciliation', 'fount' over 'fountain', 'laud' over 'praise', 'participate' over 'share', 'regeneration' over 'being born again', 'replenished' over 'nourished', 'solace' over 'consolation', 'supplication' over 'prayer', 'wondrous' over 'wonderful'.[24] Introducing 'oblation' rather than 'offering' or 'sacrifice' can leave hearers wondering whether the priest has stumbled over the word 'ablution'. One can understand why 'oblation' no longer has currency in contemporary English. In the Creed 'consubstantial' (straight from the Latin 'consubstantialis') has replaced the genial translation 'of one being'. We return to this below. The 2010 translation clearly favours old-fashioned English words that hardly belong to contemporary written or spoken English. Did the translators believe that such old-fashioned English, which they may have claimed to be 'timeless English', was the appropriate language in which to address God?

'Prevenient grace' belongs to a theological treatise rather than to a liturgical translation. But there it is in the prayer over the offerings that 'Vox Clara' offered in the 2010 *Missal* for the feast of the Immaculate Conception.

> Graciously accept the saving sacrifice which we offer you,
> O Lord, on the Solemnity of the Immaculate Conception

---

24 Such 'sacral' language belongs to the 'pseudo-sacred', distinguished by its 'remote air of pomp and circumstance': Josef Pieper, *In Search of the Sacred: Contributions to an Answer*, trans. Lothar Krauth (San Francisco: St Ignatius Press, 1991), p. 21.

of the Blessed Virgin Mary, and grant that, as we profess her, on account of your prevenient grace, to be untouched by any stain of sin, so through her intercession, we may be delivered from all our faults.

Set this endless, Latinized period over against what the 1998 *Missal* proposed:

> In your goodness, Lord, receive the sacrifice of salvation which we offer on the feast of the immaculate conception.
> We profess in faith that your grace preserved the Virgin Mary from every stain of sin; through her intercession deliver us from all our faults.

There is no competition. 'Your grace preserved' catches the meaning of 'prevenient grace', and the 1998 translation of the *Missal*—with its two sentences and the second one broken by a semicolon— follows the rhythm of spoken English. The 2010 translation seems to have disassembled the long Latin sentence, substituted English words on a one-to-one basis, and then reassembled the lot in a jerky, breathless whole.[25]

(2) Second, where Jesus told us to address God in a childlike, straightforward fashion, the 2010 translation of the *Missal* relentlessly pursues the unctuous or fulsome path, with 'graciously' incessantly introducing prayers: 'graciously grant', 'graciously accept', 'graciously choose', and so forth. 'We pray' is likewise regularly inserted. It is not enough to say 'Look, O Lord, on the offerings we make'; this must become 'look, we pray, O Lord, on the offerings we make'. It is not enough to say 'May your sacraments, O Lord, perfect in us what lies within them'; this must become 'may your sacraments, O Lord, we pray, perfect in us what lies within them'. (Both examples are taken

---

[25] The Latin original reads: 'Salutarem hostiam, quam in solemnitate immaculatae Conceptionis beatae Virginis Mariae tibi, Domine, offerimus, suscipe dignanter, et praesta, ut, sicut illam tua gratia praeveniente ab omni labe profitemur immune, ita, eius intercessione, a culpis omnibus liberemur'.

from the thirtieth Sunday in ordinary time.) Persistently, even though the celebrant is obviously engaged in prayer with God, 'grant' must be lengthened to 'grant, we pray'. Such redundancy is not good English, nor does it correspond to what Jesus said about being simple in prayer and not multiplying unnecessarily what we say (Matthew 6: 7–8).

Addressing the divine persons becomes too often a formal affair, which assumes an inappropriate 'you who' shape. See, for instance, the opening words of the prayer said by the celebrant after the Our Father: 'Lord Jesus Christ, who said to your Apostles'. If I were speaking to Barack Obama, I might begin: 'Mr President, you said last year…', but it would sound very odd to say: 'Mr President, who said last year…'

Over and over again, the translation of the collects in the 2010 translation take the 'you who' form and open by saying: 'O God, who on this day revealed…' (the Epiphany of the Lord) instead of the correct English: 'O God, on this day you revealed…' That collect requires a deep breath from the celebrant as it is one long sentence: 'O God who on this day revealed your Only Begotten Son to the nations by the guidance of a star, grant in your mercy that *we, who* know you already by faith, may be brought to behold the beauty of your sublime glory' (emphasis added). The 1998 translation, as far as I can see, never opens with 'O God who' form of address. Its rendering of the Epiphany collect, for instance, runs: 'God of mystery, on this day you revealed your only Son to the nations by the guidance of a star. We know you now by faith; lead us into that presence where we shall behold your glory face to face.' This translation avoids the clumsy 'we who' that turns up here and elsewhere in the 2010 translation. It is also much easier to say—with two sentences, and the second broken by a semicolon—and avoids the roundabout 'grant in your mercy that we may be brought' with a simple 'lead us' that parallels the language of Jesus himself.[26]

---

26 In the original Latin of the 1970 *Missal* the collect runs: 'Deus, qui hodierna

(3) A third deficiency of the 2010 translation, noted by many, is its refusal to use consistently inclusive language. Translating the Latin 'et in terra pax hominibus bonae voluntatis', the second line of the *Gloria* says: 'and on earth peace to people of good will'. This respects the fact that the Latin 'homines', unlike 'viri', is not gender specific. But in the Nicene Creed the translation renders 'propter nos homines' as 'for us men'. What about 'for us women'? One could translate the Latin as 'for us human beings'; the 1998 translation implies this inclusive meaning by saying simply 'for us'. The 2010 translation notoriously maintains gender exclusive language in its rendering of the Fourth Eucharistic Prayer: 'You formed man in your own image and entrusted the whole world to his care, so that in serving you alone, the Creator, he might have dominion over all creatures', and so forth. Apart from flouting the Genesis teaching about God creating 'male and female' in the divine image, this translation could have avoided offence by rendering the Latin: 'You formed us in your own image and entrusted the whole world to our care, so that in serving you alone, the Creator, we have dominion over all creatures'. The 1998 *Missal* translates: 'You formed man and woman in your own likeness and entrusted the whole world to their care, so that in serving you alone, their Creator, they might be stewards of all creation'. (Here 'stewards of all creation' is better English than 'have dominion over all creatures', and a happier translation theologically.)

(4) Catholics value in a special way the Nicene-Constantinopolitan Creed, since they share it with all Christians; it is the official creed on which the World Council of Churches was founded. The original English translation of the 1970 *Missal* introduced several brilliant features in its version of the Creed. The 1998 translation followed suit.

---

die Unigenitum tuum gentibus stella duce revelasti, concede propitius, ut, qui iam te ex fide cognovimus, usque ad contemplandam speciem tuae celsitudinis perducamur '.

First, it went back to the original ('we believe' of the Greek text of 381 AD), instead of retaining the traditional Latin ('credo' or 'I believe'), which was not faithful to the Greek. If we continue to speak of the 'Nicene Creed', we should true to the text of 381. Second, the traditional Latin translation ('ex Patre natum ante omnia saecula' and 'genitum, non factum') was also unfaithful to what the original Greek had said; it used the same verb each time: 'eternally *begotten* (*gennēthenta*) of the Father' and 'begotten (*gennēthenta*), not made'. The 1998 translation, like its 1975 predecessor, maintained the double use of 'begotten'. The 2010 translation, ignoring the original Greek, renders the two phrases: 'born of the Father before all ages' and 'begotten, not made'. This loses the parallelism that the original Greek expressed by twice using '*gennēthenta*'; it follows the Latin version by misleadingly translating in different ways the same participle that occurs twice within a few lines. Third, the 1975 English translation rendered as 'of one Being with the Father' the Greek phrase '*homoousion tō patrī*', and the 1998 translation did the same. This translates more accurately the Greek than the traditional Latin 'consubstantialem Patri', and is more readily understood than the transliterated 'consubstantial with the Father' of the 2010 translation.

Unlike the 2010 translation and also unlike the 1975 translation, the 1998 version of the Nicene Creed was properly inclusive. It confessed the incarnation 'for us and for our salvation', and avoided possible misconceptions by not referring to the Holy Spirit as 'he': 'We believe in the Holy Spirit, the Lord, the giver of life who proceeds from the Father and the Son, who with the Father and the Son is worshiped and glorified, who has spoken through the prophets'.

(5) In translating the Creed, the Gloria, and other parts of the Eucharist, the 2010 translation left behind any desire to use translations shared in common with other Christians. The result is that Catholics, who attend other Christian services can find themselves saying what they, as Catholics, *used to say*: for instance, 'and also with you' as a

response to 'the Lord be with you'. The 2010 translation vividly lacked any ecumenical sensibility, or the conviction that shared forms of prayer could help the cause of Christian unity.

(6) Sometimes the translation offered by the 2010 *Missal* is misleading. Take, for example, the prayer after Communion for the thirtieth Sunday in ordinary time. The Latin text of the *Missale Romanum* of 1970 runs: 'perficiant in nobis, Domine, quaesumus, tua sacramenta quod continent, ut quae nunc specie gerimus, rerum veritate capiamus'. The 2010 translation of the *Missal* renders this: 'May your Sacraments, O Lord, we pray, perfect in us what lies within them, [so] that what we now celebrate in signs we may one day possess in truth.' Here one may hear an unfortunate contrast between 'now celebrating in mere or even empty signs' with 'one day possessing in truth'. The 1998 translation gives proper weight to 'specie' and has: 'Lord, may your mysteries accomplish within us the salvation they embody, [so] that we may come to possess in truth what we celebrate now under sacramental signs'. With this appropriate weight given to what 'specie' means in the tradition as 'sacramental signs', the translation introduces 'mysteries', an alternate translation for 'sacramenta', so as to avoid a jarring repetition: 'sacraments' and then 'sacramental signs'.

At times the 2010 translation is simply mistaken. Take, for instance, the prayer after Communion for the First Sunday of Advent. The Latin text of the 1970 *Missale Romanum* runs: 'prosint nobis, quaesumus, Domine, frequentata mysteria, quibus nos, inter praetereuntia ambulantes, iam nunc instituis amare celestia et inhaerere mansuris' The 2010 translation of the *Missal* renders the prayer: 'May these mysteries, O Lord, in which we have participated, profit us, we pray, for even now, as we walk amid passing things, you teach us *by them* to love the things of heaven and hold fast to what endures' (emphasis added). English-speaking readers naturally take 'by them' to refer to the 'passing things', whereas the sense of the

Latin is clear: we are taught by the 'mysteries' and not by the 'passing things'. The 1998 ICEL translation avoids this mistake and expresses the prayer in elegant and attractive English: 'Lord our God, grant that in our journey through this passing world we may learn from these mysteries to cherish even now the things of heaven and to cling to the treasures that never pass away'. Here, as so often elsewhere, there is no competition between the two translations.

One could pile up further deficiencies in the 2010 translation. Chapter 2 above has discussed the unfortunate use of 'for you and for many' in the words of institution. Then a proper sensitivity to the St Paul's teaching on justification should have ruled out occurrences of 'meriting' in the 2010 translation that do not respect orthodox Christian faith.[27] In the Apostles' Creed 'descended into hell' replaces 'descended to the dead (descendit ad inferos)'.[28] Eastern icons show the difference: Christ has descended to save the just ones who are long dead and waiting for him as their Redeemer in the 'limbo of the fathers (*limbus patrum*)'. He is not consorting with Satan, the devils, and human beings condemned to hell, as if he were prefiguring Dante's visit to the 'Inferno'.

Often the 2010 version uses 'that' where proper English cries out for 'so that'. Take the translation of 'libera nos': 'Deliver us, Lord, we pray, from every evil, graciously grant peace in our days, that, by the help of your mercy, we may be always free from sin', and so forth in one long, breathless sentence. Surely it should be 'so that, by the help of your mercy'? Surely, incidentally, there should be at least a semicolon after 'from every evil'? Or should 'and' be inserted: 'and graciously grant'?

Since returning to live in Australia, one great shadow over my life

---

27 See e.g. the Prayers over the People for Friday after Ash Wednesday and for the Friday of the Second Week of Lent.
28 In the Fourth Eucharistic Prayer the 2010 translation speaks, however, of Christ's 'descent to the dead (descensum ad inferos)'.

as a priest has been the imposition of a clumsy, Latinized translation of the liturgy—made even more painful because there was a revised and intelligible version already available in the 1998 'Missal that never was'. My main consolation comes from regularly celebrating Mass in Italian for a group of old Italians. Their translation has not been messed about by ideologues and reads like contemporary, genuine Italian at its graceful and beautiful best.

With the hope of remedying a sad situation, I wrote an open letter to the English-speaking bishops, published on 7 March 2014 in the London *Tablet*:

> One of the great blessings in my life has come from teaching (and learning from) many of you when you were seminarians and young priests and took courses with me in Rome (1973–2006) and elsewhere. Some of you came to me for the sacrament of reconciliation.
>
> Many of you have invited me to lecture or lead retreats in your dioceses and welcomed me when I came. I have treasured your friendship and been encouraged by your example.
>
> My hope now is that you will act quickly to help English-speaking Catholics participate more effectively in the liturgy—a central recommendation in Vatican II's very first document. You all know that your episcopal conferences approved a revised translation completed after seventeen years of work by the International Commission on English in the Liturgy. You also know that the 1998 translation, when sent to the Congregation for Divine Worship, was simply rejected without any dialogue. Roman authorities set up a committee called Vox Clara ('a clear voice') which was largely responsible for a 'revised' translation in 2010 which came into force in November 2011. Ironically, the results produced by Vox Clara were too often unclear and sometimes verging on the unintelligible. This new 2010 translation regularly sounds like Latin texts transposed into English words rather than

genuine English. A notable English writer and translator, Monsignor Ronald Knox, like many others before and after him, wanted translations that 'read like a first-rate native thing'. Who could say that of our present *Missal*? Over and over again it reads like trans-literalized Latin or Latin texts simply transposed into English words.

Those who prepared the 2010 *Missal* aimed at a 'sacral style'—something that is alien to the direct and familiar way of speaking to God and about God practised by the psalmists and taught by Jesus. He never encouraged us to say: 'graciously grant, we pray, that you give us our daily bread', or 'may thy will, we pray, O Lord, be done through your prevenient grace'. He asked us to pray simply and directly to God: 'thy will be done; give us this day our daily bread'.

What would Jesus say about the 2010 *Missal*? Would he approve of its clunky, Latinized English that aspires to a 'sacral' style which allegedly will 'inspire' worshippers?

Many of you have copies of the 'Missal that wasn't', the 1998 translation summarily dismissed by the Congregation for Divine Worship. If not, you can easily download one from the internet. Set it alongside the 2010 *Missal*, and there should be no debate about the version to choose. Like the Lord's Prayer and like the Psalms, which fed the prayer life of Jesus, the 1998 translation is straightforward. As an example of genuine English, it is incomparably better than that imposed on English-speaking Catholics in November 2011.

Remembering the blessing of your long-standing presence in my life, I yearn for a final blessing, a quick solution to our liturgical woes. The 1998 translation is there, waiting in the wings. Please pass on now to English-speaking Catholics the 1998 translation that you or your predecessors voted for only a few years ago

The Background to Pope Francis

What the Congregation of Worship did to the eleven bishops' conferences of the English-speaking world is yet another example of power being misused by the Roman Curia. When, only ninety days after his election to the papacy, John XXIII called the Second Vatican Council (1962–65), he had two major aims in mind: (a) updating internally the Catholic Church, and (b) improving relations with other Christians and, indeed, with all people. In part, (a) included reforming the Curia, which, as an historian, he knew had little theological justification for its power, let alone for the size of its existence. In the event, the members of the Curia more than doubled: from 1,322 in 1961 to 3.146 in 1977, the year before the death of Pope Paul VI.[29]

Even before Vatican II opened or at least when they arrived for the Council in October 1962, many diocesan bishops showed their anger at the Curia and desire for its reform. Over the years it had appropriated responsibilities from the bishops. When through a *motu proprio*, *Pastorale munus* (30 November 1963), Paul VI partly reformed this situation, Yves Congar remarked in his diary: 'A list was read this morning of the faculties the Pope grants to bishops: "*concedimus* [we grant]", *impertimur* [we impart]. In reality, all he is doing is to give back—and not graciously—a part of what had been stolen from them over the centuries'.[30] Vatican II's Decree on the Pastoral Office of the Bishops in the Church, *Christus Dominus* of 28 October 1965, looked for a reform of the Curia, in particular, through its becoming internationalized (nos. 9–10).

In the Dogmatic Constitution on the Church (*Lumen Gentium*)

---

29 For a full account of modern attempts to reform the Roman Curia, see Massimo Faggioli, 'The Roman Curia at and after Vatican II; Legal-rational or Theological Reform', forthcoming in *Theological Studies*. See also G. O'Collins, *Living Vatican II: The 21st Council for the 21st Century* (Mahwah, NJ: Paulist Press, 2006), pp. 19–40, and, in particular, 37–38.

30 Y. Congar, *My Journal of the Council*, trans. M. J. Ronayne and M. C. Boulding (Collegeville, Minn.: Liturgical Press, 2012), p. 465.

Vatican II taught that the bishops around the world share responsibility with the Pope and make up a college 'with and under Peter' (nos. 22–23). An original apostolic college, which now serves as a model for the Bishop of Rome in his relations with other bishops, was not understood to include such members of Peter's entourage as Sylvanus and Mark (1 Peter 5:12–13), who might be thought of as precursors of the Roman Curia.[31] As we have seen above, the English-speaking bishops' collegiate responsibility for providing an appropriate translation of the liturgy was thwarted by members of the Roman Curia. In 1998, the year when their new translation of the *Missal* was presented for confirmation, John Paul II by a *motu proprio*, *Apostolos Suos*, limited the powers of all Western bishops' conferences by decreeing that, for their doctrinal declaration to be authentic teaching, such conferences need the unanimous agreement of all the bishops, or—in the case of a two-thirds majority—the approval of the Holy See. Here one should recall that at Vatican II, despite overwhelming votes for the final texts, no doctrinal document was approved unanimously or literally by all the bishops. There were always at least a very few who voted 'no'. The Pope and his Curia required from bishops' conferences a higher standard than that reached at the Council!

Paul VI, in his attempt to rein in the Roman Curia, seems to have imagined that it could be counter-balanced by two bodies: by the synods of bishops (meeting in Rome) that he introduced after the Council and by periodic meetings of the College of Cardinals. However, these two bodies enjoyed as such only affective authority and not the effective power to reform matters and bring about changes. The Secretariat of State, led by Cardinal Jean-Marie Villot, the first non-Italian to

---

31 From Romans 16 and other passages in other letters, we know much more about those who worked 'with and under' Paul. But, both in the ancient church and today, collegiality concerns apostolic leaders and not as such their entourage and administrative collaborators. On the collegial authority of the bishops, see G. O'Collins, *The Second Vatican Council: Message and Meaning* (Collegeville, Minn.: Liturgical Press, 2014), pp. 192–96.

hold that position since the Spaniard Merry Del Val (Secretary of State 1903–1914), included under Paul VI Archbishop (later Cardinal) Giovanni Benelli, a powerful and authoritarian 'sostituto' in charge of the day-to-day work of the Vatican.

Under the charismatic style of government of John Paul II (pope 1978–2005), the Congregation for the Doctrine of the Faith (CDF) regained its pivotal role as the 'supreme congregation'. Frequent bishops' synods (six 'ordinary' synods, the 'extraordinary' synod of 1985, and eight special continental or national assemblies) and 'extraordinary' consistories of cardinals (1979, 1982, 1985, 1991, 1994, and 2001) never curbed the power of the Roman Curia, which the Pope himself seemed uninterested in controlling.

To be sure, John Paul II did some reorganizing of the Roman Curia through a 1988 apostolic constitution *Pastor Bonus* that revised the 1967 reform under Paul VI. While Vatican II in *Christus Dominus* had spoken of the Curia functioning for 'the good of the churches' and 'in the service' of the bishops (no. 9), *Pastor Bonus* saw the Curia serving directly only the Pope and thus being only indirectly at the service of others in the Church. Where Paul VI wanted positions in the Curia to last only five or at most ten years, under John Paul II they could last for decades: for instance, Cardinal Gantin as prefect of the Congregation for the Bishops (1984–1998); Cardinal Ratzinger as prefect of the Congregation for the Doctrine of the Faith (1981–2005); Cardinal Tomko as prefect of the Congregation for the Evangelization of Peoples (1985–2001); Cardinal Martinez Somalo as prefect of the Congregation for Institutes of Consecrated Life and Societies of Apostolic Life (1992–2004), and Cardinal Grocholewski as prefect of the Congregation for Catholic Education (1999–2015). Members of these congregations or consultors to them could also remain there for fifteen years or more—a practice that encouraged investing their own opinions with false authority.

Benedict XVI (pope 2005–2013) extended the power of the

Roman Curia over bishops and bishops' conferences, and made an unfortunate choice for his Secretary of State, Cardinal Tarcisio Bertone. An Italian bishop who had come from the Diocese of Vercelli to serve under Ratzinger at the CDF and then become Archbishop of Genoa, Bertone had no diplomatic experience, spoke only Italian, and was dismissed by the Curia as an unqualified outsider.[32] Pope Benedict paid a heavy price for this appointment, the climax of his habit of choosing collaborators who could lack qualifications but with whom he felt at ease.

The Curia, already a body blighted by careerism, became even more riddled with infighting and financial irregularities connected with the Vatican Bank (euphemistically named the 'Istituto Opere Religiose' or Institute of Religious Works). The climax of the 'mess' arrived with the trial and conviction of Pope Benedict's butler, Paolo Gabriele, who had leaked confidential documents exposing the Vatican power struggle. Already worn out physically and mentally, the Pope resigned—a humble and courageous decision. On 13 March 2013, a conclave of 115 voting cardinals elected Cardinal Jorge Bergoglio of Buenos Aires, the first Latin American to become pope. The choice reflected an widespread concern for a radical reform of the Curia and the desire for a pope without links to an establishment widely seen as dysfunctional and even corrupt. In interviews that followed his election, Pope Francis spoke of the mandate to reform he had received, characterising the Curia as 'self-referential', 'narcissistic', and even 'the leprosy of the papacy'. In a pre-Christmas address to the Curia in December 2014, he spelled out the spiritual self-reformation that he expected of them. Without such a deep conversion, any changes will remain merely cosmetic.

---

32 Bertone could read French and Spanish, but his attempts as Secretary of State to speak those two had disastrous results. His successor as Secretary of State under Pope Francis, Cardinal Pietro Parolin is also an Italian, but he is an experienced diplomat who speaks English, French, Spanish, and some German.

Pope Francis: some reflections

Through his choice of name, Francis had sent a powerful message, even before he appeared on the balcony of St Peter's. St Francis of Assisi was a saint of poverty, a saint of peace ('Make me a channel of your peace', as a modern hymn expresses his deep desire), a saint who cherished the poor, and a saint who loved and protected the created world.

Pope Francis, by what he began doing, also reminded people of St Francis' famous advice: 'Preach the Gospel always and use words when necessary'. A few weeks after being elected Pope Francis continued the papal tradition of washing feet on Holy Thursday. But he did so in an unprecedented way: he went to a prison for young offenders, and washed the feet of twelve inmates, including two women: one a Serbian Muslim and the other an Italian Catholic.

The Pope's option for the poor became blatantly clear when, in July 2013, he made his first official journey out of Rome by heading south to visit Lampedusa. Shortly before he arrived, a boat carrying 165 asylum seekers from Eritrea pulled into the harbour of that tiny island. Francis celebrated the Eucharist in a sports field, which serves as a reception centre for thousands of desperate people fleeing across the Mediterranean. His chalice had been carved out of the wood of a migrant boat, and the altar was small painted boat. After Mass he laid a wreath in the harbour to remember the thousands of migrants who have drowned trying to reach Lampedusa.

What we might call 'the Francis programme' is set out in his November 1913 apostolic exhortation, *Evangelii Gaudium* (the Joy of the Gospel, EG). He invites 'all Christians' to open themselves to 'a renewed personal encounter with Jesus Christ'(no.3). Jesus 'speaks to the deepest yearnings of people's hearts'; he is 'a treasure of life and love that cannot deceive' (no. 265). So much of the exhortation's Jesus-centred message reflects what Pope Francis has himself personally experienced: 'Life grows by being given away…those who enjoy life most are those who leave security on the shore and become excited by the mission of communicating life to others' (no. 10). He repeatedly witnesses to his own service of the Gospel: 'we achieve fulfilment when we break down walls, and our heart is filled with faces and names' (no. 274).

If we reflect on EG in the light of the teaching of the Second Vatican Council, at times we find the Pope calling for that teaching to be implemented adequately. A glaring failure in its implementation has come from the Vatican's opposition to the practice of 'collegiality', which would involve a shared, decentralised leadership. Francis writes: 'it is not advisable for the Pope to take the place of the local bishops in the discernment of every issue which arises in their territory…I am conscious of the need to promote a sound "decentralisation"' (no. 16). In the opening years of Francis' papacy, we are still observing the working out of such decentralisation and true collegiality.

Sometimes EG represents a development of teaching that builds on but goes beyond Vatican II. Let me mention four areas. First, the Council's documents, and not least the Pastoral Constitution on the Church in the Modern World (*Gaudium et Spes*), feature clearly the need to pursue truth and practice goodness or justice. Without denying the role of beauty in the life of faith, Vatican II, even in *Gaudium et Spes*, hardly mentions beauty and, in particular the divine beauty (e.g. nos. 57, 76). EG, however, has much to say about beauty, starting from the beauty of the Church (no. 14) and her liturgy (no. 24). Pope Francis is at his eloquent best on the 'way of beauty' and 'the inseparable bond between truth, goodness and beauty'. He could have been speaking of himself when he wrote of 'beauty which shines forth in the life of fidelity to the Gospel' (no.167). Nos. 34–36, 42, 257, and 265 have more to add on the divine beauty revealed in Christ and his message.

Secondly, Vatican II underlined the responsibility of wealthier nations, groups, and individuals to assist the poor. It cited effectively the parable of the rich man and Lazarus (*Gaudium et Spes*, 27). Pope Francis moves such official teaching forward (EG, 186–214) and not least through insisting that the poor 'have much to teach us': 'we are called [not only] to find Christ in them, to lend our voice to their causes, but also to be their friends, to listen to them, to speak for them, and to embrace the mysterious wisdom which God wishes to share with us through them' (EG, 198).

Thirdly, instead of continuing the Vatican II language about other Christians as 'separated brethren', Pope Francis writes of 'pilgrims journeying alongside one another'. He speaks too of 'what the Spirit has sown in them, which is also meant to be a gift to us' Catholics. He provides a pertinent example of learning from 'our Orthodox brothers and sisters' more about 'the meaning of episcopal collegiality and their experience of synodality' (EG 244–46). Such learning is all the more necessary, since the implementation of the Council's teaching on such collegiality has been widely thwarted and the impact of numerous bishops' synods in Rome has been largely muted.

Fourthly, in *Lumen Gentium* (no. 16) and in the Declaration on the Relation of the Church to non-Christian Religions, *Nostra Aetate* (nos. 4–5), Vatican II became the first general council in the history of the Catholic Church to offer some positive teaching about the Jewish people. Pope Francis would not place them in a document on 'non-Christian religions': 'as Christians, we cannot consider Judaism as a foreign religion'. He insists that 'dialogue and friendship with the children of Israel are part of the life of Jesus' disciples'. The Church at large 'is enriched when she receives the values of Judaism' (EG, 247–49).

Conclusion

As this book draws to an end, I am more conscious than ever that it does not mention many relatives and friends who are very close and dear to me. They have shared and made possible my journey from 2009 to 2014. For that I remain deeply grateful. I am also aware that volume three of my memoirs—and not least in the appendices—offers views on a larger scale than the previous two volumes.

For months through 2014 I set myself to move slowly through the fresh translation of Dante's *Divine Comedy* that Clive James spent years in producing. In the past I had read, often in the original Italian, large chunks of the *Comedy*. But this was the first time that I had read the masterpiece from the beginning right through to the final words about 'the love that moves the sun and the other stars'. That divine love has carried me through life. May it save me from the 'inferno', and take me through my 'purgatorio' to share in the eternal light and life of 'paradiso'.

APPENDIX 1

Spe Salvi (Saved by Hope)

'Pope Attacks the Cruelty of Atheism' and 'Pope Benedict Replies to *The God Delusion* by Richard Dawkins' were two of the headlines that greeted Benedict XVI's second encyclical, *Saved by Hope*. An Anglican bishop was more on target when he told me: 'I welcome this encyclical on Christian hope. Hope is essential, but too often it's been neglected. I'm very glad to find a papal encyclical for the first time taking hope as its theme.'

What are the surprises in this encyclical? Do parts of it take us beyond the Pope's first encyclical, *God Is Love*? Does this second pastoral letter show any links to *Eschatology: Death and Eternal Life*, a book on hope that Joseph Ratzinger first published in 1977? Are there any significant omissions?

The Letter's Content

The Pope's message combines a pastor's concern for his people with a scholar's use of Scripture and an effective appeal to some great voices in the Catholic tradition— from Augustine of Hippo to Cardinal Nguyen Van Thuan, a prisoner for 13 years, nine of them spent in solitary confinement. The encyclical is peppered with references and insights of every kind: biblical, doctrinal, spiritual, philosophical, historical, and artistic.

'Young people', the Pope writes, 'can have the hope of a great and satisfying love, the hope of a certain position in their profession, or of some success that will prove decisive for the rest of their lives.' But even when such hopes are fulfilled, it becomes evident that 'only something infinite' will satisfy a 'great hope' that is something more than we can 'ever attain' or achieve for ourselves (nos. 30, 31). One hears an echo of the words with which Augustine begins his *Confessions*: 'Our heart is restless until it finds rest in you, O Lord.' Pope Benedict draws on Augustine to underline our primordial hunger for true and lasting happiness, for that eternal life in which we will experience a totally satisfying fullness and be 'plunged into the ocean of infinite love' (nos. 11, 12).

The Pope appreciates 'the experience of a great love' that can give 'a new meaning' to our existence. Yet by themselves such experiences remain 'fragile' and will, in any case, be 'destroyed by death'. We need the 'unconditional love' (no. 26), which St Paul described luminously in cosmic language: 'neither death, nor life, nor angels, nor principalities, nor things present, nor things to come, nor powers, nor height, nor depth, nor anything else in all creation will be able to separate us from the love of God in Christ Jesus our Lord' (Rom 8:38–39).

Almost half the encyclical (nos. 32–48) is dedicated to what the Pope calls 'settings for learning and practising hope'. He names prayer as the 'school of hope'. An 'exercise of desire', prayer also entails 'a process of inner purification which opens us up to God and thus to our fellow human beings'. There is an 'intimate relationship between prayer and hope'.

Pope Benedict recalls what Cardinal Van Thuan wrote in *Prayers of Hope*: 'During thirteen years in gaol, in a situation of seemingly utter hopelessness, the fact that he could listen and speak to God became for him an increasing power of hope, which enabled him, after his release, to become for people all over the world a witness to hope—to that great hope which does not wane even in the nights of solitude' (nos. 32–33).

'All serious and upright human conduct', the Pope insists, 'is hope in action'. But, as well as practising hope through working 'towards a brighter and more humane world' (no. 35), we can grow in hope through the things we suffer. We must 'limit' and 'fight against suffering', but 'we cannot eliminate it'. Benedict adds: 'It is not by sidestepping or fleeing from suffering that we are healed, but rather by our capacity for accepting it, maturing through it, and finding meaning through union with Christ, who suffered with infinite love'. The Pope then quotes a vivid passage from a letter by the Vietnamese martyr Paul Le-Bao-Tinh (d. 1857) that illustrates the 'transformation of suffering through the power of hope'. It was a 'letter from Hell' that described the hideous conditions of a prison where tyrants abused and brutalized their victims. Yet the martyr wrote: 'In the midst of these torments which usually terrify others, I am, by the grace of God, full of joy and gladness, because I am not alone—Christ is with me' (no. 37).

The Pope looks beyond the suffering embodied in Christian martyrdom to broader issues: 'The true measure of humanity is essentially determined in relationship to suffering and to the sufferer. This holds true both for the individual and for society.' A society that 'is unable to accept its suffering members and incapable of helping to share their suffering and to bear it inwardly through compassion is a cruel and inhuman society.' Yet society at large will not support suffering members in their trials, unless 'individuals are capable of doing so themselves' and personally 'able to find meaning in suffering' (no. 38). In effect, the Pope challenges both the public and every individual with the questions: Do you find any meaning in suffering? How do you relate to those who suffer? What do you do for them? Real Christian hope is always hope for others—and, especially, an active, compassionate hope for those who suffer.

Along with the role that prayer and suffering should play here and now as settings for learning and practising hope, the Pope turns to the future and recalls the expectation that the risen Christ 'will come again in glory to judge the living and the dead'. On the east end of ancient churches it became customary to depict the Lord returning as king, while the west wall 'normally portrayed the Last Judgement as a symbol of our responsibility for our lives'. This was the 'scene which followed and accompanied the faithful as they went out to resume their daily routine'. Unfortunately, as the iconography of the Last Judgement developed, 'more and more prominence was given to its ominous and frightening aspects, which obviously held more fascination for artists than the splendour of hope, often all too well concealed beneath the horrors' (no. 41). Benedict XVI emphasizes that 'the image of the Last Judgement is not primarily an image of terror but an image of hope'. Even though it is also 'an image that evokes responsibility', it remains an image of hope, even a 'decisive image of hope' (no. 44).

In making his case for recognizing the splendour of hope to be found in the image of the Last Judgement, the Pope engages in a fascinating dialogue with two acclaimed Jewish philosophers and sociologists of the Frankfurt School: Max Horkheimer (1895–1973) and Theodor Adorno (1903–69). They insisted that the horrible injustices of history should not have the final word. There must finally be justice. But that, in the words the Pope quotes from Adorno, would require a world 'where not only present suffering would be wiped out, but that which is irrevocably past would be undone'. Yet this would mean, the Pope points out, something foreign to the thought of Adorno: the resurrection of the dead (no. 42).

There will be, the Pope declares, 'an undoing of past suffering, a reparation that sets things right'. 'For this reason', he adds, 'faith in the Last Judgement is first and foremost hope'. Personally he is convinced that 'the question of justice constitutes…the strongest argument in favour of faith in eternal life'. It is only because 'the injustice of history' cannot be 'the final word' that 'the necessity for Christ's return and for new life become fully convincing' (no. 43). Hence he can state firmly: 'God is justice and creates justice. This is our consolation and our hope' (no. 44).

The encyclical ends with a touching address to the Blessed Virgin

Mary, the 'Star of Hope' (no. 50). Here Pope Benedict follows a practice of his predecessor, who often closed his official texts with a prayer to the Virgin Mary. I find Benedict's prayer even more effective than those of John Paul II. In an affectionate and effective way, it follows the journey of hope that was the life of Mary.

The encyclical remains in steady dialogue with the modern world in all its technological progress, dreadful upheavals, and material hopes. The Pope recognizes, for instance, how at one level 'the laws of matter and of evolution' govern the world. But they do not 'have the final say'. That belongs to the personal, loving God who governs the universe (no. 5).

The Pope recalls the progress signalled by 'the discovery of America and the new technical achievements' encouraged by the thought of Francis Bacon (1561–1626). 'He even put forward a vision of foreseeable inventions—including the airplane and the submarine' (no. 17). Reason and freedom fuelled faith in progress and a hope for a new Jerusalem that progress might bring into his world. After the French Revolution, 'the nineteenth century held to its faith in progress as the new form of human hope' (no 20). Marx and Engels envisaged the proletarian revolution, which came 'in the most radical way in Russia'. The supposedly 'interim phase of the dictatorship of the proletariat' did not usher in 'a perfect world' but left behind 'a trail of appalling destruction' (no. 21).

As Adorno warned dramatically, 'progress, seen accurately, is progress from the sling to the atom bomb'. The Pope cites these words to illustrate 'the ambiguity of progress'. Unquestionably 'it offers new possibilities for good, but it also opens up appalling possibilities that formerly did not exist'. In words that echo Albert Einstein, he warns: 'if technical progress is not matched by corresponding progress' in the 'ethical formation' of human beings, 'then it is no progress at all, but a threat' for humanity and the world (no. 22).

We cannot simply 'be redeemed through science. Such an expectation asks too much of science'. To be sure, 'science can contribute greatly to making the world' more human. Yet 'it can also destroy' the human race and the world, 'unless it is steered by forces that lie outside it' (no. 25). Without opening themselves to truth, love and what is good and making 'a right use of creation which comes to us as a gift', human beings can destroy 'the present and the future' (no.35).

Pope Benedict sums up the dramatic state of the human race. While, on the one hand, there is 'incremental progress' in the material sphere, a 'continuous progress towards an ever greater mastery of nature', on the other hand, human freedom 'is always new', and 'decisions can never simply be made for us in advance by others'. In 'fundamental decisions, every person and every generation are a new beginning'. New generations 'can build on the knowledge and experience of those who went before, and they can draw on the moral treasury of the whole of humanity. But they can also reject it' (no. 24).

In developing his encyclical, the Pope draws on a rich variety of sources and examples. After an opening section on the teaching of the New Testament, he moves to the heroic life of the Sudanese saint Josephine Bakhita. Born in Darfur, she was kidnapped at the age of nine, sold five times in slave markets and flogged repeatedly. Bought by an Italian merchant, she was taken to Italy, set free, and received into the Catholic Church by the Patriarch of Venice. As a Canossian sister, she set herself to extend to others the 'liberation' and the hope she 'had received through her encounter with the God of Jesus Christ' (no. 3).

The Pope cites from the tradition such major voices as Ambrose of Milan, Maximus the Confessor, Bernard of Clairvaux, Thomas Aquinas, and Henri de Lubac (but not his friend Pierre Teilhard de Chardin, who combined a Christ-centred hope with a profound sense of evolutionary progress towards the final future). The Pope repeatedly uses texts from Augustine of Hippo to illuminate the theory and practice of Christian hope. Augustine and other church fathers understood 1 Corinthians 3:12–15 to express a fiery judgement facing every individual; it became a classic passage supporting the existence and function of Purgatory (no. 40). This interpretation, however, went far beyond what Paul himself had in mind: the judgement that missionary preachers would experience.

Pope Benedict draws on two essays of Immanuel Kant to exemplify this great philosopher's disillusionment as the progress promised by the French Revolution lapsed into violence and terror (no. 19), and from Plato's *Gorgias* and Dostoevsky's *The Brothers Karamazov* to illustrate the meaning of final justice (no. 44). In highlighting 'the innumerable interactions' that link the lives of all people, the Pope echoes John Donne: 'No man is an island' (no. 48).

Even more than *God Is Love*, this second encyclical cites a rich range of witnesses from beyond the Catholic tradition. The Pope's respect for Adorno, Bacon, Dostoevsky, Horkheimer, Kant, and Plato sets the encyclical in a broad context of human thought and culture. *Saved by Hope* reads seamlessly, unlike *God Is Love*, of which the first part came from Pope Benedict himself while the second part comprises reworked themes on charity and justice inherited from his papal predecessor. John Paul II broke new ground in papal teaching by considering repeatedly and at length the question of human and Christian suffering. *Saved by Hope* also takes up suffering and its possible meaning.

Like Ratzinger's 1977 book, this new encyclical draws on Adorno's thought in maintaining justice to come though the resurrection of the dead, and reflects on an 'intermediate state' of purification after death. But unlike that book, it neither develops a theology of death nor attends to the precise theme of the immortality of the soul.

For all its richness, Pope Benedict's second encyclical does not include everything one might expect. It does not invoke the Second Vatican Council, which concluded by issuing its longest document *Gaudium et Spes* (Joy and Hope) and declaring: 'The future of humanity lies in the hands of those who are strong enough to provide coming generations with reasons for living and hoping' (no. 31). Nor does the encyclical mention the Holy Spirit, whose powerful presence is at work to bring all things to final salvation (Romans 8:23). These are two surprising omissions.

Nevertheless, Pope Benedict has published a timely and welcome appeal to refresh our life of hope. May his new encyclical give much light and encouragement to the Church and the world.

This appendix was originally published in *America* magazine for 21–28 January 2008, and is reproduced with permission.

APPENDIX 2

ECUMENISM IN ADVENT

Soon we move into the season of Advent, and Christmas will be less than a month away. When Christmas comes around, we Christians do many of the same things.

We send Christmas cards to our family and friends. We put up cribs in our churches, schools, and homes. Many of us will attend a service of nine lessons and carols, a practice introduced in 1880 by Bishop Edward White Benson, later Archbishop of Canterbury. This Anglican service has been widely adopted by Christian churches around the world.

As for the carols themselves, Christians everywhere sing more or less the same repertoire during Advent and at Christmas. Through our carols we share together the same deep delight at the birth of a poor child who became the Saviour of the world.

The carols are wonderfully ecumenical in their origins. Four verses and the tune of *Adeste fideles* (O come all ye faithful) go back to an eighteenth-century Roman Catholic layman, John Francis Wade. *Angels we have heard on high* is a traditional French carol, now commonly sung to a tune arranged by Edward Shippen Barnes (1887–1958), an American organist and composer. The text of *Hark the herald angels sing* comes from Charles Wesley; its widely used melody is taken from Felix Mendelssohn, who was born into a Jewish family and brought up a Lutheran. Isaac Watts, a non-conformist, composed the words of *Joy to the world*. The music, though often attributed to George Frederick Handel, seems to be of English origin.

An Episcopalian bishop, Phillips Brooks, wrote *O little town of Bethlehem*, and the tune normally heard in England is due to Ralph Vaughan Williams. *Ding dong merrily on high* is sung to a dance tune from sixteenth-century France; the text comes from an English enthusiast for carols, George Ratcliffe Woodward (1848–1934). We owe *Away in a manger* to a nineteenth-century children's book used by American Lutherans. The words for *See amid the winter's snow* were written by Edward Caswall, a convert who joined John Henry Newman in the Birmingham Oratory. Sir John Goss, an Anglican organist and composer, provided the musical setting.

Silent night, holy night was the work of two Austrian Catholics, the priest and organist of a country church. An Irish Protestant, Nahum Tate, probably composed the text for *While shepherds watched their flocks at night*, which is often sung to a melody taken from Handel.

These and other familiar carols have been composed by members of different Christian communities who lived in various parts of the world. The carols have also proved splendidly ecumenical in their use. No other hymns are sung so widely by Christians when they celebrate one of the two central feasts of their liturgical year.

With a happiness that shines on their faces, Christians sing together the carols. With the birth of Christ, light has replaced darkness and true freedom has taken over from sin. The beautiful *Sussex Carol* catches the common joy of Christian believers: 'On Christmas night all Christians sing/To hear the news the angels bring./News of great joy, news of great mirth./News of our merciful King's birth.' The words of this carol go back to a seventeenth-century Irish bishop, Luke Wadding. In the early twentieth century, Vaughan Williams discovered the text and the tune we use today, when he heard it being sung at Monk's Gate in Sussex. Hence it is called *The Sussex Carol*.

Such carols unite Christians around the Christ Child in the manger. They blend beautifully text and music to unite us and lift our spirits at Christmas. But they also remind us that the shadow of the cross falls across the birth of Jesus.

Some carols foreshadow the suffering which the Christ Child

will endure for all human beings. Thus the penultimate verse of the traditional English carol, *The first Nowell*, declares: 'and with his blood mankind has bought'. *In dulci jubilo*, a medieval German carol, arranged by J. M. Neale and entitled *Good Christian men, rejoice*, subtly links Bethlehem and Calvary when the second verse repeats: 'Christ was born for this'.

In a special way the carols that feature the Magi and one of the gifts they offer foretell the passion of Christ. Myrrh is an aromatic resin that was widely used in the Middle Ages to embalm corpses. From early times Christians understood that gift to symbolize the death and resurrection of Jesus. *We three kings of Orient are*, a nineteenth-century Christmas carol from Pennsylvania, devotes a whole verse to the gift of myrrh: 'Myrrh is mine, its bitter perfume/breathes a life of gathering gloom,/sorrowing, sighing, bleeding, dying,/sealed in the stone-cold tomb.' Such carols bring Christians together with the Magi in worshipping the Christ Child, whose birth is already overshadowed by the cross.

There is an edge of sadness to the great joy we share at the birth of Jesus. While uniting us in happy song, Christmas reminds us of the pain that surrounds the ecumenical movement, a movement that prays and works in a world of pervasive suffering.

By all means we should join *The Sussex Carol* in singing; 'When sin departs before his grace,/Then life and health come in its place./Angels and men with joy may sing,/All for us to see the new-born King.' But we should not forget the Magi, their gift of myrrh, and the painful meaning it symbolized. *We three kings of Orient are* and *The first Nowell* add their sombre note. So too does W. H. Auden in *For the Time Being: A Christmas Oratorio*. He pictures Mary gazing at the child Jesus in the manger and wondering: 'How soon will you start on the Sorrowful Way?'

When we sing our favourite carols this Advent and Christmas, let us rejoice in their very ecumenical origins and in their use by Christians everywhere. But may we also remember how the shadow of the cross fell over the Christ Child, and how relations between Christians bear their own suffering in a world of great pain.

[This version of a lecture, given to the Friends of the Anglican Centre (Rome) in the Jerusalem Chamber, Westminster Abbey (4 December 2007), appeared in *The Pastoral Review* for March/April 2011, and is reprinted with permission.]

APPENDIX 3

THE CONGREGATION FOR THE DOCTRINE OF THE FAITH EXPLAINS AND COMMENTS

[In June 2007, as I mentioned in Chapter 3, the CDF sent the presidents of episcopal conferences a document, the *Responsa* (*Responses to Some Questions Regarding Certain Aspects of the Doctrine of the Church*, replies to five questions the CDF put to itself), accompanied by an official *Commentary*, explaining the 'authentic' meaning of certain expressions they had used in earlier texts. At his request, I wrote the following comments for Cardinal Cormac Murphy-O'Connor, in a letter dated 21 June 2007, adding 'I cannot imagine that Cardinal Walter Kasper had a hand in this business. Did he ever see the *Responsa* and have a chance of correcting the text?' At the time Kasper was not only President of the Pontifical Council for Promoting Christian Unity but also a member of the CDF.]

The *Responsa* concentrates on one issue: the interpretation of the Latin verb 'subsistit' (see Vatican II, *Lumen Gentium*, 8). It is pretty clear that among the principal 'targets' (i.e. those who are said to be creating confusion by their 'incorrect' interpretation of 'subsistit') are Giuseppe Alberigo (who died last week) and Frank Sullivan, SJ, (now at Boston College). In an article that appeared in *Theological Studies* in 2006, Sullivan took issue with what Karl Josef (later Cardinal) Becker, SJ, had published about 'subsistit' in the *Osservatore Romano*. That exchange is the obvious background to much of what is said in the *Responsa* and its *Commentary*.

Where LG simply teaches that 'the one Church of Christ' 'subsists in the Catholic Church', the *Responsa* interprets the Council's text to mean 'subsists *only* in the Catholic Church'. The CDF claims that the word 'subsists' can '*only* be attributed to the Catholic Church *alone*' (reply to second question; emphasis mine)—a claim that is incompatible with the teaching of the Vatican II.

In the context of Vatican II, the Latin word 'subsistit' means 'continues to exist'. In the teaching of Vatican II, to say that the Church of Christ continues to exist fully in the Catholic Church went along with the recognition that this same Church continues to exist, but not so fully, in other churches. Vatican II called the separated Eastern churches 'true particular churches'; the universal Church also exists 'in and out of' particular churches that are not in full communion with the Holy See. To recognize Orthodox Christianity as being constituted of 'true particular churches' entails recognizing that the universal Church of God is wider and more inclusive than the Roman Catholic Church. See, for instance, what *Unitatis Redintegratio* (the Decree on Ecumenism) says about the celebration of the Eucharist among the Orthodox, a celebration through which 'the Church of God is built up and grows in stature' (no. 15). Obviously the Council was not speaking of a second Church of God. There is only one Church, and that Church of God continues to exist (subsists), albeit not fully, also in these other particular churches.

In reply to its fifth question, the CDF introduces offensive terminology about the Christian communities born out of the Reformation: they are not to be called 'Churches in the proper sense'. Authors of this offensive language, which is not used by Vatican II but is found in the CDF's document of 2000, *Dominus Iesus*, are still very much involved in the CDF. They want to insist on being right, even after the reaction this language drew from Cardinal Kasper and others. The theology behind this particular response plays down the baptismal basis for Christian unity.

In replying to their second question, (a) the CDF tells the reader correctly that 'subsistence' in LG means 'perduring historical continuity'. But then it refers in a footnote to the 1985 CDF notification on a book by Leonardo Boff. In that notification the CDF endorsed a rather Platonic notion of subsistence as an idea being realized in history in one, unique, historical existence. (b) The *Commentary* reveals a similar confusion. Apropos of the second question, it obviously takes up again the philosophical sense of subsistence endorsed by the CDF in its 1985 notification But, in dealing with the fifth question, the Commentary goes back to the correct meaning of 'subsistit': namely, 'continues to exist'. Thus a remarkable inconsistency over the meaning of 'subsistit' emerges in both the *Responsa* and the *Commentary*. Readers can only shake their heads and ask: who is creating confusion?

Furthermore, in the *Commentary*, apropos of the first question, the claim is made that *Dominus Iesus* 'merely reaffirmed the conciliar and post-conciliar teaching without adding or taking anything away'. This claim does not stand up when one analyses some of the details. For instance, DI presents the followers of other religions as being able to reach only 'beliefs' and not 'faith': Christians receive the gift of faith but these others do not (DI, 7). Vatican II, however, recognized that God calls those who, through no fault of their own, do not know the Gospel to that *faith* 'without which it is impossible to please God' (*Ad Gentes*, 7, citing Hebrews 11:6). A second example: Vatican II's *Dei Verbum* spoke of the *fullness* of the historical revelation brought by Christ in his life, death, and resurrection (along with the coming of the Holy Spirit), but never called that revelation *definitive* and *absolute*—dangerously inaccurate language used repeatedly in DI and language that is incompatible with the New Testament's doctrine about revelation being consummated at the end (e.g. 1 Corinthians 13:12; 1 John 3:2; 1 Peter 1:5, 13).

Finally, the *Commentary* in dealing with the third question boldly asserts what 'was intended' and what 'the Council intended' by the choice of 'subsistit' over 'est'. The Council had rejected 'est' in a draft which stated that 'the Church of God is the Catholic Church'; that rejection was clearly intended. But in a search for an alternative verb, the possibility came up of using 'adest' (is present in), and finally 'subsistit' slipped quietly into the text, without any clearly elaborated intention being involved. See the article by Frank Sullivan and the published research by Alexandra von Teuffenbach, as well as her ongoing publication of the Council diary authored by Fr Sebastian Tromp, SJ.

[The original (Latin) text of the *Responsa*, dated 29 June 2007, is found in the *Acta Apostolicae Sedis* 99 (2007), pp. 604–08; see *Origins* 37/9 (19 July 2007), pp. 134–36, for an English translation. The same number of *Origins* adds a translation of the *Commentary*, pp. 136–39. The next appendix, Appendix Four, offers a more accessible reflection on the *Responsa* and its *Commentary*, written for but not published by *The Tablet*.]

Appendix 4

One Little Word

Right from the early centuries of Christianity, councils and synods have often been clearer about what they 'rule out' than about what they 'rule in'. At the Second Vatican Council, for instance, a majority of bishops did *not* want to say that the Church of Christ *is* ('est') the Catholic Church, which would mean simply identifying the Church of Christ with the Catholic Church. For the final text of the Constitution on the Church (*Lumen gentium*) they changed the word *est* to *subsistit in* (subsists in). But what does this verb mean in its context? What might it entail for ecumenical relations? How should one understand and assess the very recent comments [the *Responsa* and its *Commentary* of 29 June 2007] on this verb from the Congregation for the Doctrine of the Faith (CDF). Let me begin with the key paragraph from *Lumen gentium* where the verb was used for the first time in an official document.

'The unique Church of Christ…subsists in the Catholic Church, which is governed by the successor of Peter and by the bishops in communion with him. Nevertheless, many elements of sanctification and truth are found outside its visible confines' (no. 8). The first point to note is that the Council did not teach, 'subsists *only* in the Catholic Church'. Nor, secondly, did it teach that 'outside the visible confines of the Catholic Church there are found *only elements* of sanctification and truth'.

The final sentence in the passage I have quoted from *Lumen gentium* received an authoritative commentary in a 1995 encyclical by John Paul II on the Catholic commitment to ecumenical work, *Ut unum sint* (that they may be one). The Pope wrote: 'the elements of sanctification and truth present in other Christian communities… constitute the objective basis of communion, albeit imperfect, which exists between them and the Catholic Church. To the extent that these elements are found in other Christian communities, the one Church of Christ is effectively present in them' (no. 11). Obviously, then, these 'many elements' carry implications for central issues: the nature of *communion* (even a communion that is less than perfect) in the One Church of Christ, the visible *presence* of that one Church, and the meaning of 'subsists in'.

But before addressing these issues, I need to recall a second document from Vatican II, the Decree on Ecumenism (*Unitatis redintegratio*). By calling the separated Orthodox churches 'particular' and 'sister' churches (no. 14), this document recognized that the universal Church of God is wider and more inclusive than the Catholic Church. Hence the decree could say that, through the celebration of the Eucharist among the Orthodox, 'the Church of God is built up and grows in stature' (no. 15). Obviously the Council was not speaking of a second Church of God. There is only one Church, and that one Church of God continues to grow and is built up *also* in the true, particular churches of Orthodox Christianity.

As it had already done in its declaration published in 2000, *Dominus Iesus*, the CDF in some but not all passages of its latest pair of documents, as we will see below, takes the word *subsistit* to have its normal Latin meaning of 'continues to exist'. Hence the corresponding noun 'subsistence' means 'perduring historical continuity' and 'permanence'. Both here and for the teaching of Vatican II, the question naturally arises: *how* does the one Church 'continue to exist' historically, remain permanently in continuity with its origins, and maintain communion or unity?

The CDF answered this question in *Dominus Iesus* by saying that it is '*only* in the Catholic Church' that the Church of Christ 'continues to exist *fully*' (no. 16; emphasis mine). The use of the adverbs 'only' and 'fully' was justified by what Vatican II taught about the Catholic Church in its Decree on Ecumenism. There the Council said: 'We believe that it [the unity which Christ bestowed on his Church from the beginning] subsists in the Catholic Church as something she can never lose' (no. 4). Apropos of this unity, the decree also said: 'our separated fellow Christians, whether considered as individuals or as communities and churches, are not blessed with that unity which Jesus Christ wished to bestow' (no. 3). Further, as regards the means of salvation, the Council taught: 'it is only through Christ's Catholic Church, which is the all-embracing means of salvation, that the fullness of the means of salvation can be attained' (ibid.).

Summing up the Council's teaching, one can say that only the Catholic Church has fully maintained the unity and fullness of the means of grace which Christ gave to his Church. Since, as the CDF has, at least in places, recognized, the Latin word *subsistere* means 'to continue to exist', one can rightly say that it is only in the Catholic Church that the Church of Christ subsists fully. This is obviously not the same thing as saying that the Church of Christ subsists only and exclusively in the Catholic Church alone—as the CDF now proposes.

Clearly this desire to limit the use of the word 'subsist' stands in tension with what the CDF's *Responsa* quotes from John Paul II's encyclical *Ut unum sint*: 'the Church of Christ is present and operative in the churches and ecclesial communities not yet fully in communion with the Catholic Church' (*Ut unum sint*, 11; *Responsa*, 2). Thus the CDF would expect Catholics to speak of the Church of God as 'present and operative' in various separated churches and ecclesial communities but not as 'subsisting' in them! Likewise, even though Catholics follow the lead of Vatican II's Decree on Ecumenism and talk of the Church of God as being 'built up' and 'growing' among the Orthodox (see above), they would be forbidden by the CDF to say that the Church of God 'subsists' (or continues to exist) in the particular churches of Orthodox Christianity. Use of the verb in this context is disqualified, whereas being 'present and operative' (or being 'built up' and 'growing') remains language that is allowable and even encouraged.

Let me put matters bluntly. If Catholics are expected to follow the CDF and say that the Church of Christ continues to exist *only* in the Catholic Church, how can they also (1) agree with Vatican II that the Church of God is 'built up' and 'grows' in the Orthodox Churches, and (2) follow John Paul II in saying that the Church of God is, to some extent, 'present and operative' in such other Christian communities?

It would have been better on the part of the CDF to speak of the Church of God subsisting *fully* in the Catholic Church and subsisting in many ways, albeit not fully, in other churches and ecclesial communities. Faith in Christ as the incarnate and risen Son of God, baptism, the Scriptures, and many other elements of sanctification and truth are found in these other churches and ecclesial communities. Much more is it to be found, of course, in the particular, sister churches of Orthodox Christianity. In short, it would have been advisable to recognize degrees in the 'subsistence' of the Church of Christ rather than endorse a kind of 'all or nothing' judgement about 'subsistence'.

Despite this less than happy limitation in recognizing 'subsists', at least sometimes the CDF understands correctly the basic meaning of the verb to be 'continues to exist': for instance, in the declaration of 2000, *Dominus Iesus*. But I have to say 'sometimes'. Both the CDF's recent *Responsa* and the accompanying *Commentary* also refer back to a 1985 CDF notification on a book by Leonardo Boff. When doing so, they apparently follow the notification in understanding 'subsists' in the rather Platonic sense of an idea realized in history and actualized (in German 'verwirklicht') in only one, unique historical existence. For those who accept this way of translating 'subsistit', the Church of

Christ is realized only once in history: in the unique existence of the Catholic Church. Seemingly they come to this conclusion simply on the basis of their way of understanding and interpreting the verb. But many scholars rightly challenge this way of rendering 'subsistit' and reject the German translation that would encourage this rendering.

Taking 'subsistit' to mean 'continue to exist' follows normal Latin usage. It also belongs squarely to what the teaching of Vatican II and John Paul II clearly implies: the Church of God continues to exist, albeit not fully, in churches and ecclesial communities other than the Catholic Church.

Appendix 5

A Challenge for Theologians: Three Puzzling Positions

In its recent notification on two works by Fr Jon Sobrino, SJ, the Congregation for the Doctrine of the Faith (CDF) recalls and re-affirms some utterly basic Christian teachings about Jesus Christ—above all, that Jesus was/is both truly divine and fully human. Such doctrines, embodied in the Nicene-Constantinopolitan Creed of 381 that is accepted by all Christian communities, require firm assent from any Catholic theologian worthy of the name.

There are, however, several particular positions adopted by the notification that seem less than convincing and have puzzled commentators. Let me give three examples, two of them theological and one of them biblical.

First, the notification takes up a point of theology that might seem somewhat arcane but does, nevertheless, lie at the heart of the teaching of the Councils of Ephesus (431) and Chalcedon (451). This is the *communicatio idiomatum* or exchange of properties (no. 6). By describing the exchange of properties as 'the possibility of referring the properties of divinity to humanity and vice versa', the notification could be misleading. It gives the impression that we would, for example, be justified in attributing to the divine nature of Christ the property of mortality and to his human nature the property of omnipotence. The meaning of the exchange of properties is entirely different.

We can name the *person* of Christ with reference to one nature (for instance, 'the Son of God') and then attribute to his *person* some property due to the other nature ('died on the cross'). Such attribution justifies the language of Christmas carols in which the Christ Child is described as 'the creator of the sun and stars'. This language names the person in reference to one nature (his humanity) and attributes to his person a property (here the power to create) that belongs to his other nature (his divinity). The *communicatio idiomatum* is not an optional extra or a game to be played by theologians alone. It essentially serves to defend the unity of Christ (at the level of his person) and his duality (at the level of two distinct but not separated natures). One may not gloss over the fact that attributions are attached to the person of Christ and go on to describe the *communicatio idiomatum* as a matter of 'referring the properties of the divinity to the humanity and vice versa [of the humanity to the divinity]'.

Second, the section where the notification deals with the self-consciousness of Jesus seems unclear about the position it intends to maintain (no. 8). On the one hand, it expounds 'the filial and messianic consciousness of Jesus' and 'his intimate and immediate knowledge' of the Father—a doctrine that is well supported by the Gospels and by the theology of Karl Rahner (which this section echoes in passing). On the other hand, the section appears to advocate a return to the view of St Thomas Aquinas: namely, that from the very first moment of his human conception, Jesus enjoyed in his earthly mind the beatific vision. This view was not included in the 1992 *Catechism of the Catholic Church*. It had already been dropped by the majority of theologians and biblical scholars. Aquinas's view does not show up in several documents issued in the 1970s and 1980s by the International Theological Commission and the Pontifical Biblical Commission. These texts assembled the information that can be gleaned from the Gospels about Christ's human consciousness of his personal identity and redemptive mission. These highly relevant documents from two official commissions fail to make an appearance in the notification. To be sure Aquinas's view of the beatific vision as experienced by the human mind of Christ was endorsed in passing by a 1943 encyclical of Pope Pius XII, *Mystici Corporis*. But that encyclical was primarily concerned with the doctrine of the Church. It certainly did not intend to determine once and for all a position on the human consciousness of Christ inherited from Aquinas.

Does the CDF ask Fr Sobrino and other theologians to agree with the already widely accepted position that Jesus, during his earthly life and in his human mid, enjoyed a unique, intimate knowledge of the Father and consciousness of his personal identity and saving mission? Or does the CDF require a return to the view that, from the very first moment of his conception, Jesus enjoyed in his human mind the vision of God enjoyed by the saints in heaven—a view that rules out the possibility of recognizing the perfect faith exercised by Jesus during his earthly pilgrimage (Hebrews 12:2)?

Third, apropos of the redemptive value of the crucifixion and resurrection, the notification rightly wishes to establish the significance that the earthly Jesus ascribed to his coming death (no. 9). It appeals to relevant texts from the Last Supper in support of this conclusion. But the notification also cites Mark 10:45: 'The Son of Man did not come to be served but to serve, and to give his life as a ransom for many'. Many mainstream scholars agree that the first part of this saying goes back to the words of Jesus. Few, however, maintain that 'giving his life as a ransom for many' derives directly from Jesus himself. These words appear, rather, to be a formulation stemming from the evangelist Mark or his sources in the Christian tradition. They express, of course, a perfectly justified theological interpretation of the significance of Jesus' violent death.

With reference to Isaiah 53, the notification holds that 'Jesus himself explained the meaning of his life and death in the light of God's suffering Servant' (no 10). Beyond question, the New Testament authors frequently echoed or cited this fourth and final 'Song of the Servant'. But many reputable scholars hold the view that Jesus himself did not necessarily have in mind this remarkable Old Testament passage when he recognized the saving value of his passion and death. It was one thing for him to indicate the redemptive and expiatory value of his imminent death. It was another for him to do so precisely in terms of Isaiah 53. There are some scholars who hold this view, but one cannot allege a consensus among mainstream biblical experts that Jesus explicitly invoked Isaiah 53.

To sum up: with the main concerns that lie behind the CDF's notification there can be or should be no argument: Jesus was truly divine and fully human. But there is clearly room for some respectful quibbles over the description offered of the *communicatio idiomatum*, the proposed return to a 'maximalist' view of St Thomas Aquinas on the human consciousness of Jesus, and the use of Isaiah 53 to support a thoroughly justified position on the saving intentions of Jesus.

[This appendix was originally published in *America* magazine for 17 September 2007, and is reproduced with permission. The original (Spanish) text of the CDF's *Notification on Two Books of Father Jon Sobrino, SJ*, (with an explanatory note), dated 26 November 2006, is found in the *Acta Apostolicae Sedis* 99 (2007), pp. 181–98; see *Origins* 41 (29 March 2007), pp. 662–69 for an English translation.]

Appendix 6

Living the Sacrament of Matrimony

Dr Eugene ('Gene') McCarthy, who died in New York on 16 September 2010 and his wife Maureen, who passed away on 3 September 1999, attracted attention wherever they went in life. Gene was always a tall, handsome presence. Maureen's bright red hair framed her green eyes that sparkled with delight over the people she met. This couple also showed me and many others how Jesus and the Holy Spirit can work in married life.

A Trappist, for years their spiritual adviser, once remarked to them: 'Every marriage has trials, and progression through those trials is the seedbed for growth in durability and love within the marriage.' Three painful crises proved the truth of this observation.

Married in 1958 and with three teenage boys, Gene and Maureen faced their first painful trial in the late 1970s. Maureen had become increasingly dependent upon alcohol and this put the marriage at risk. But she entered an AA programme and went on to assist many others on their own path to sobriety. She turned into what Gene called the 'den mother' for AA members on the Upper East Side of New York. Increasingly aware of the sacramental grace of their married vocation, he acknowledged his own part in causing her disease through his extremely busy life as a professor of public health.

When their eldest son Joe, a gentle and lovable giant, was a sophomore at St John's College, Queens, in 1980/81, he became involved with a drug crowd and this triggered the onset of paranoid schizophrenia. 'Maureen and I', Gene recalled, 'now had a son suffering from a mental illness which was to prove fatal'. But, 'thanks to the sacrament of our marriage, this experience united us even more as one in Christ'. Joe was in and out of hospital, joined AA, related well to other members, spent a final Thanksgiving with his parents in 1984, and died the following Saturday. He had found some liquor, started to drink again, and died when he aspirated some of his own vomit into his lungs. The death of Gene's and Maureen's first born followed quickly on the heels of her own struggle with alcoholism.

They both took time out to make twenty-one day retreats and considered the possibility of going into monastic life, Gene into the Trappists and Maureen into the Trappistines. But a Trappist priest, who had trained as a psychoanalyst under Carl Gustav Jung, rocked back and forth in his chair as he listened to the proposal and finally said: 'Gene, you're married. That's all I have to say. You're married!' On another occasion Gene asked the same old friend about St Teresa of Avila and the 'spiritual rooms' in *The Interior Castle*. He wanted to know what room he was in, but was told: 'You're just across the drawbridge, McCarthy!'

More realistic now about the future direction of their lives and responsibilities towards their sons John and Paul, Gene and Maureen took to reciting the Daily Office and did that together, if possible. 'You and I are a community', Maureen often said. They also attended daily Mass, either together or separately, according to their schedules. They continued to draw much strength from an annual retreat made during Holy Week, and started going each year on pilgrimage to Lourdes.

On their first visit to Lourdes, they continued on to Rome and came by my office at the Gregorian University. They were looking for effective ways for helping those who studied and taught at the Church-affiliated institutions in the eternal city. That was the first time we had met, and I was at once impressed by their matter-of-fact approach to finding out what they might support financially and personally.

At the Gregorian we already had the practice of enriching our programmes for graduate students in theology by securing visiting professors who offered courses for six weeks or even a whole semester. But it was a somewhat hand-to-mouth affair, which depended on juggling available funds within a tight budget. Thanks to the McCarthy Family Foundation, we could now issue regular invitations on a firm basis.

Gene proposed that these visiting stars should also deliver a public lecture, which was to be published in our quarterly, the *Gregorianum*. One of the most memorable of these lectures was delivered by Bishop Eduard Lohse, a New Testament scholar and retired Lutheran bishop. Lohse presented very positively what we can glean from the New Testament about St Paul's view of the ministry of St Peter. The huge audience included in the front row, sitting alongside Gene and Maureen, a weary Cardinal Joseph Ratzinger, who occasionally nodded off. In April 2005 he was to be elected Pope and succeed to the chair of St Peter!

Each year Maureen asked a Trappistine friend to prepare a beautiful scroll to be presented to the current McCarthy Professor. Written by hand in blue and gold, these were the most beautiful academic parchments I have ever seen. Before each of the public lectures, Maureen prepared a large display of flowers to decorate the podium. After the lecture and the discussion ended, she would come forward to speak and present the scroll. For the dinner that followed, she looked after the seating arrangements with the eye of a practised hostess.

The visits to Rome allowed Gene and Maureen to meet another remarkable couple, Prince Frank and Princess Orietta Doria Pamphilj, whose palace is only a very short walk from the Gregorian. On one unforgettable Sunday evening, when their chef was enjoying his regular day off, Orietta insisted on cooking a meal for Gene, Maureen, Frank, and myself. She made Gene and me sit down with Frank, while she and Maureen served. At that stage Maureen already had one major operation for cancer behind her, while Orietta was suffering from a slow-moving, malignant disease. Between courses, the two ladies limped around the table in the wonderful dining room of the Palazzo Doria. It was embarrassing for Gene and myself not to be allowed to get up and do the serving. But the Princess Doria and Maureen insisted!

Gene and Maureen encouraged and financially supported me and various colleagues in setting up four international conferences (we called them 'summits'), which were held at St Joseph's Seminary, Yonkers, just after Easter 1996, 1998, 2000, and 2003. These meetings drew together specialists from various disciplines and Christian denominations to present papers on central themes: Christ's resurrection (1996), the Trinity (1998), the incarnation (2000), and redemption (2003). In each case the proceedings were published by Oxford University Press.

On the occasion of the first 'summit', Kenneth Woodward wrote a cover story on the resurrection for *Newsweek*. That issue not only sold extraordinarily well but also encouraged the press and television networks to cover our meeting. ABC, CNN, and NBC could not have done more for us.

From the time we first met, I gradually learned more about the earlier life of Gene and Maureen: her studies at Lesley College (Boston), and his studies at Boston College (where he was the valedictorian for his class), at Yale Medical School, and at Johns Hopkins (for a Master's in public health). They were on the road campaigning when John Kennedy ran for president. Later Gene was to work as a health adviser for Senator Robert Kennedy in implementing Medicare and Medicaid, and Maureen enjoyed a warm friendship with Ethel Kennedy.

In 1961 they flew down to Asunción, Paraguay. With her mastery of Spanish, Maureen flourished during their three years in Latin America. Appointed by USAID as a public health adviser, Gene was responsible for programmes in rural towns and villages. They both worked effectively to reduce the incidence of tuberculosis. Maureen received a gold medal from the Paraguay School of Nursing and Midwifery in recognition of her work.

They went home to the USA in late 1964 and Gene took up an appointment with the School of Public Health at Columbia University and then with the Department of Public Health at Cornell Medical School (also in New York). Gene left an enduring mark through his research and advocacy for the health benefits of 'the second opinion'. He persuaded health insurers and pension and welfare associations of the need to have an opinion from a second doctor before undergoing elective surgery and other major medical treatment. Many groups made that requirement mandatory.

Over the years I became more and more aware of the wide range of institutions and individuals that Gene and Maureen quietly supported, both personally and financially. Their spiritual networking included many diocesan priests and bishops, Benedictines, Carmelites, Jesuits, Passionists, Trappists, Trappistines, and others.

An intellectual who also knew how to act in very effective ways, Gene was less skilled with words than Maureen. She published two volumes of fresh, lyrical poems about human and divine love: *Catching the Spirit: Songs of Light and Shadow* (1994) and *Prelude to Passion: Journey of Love* (1999). A painter as well as a poet, she became an unofficial spiritual director to many. She had great ease in talking about divine and human affairs with a great range of people, including those in the priesthood and religious life. They drew much from her affectionate support, palpable love for Jesus, and willingness to be led by the Holy Spirit.

Gene and Maureen plunged into their third and final trial in September 1996. An operation on Maureen's knee revealed a synovial sarcoma. Over the next three years the cancer spread and she faced repeated surgery and chemotherapy programmes. She constantly drew strength from the Eucharist, *lectio divina* (or meditative reading of the Scriptures), ministering to other patients, especially the terminally ill, and contacts with her friends and family—in particular, her two grandchildren. She learned centring prayer from Abbot Thomas Keating, and turned constantly to the Lord: 'Be my food for my passage through death, O good and loving Jesus'. When others anxiously asked her about her physical and emotional travail, she would say simply: 'Jesus carries me'.

Gene became her '100 per cent caregiver', as he put it. One could see them growing closer and closer in that terrible challenge of her final illness. A profound spiritual peace flowed from them, and communicated to others so much love and compassion.

During their lifetime Gene and Maureen sometimes teased each other in religious terms. He would call her 'Mother Superior', and she would speak to him as 'My Abbot'. Behind this jesting, a tried and tested spirituality, in which they ministered to each other the sacrament of matrimony, made them true contemplatives in action. Like innumerable others, I was deeply blessed to have known them.

[This appendix was originally published in *The Pastoral Review* for January/February 2011, and is reproduced with permission.]

Appendix 7

Interpreting the Documents of Vatican II Integrally

In a study of literary theory that first appeared in 1967 and so two years after the close of Vatican II, Eric Donald Hirsch argued that a text means only what its author intended to communicate. Although generally unaware of Hirsch's *Validity of Interpretation*, many commentators on the sixteen documents produced by the Council, have followed suit. Often without thinking through any theory of interpretation, they have understood these four constitutions, nine decrees, and three declarations to mean only what the Vatican II authors consciously wanted to convey.

We have abundant information about what the bishops and others who served on the conciliar commissions intended to communicate in the texts they composed and then revised. In a kind of committee authorship they evaluated what ideas were to be included, how they were to be expressed, and on what basis they should be endorsed. When they distributed the texts to those attending Vatican II, they justified their sources and formulations through the 'notes' provided and the 'relations' delivered in plenary sessions of the Council.

All of this can be studied in the acts of Vatican II, the unpublished records from the commissions, scholarly studies of particular documents, diaries, and other personal records that have become available.

Those who, like Hirsch, over-emphasize the intentions of authors limit themselves to establishing what was in the minds of the Vatican II commissions. Valid interpretation then becomes a matter of meaning being conveyed from one set of minds, primarily the members of those commissions, to the minds of current readers. The Vatican II texts function as a bridge between the minds of the authors and those of the readers. The latter have the role of grasping and restating what the authors consciously wished to convey.

Such a Hirsch-style approach to the documents of Vatican II stands in tension with the views of innumerable literary critics and, one must add, philosophers. Yes, by all means let us study the evidence that illuminates the intentions of the Council's authors. But we need an integral view that also attends to the texts themselves and how they have been received and implemented by countless readers around the world. It is a commonplace among literary critics and philosophers that texts, once published, enjoy a certain independence from their authors. When texts are read in new cultural and historical contexts, meanings contained in the texts come to light and can go beyond what the original authors ever consciously intended. In short, any adequate interpretation of the Vatican II documents requires attention not only to the authors but also to the history of the texts and their readers.

Authors are not necessarily the most reliable guides to interpreting what they compose. Famously T. S. Eliot refused to comment on the meaning of his works. When Robert Schumann composed and played a new piece, someone asked him what it meant. Schumann did not say a word. He simply sat down again at the piano and played the piece a second time.

As much as any writers or composers, the Vatican II authors could hardly foresee how their texts would be received, interpreted, and practised. Here the Declaration on the Relation of the Church to Non-Christian Religions, *Nostra aetate*, offers an intriguing example. The shortest of all the Vatican II documents and the one that had the most troubled passage to its final form, it was given the lowest grade of authority as a 'mere' declaration. But its subsequent, very positive reception by Catholics and others continues to give this text a meaning and significance far beyond what its authors ever imagined.

Nostra aetate opened the door for a reconciliation with the Jewish people practised, often dramatically, by St John Paul II and now by Pope Francis. His pilgrimage to the Holy Land and dialogue with Shimon Peres (the Israeli President) and Mahmoud Abbas (the Palestinian President) in the Vatican gardens add to the meaning of *Nostra aetate*. Moving beyond the declaration's renunciation of centuries of anti-Semitism, Pope Francis has stated: 'as Christians, we cannot consider Judaism as a foreign religion… Dialogue and friendship with the children of Israel are part of the life of Jesus' disciples' (*The Joy of the Gospel*, 247–48).

Interpreters of the Council's documents would well be advised to follow those engaged with biblical studies. In his 1943 encyclical *Divino afflante Spiritu*, Pope Pius XII encouraged the 'historical-critical method,' which aims to establish the meaning intended by the authors of the sacred texts. Nevertheless, as a 1993 document of the Pontifical Biblical Commission, *The Interpretation of the Bible in the Church*, spelled out, interpreters of the scriptures need to go beyond the intentions of the original *authors*. They should also approach the *texts* through the history of their reception, as well as apply methods that yield fresh meanings from the *readers* of scripture.

Finally, the sixteen documents of Vatican II do not form a code of canon law. But those who interpret them should learn not only from literary critics, philosophers, and biblical scholars but also from legal theory and practice. The interpretation of statutes looks beyond the intentions of those who originally framed them to construe what the texts, their language, and their purpose (to be determined by context and history) mean.

A legal friend remarked to me: 'The idea of a law frozen in amber according to the mind of its makers finds little support in the 1983 Code of Canon Law or elsewhere.' He recalled canon 17 of the Code. 'The mind of the legislator' should be considered only if 'recourse to the text and its purpose have failed.' It comes not first but only at the very end of the canon:

> Ecclesiastical laws are to be understood according to the proper meaning of the words considered in their text and context. If the meaning remains doubtful or obscure, there must be recourse to parallel places, if there be any, to the purpose and circumstances of the law, and to the mind of the legislator.

For good measure, my friend pointed to canon 27. 'Custom,' and not the mind of the legislator, 'is the best interpreter of laws.'

Legal studies, like literary, philosophical, and biblical studies, form areas of research and knowledge that are distinct from the study of councils. But they are not so distinct as to exclude some general principles and methods of interpretation that apply, at least analogously, to all four areas.

It is high time that many commentators on the Council's texts caught up with the principles and methods of interpretation practised elsewhere. The reception of the Vatican II *texts* (or failure to receive them) in the post-1965 history of the church influences current *reading* of these documents. Our search for their meaning should take us beyond the intentions of the original *authors*.

The publication of *Nostra aetate* in 1965 signalled the start of serious official Catholic engagement with Judaism, Islam and other living faiths. Subsequent statements on Christian-Jewish and Christian-Muslim relations, not to mention the actions of John Paul II, Pope Francis, and countless other Christian leaders and believers, have created the new context in which we read, interpret, and apply the declaration on the church's relations to other living faiths.

Nostra aetate presents a spectacular case of how the interpretation and implementation of Vatican II texts have pressed beyond the authorial intent of the original drafters to unfold the meaning that the texts have also received from successive generations of readers. Those who continue to privilege unilaterally the minds of the committees that framed the Council's documents should pause to take advice from literary critics, philosophers, biblical scholars, and canon lawyers.

[This article is published here for the first time.]

APPENDIX 8

SIX OBITUARIES

Prince Frank Pogson Doria Pamphilj (1923–1998)

It was no accident that I first met Frank and Orietta Pogson Doria Pamphilj through a young American who was writing his thesis with me. The priest belonged to those generations of students who came from all around the world to study in Rome and enjoyed a delicious surprise: the relaxed and unassuming friendship of Frank and his marvellous wife. To borrow the language of Tagore, many who briefly visited the eternal city or stayed for years could say to the Dorias: 'I came as a stranger; you received me as a guest; and now I am departing as a friend'.

Year by passing year, the Christmas carols in the Palazzo Doria were vividly memorable occasions when Frank and Orietta brought together family and friends around the piano in their home. Led by a student from the English College, we had to sing our way through a booklet before being allowed to move on to supper. At buffet meals, I frequently gravitated towards Frank, unless first summoned there by his incomparable butler, Mario.

Frank was always happy to talk about his years at sea during the Second World War. I knew that he had a special interest in the techniques for mine-sweeping. Courageous man that he was, he never spoke of the dangers but recalled the friends he made in the armed forces. He was always a great teaser, and he joked about my persistent failure to distinguish between being 'in' a ship or 'on' a ship. I never knew him to tell set-piece jokes, but he inserted brilliantly funny remarks into conversations going on around him.

He could also laugh at himself. When we were rehearsing his

daughter's wedding in the Doria church, St Agnes on the Piazza Navona, the short aisle meant that he walked her from the door to the altar in a minute or so. 'Frank, let's have that again', I told him. 'You'll have to take it more slowly with Gesine.' With a laugh he excused himself: 'I'm trying to get rid of her quickly. Can't you see that?'

Memory brings back many pictures of him, always surrounded by family and friends. If anyone deserved the title of a 'people's person', it was Frank. The people extended beyond his loving family to old colleagues from the war, bishops and students, distinguished scholars, Italians of all kinds, the English-speaking colony in Rome, diplomats and other visitors from outside Italy, right through to small children. One of my last memories of him is his warm welcome to little Abigail, an 11-year-old on her first visit to Rome with her parents.

Early last year, when a heart condition meant that Frank could only move around in a wheelchair, I started coming each week to say the Sunday Mass for him and Orietta in their sitting room. 'You are the specialist in St Paul', I told him, and always asked him to take the second reading. From his wheelchair he proclaimed the apostle's words with care and concentration. His quiet devotion touched me over and over again. Then in the minutes after Communion when the three of us, sometimes joined by visitors, sat in silence gave me a fresh sense of how we experience the communion of saints in the presence of Christ.

For me and for so many others Frank was love, loyalty, friendship and fun personified. He was all that for his wife, their children Jonathan and Gesine, his sister Margaret, and the rest of the family. *The Tablet* has lost a great friend and supporter, and so have many in Rome. I think of Mario and his wife, of Frank's incredibly competent nurse Annette, of her student daughter Clarissa, and others who make up the village which is the historic centre of Rome. After years of struggling with ill health, our friend Frank has gone to heaven. We mourn his passing, give thanks for his life, and know that we will all be merry together with him at home with our God.

[*The Tablet* for 10 October 1998 carried an obituary by George Bull, to which the journal appended the above remarks.]

Princess Orietta Pogson Doria Pamphilj (1922–2000)

Daughter of a Doria prince and a Scottish mother, Princess Orietta Pogson Doria Pamphilj inherited the patrimony of one of Italy's greatest families. For many years she and her husband were at the heart of the English community in Rome.

It was after the liberation of the city in June 1944 that she first met the English naval officer Frank Pogson whom she was to marry. He had docked his minesweeper in Ancona where she came to work in a canteen as a volunteer for the Catholic Women's League. She had just emerged from hiding out in Rome with her parents during the Nazi occupation of the eternal city.

Months earlier when German soldiers raided the Doria Palace, Prince Filippo Andrea, Princess Gesine, and their daughter hid in a lavatory behind a sliding bookcase listening to the soldiers clumping around the gigantic building. The parish priest of Santa Maria in Trastevere hid the three Dorias for months and shared his food (mainly vegetables) with them. Everyone went very hungry and lived in constant fear.

Orietta's father, the Prince Doria, continued working secretly with Mgr Hugh O'Flaherty, a Scarlet Pimpernel figure who organized hiding places and food for Allied soldiers, Jews, and others on the run from the enemy forces. In 1943–44 there was a high price on the Prince's head.

Born in 1922, Orietta divided her education between Rome, England, and Switzerland. Her father's chronically poor health involved a long stay in the Swiss mountains in 1938–39 with his wife and daughter. In Switzerland Orietta developed her love for mountaineering and skiing. Her education may have been fragmented, but she grew up speaking excellent French as well as Italian and English.

She had a great affinity with her father. When Prince Filippo came out of hiding in June 1944, the Allied authorities appointed him mayor of Rome and he led the city well until democratic elections could once again be held. Orietta shared deeply his sense of service. She handled motor vehicles with skill, and from the 1940s to the end of her life had a truck driver's licence. That licence also let her drive vehicles for the girl guides, an organization which she supported with energy and generosity.

When she married Frank in 1958, her father had given his full blessing to their union but, sadly, died a few months before the wedding took place. Mean-minded gossips among the Roman nobility falsely suggested that Prince Filippo opposed the marriage—something that in any case he was unlikely to do since he had himself married a Scottish nurse and was related to the Dukes of Newcastle and the Earls of Shrewsbury. Orietta felt deeply let down by the gossip coming from the Roman families, some of whom had already compromised themselves by earlier accepting Mussolini's fascist regime. In any case she had the strength and wisdom to adapt to the post-war world, which was very different from the one in which she had been raised as the only child of an immensely wealthy, aristocratic family that spent its summers in the Villa Doria Pamphilj on top of the Janiculum and its winters in their 1,000-room palace at the heart of Old Rome. She could never identify with the nobility who pretended that everything had remained just the same. One only needed to see Orietta riding her bicycle around the city or hear her talk with shopkeepers to realise how she identified with ordinary people.

She never agreed with the post-war critics who attacked Pius XII for deciding that it would be counter-productive for him publicly to denounce the Nazi genocidal persecution of the Jews. Yet Orietta had little time for some who worked later in the Vatican. 'They're a dreadful lot', she remarked to me more than once.

She and Frank, both devout Catholics with a life of daily prayer, gave strong support to inter-church relations when Pope John XXIII called the Second Vatican Council. In their palace overlooking the Piazza Navona they made available a meeting-place for non-Catholic observers who attended the Council. Part of that palace became Foyer Unitas, a residence for non-Catholic visitors administered with skill and devotion by the Ladies of Bethany. The Franciscan Friars of the Atonement were welcomed and continue to run there the Centro Pro Unione, one of the world's most important ecumenical study-centres. On the Via del Corso the Palazzo Doria itself came to house the Anglican Centre, the fruit of a 1966 meeting between Pope Paul VI and the Archbishop of Canterbury, Michael Ramsey. When Archbishop Robert Runcie came to Rome, Orietta and Frank offered him a wonderful reception in their home. In protest against Runcie's visit, Ian Paisley stood across the Corso from the palace door. It was also in the Palazzo Doria that I renewed my friendship with George Carey when he returned to Rome as Archbishop of Canterbury.

Orietta was a Roman to the core. One memorable Sunday she joined me and Frank for a day of prayer out at the Villa Cavalletti in the Alban Hills. When we turned a corner on the Via Quattro Novembre and drove down the hill towards the Piazza Venezia, I felt a little bump. 'That hole has been there since the war', Orietta explained. She cherished her city right down to minor potholes and the sheep driven at night down the Via del Corso.

Frank and Orietta were a great twosome; his sense of fun checked her tendency to over-seriousness. After she underwent a serious operation in the Roman hospital of Salvator Mundi, I came one afternoon, found her alone, and blurted out something that I had been waiting to say for years: 'I find it very touching to see how much Frank loves you and misses you right now'. In her usual matter-of-fact style, she brushed my remark aside but could not help letting me see how I had caught the heart of her existence.

For years the prayerful princess struggled against cancer with cheerful courage and never a hint of self-pity. She is survived by her loveable children, a charming son-in-law, the two grandchildren who were the joy of her old age, a butler *par excellence*, his wife who cooks with such skill, and so many other friends who form the Doria village in the historic heart of old Rome.

Only a month before she died, Orietta was invested by Her Majesty the Queen with an OBE and a few hours later attended the pre-lunch drinks party for the Queen in the Anglican Centre, now housed in splendid new quarters above the Doria Gallery. It was Oriettta's final and most fitting public appearance.

[This obituary appeared in *The Tablet* for 25 November 2000, and like the previous obituary is reproduced with permission.]

Cardinal Avery Dulles (1918–2008)

A final lecture delivered by Cardinal Avery Dulles was a moving testimony to his life as a theologian and a Jesuit. 'There is no one on Earth with whom I would want to exchange places', he said. 'It has been a special privilege to serve in the Society of Jesus, a religious community specially dedicated to the Saviour of the world'.

Cardinal Dulles was already stricken with health problems, resulting from an attack of polio when serving in the American navy during the Second World War. He had occupied the McGinley Chair in theology at the Jesuit-run Fordham University in New York since 1988. The previous 38 McGinley Lectures had already been published in a handsome volume, which he presented to Benedict XVI on his visit to the United States.

By the time he delivered the thirty-ninth lectures he was becoming increasingly disabled, yet he remarked: 'I can identify with the paralytic and mute persons in the Gospels, grateful for the loving and skillful care I receive and for the hope of everlasting life in Christ. The Lord now calls me to a period of weakness. I know well that his power can be made perfect in weakness.' The period lasted only a few months. He reached his ninetieth birthday on 24 August and died on the morning of 12 December.

The son of John Foster Dulles, Secretary of State under President Eisenhower, Cardinal Dulles was raised in the Presbyterian Church and did his undergraduate studies at Harvard University. He was desperate to know whether there was anything worth living or dying for. As he explained in *A Testimonial to Grace*, that desperation led through ancient Greek philosophy to the Catholic Church, which he joined in 1940. Conscious of the emptiness of a life based on the pursuit of pleasure, he had come to see that happiness is the reward for holding to what is 'truly good and important'.

In 1946 he entered the Society of Jesus and completed his studies with a doctorate in 1960 at the Gregorian University in Rome. There he met Fr Jacques Dupuis, and years later contributed a chapter to *In Many and Diverse Ways*, a volume published for Dupuis's eightieth birthday in 2003. Specialising in the doctrine of revelation and the Church, Dulles taught at Woodstock College in Maryland and New York and at the Catholic University of America before going to Fordham.

He was also visiting professor at many academic centres, including the Gregorian University and Oxford University where his Martin D'Arcy Lectures appeared as *The Catholicity of the Church* in 1985. In Catholic theology Dulles pioneered the use of models or elaborated images with two landmark books: *Models of the Church* (1974) and

Models of Revelation (1983). He served on the Lutheran-Roman Catholic Dialogue in the United States for 20 years.

Tall, gaunt and courageous, he had an infectious chuckle, a loyal love of friends, and a conservative streak. A deep integrity shone out of him. He made no fuss about joining others in celebrating the life of Dupuis, even though the Congregation for the Doctrine of the Faith had issued a 'notification' warning about 'ambiguities' in Dupuis's *Toward a Christian Theology of Religious Pluralism* (1997). 'I've read the book twice', Dulles said, 'and can't see what's wrong with it'.

After seven years as a consultor for the Secretariat for Dialogue with Non-Believers and five years on the International Theological Commission, his work for the Church and the world was fully recognized when Pope John Paul II created him a cardinal in 2001.

'Uncle Avery', as I called him, was always a delightful companion. On a drive around Washington we were deep into theological discussion when I reminded him that the car had previously belonged to his uncle, Allen Dulles, a long-time director of the CIA. 'The Russians may have bugged this car', I suggested. 'Don't worry', Uncle Avery retorted, 'they won't understand a word of what we've saying'. Years later, in the aftermath of 9/11, airport security insisted that he take off his boots. Well into his eighties, he was suffering from the long-term effects of polio. 'Doesn't that bother you?', I asked. 'Not much', he replied. 'I always bring a long shoehorn with me'

Last July I visited him in the infirmary of Fordham University. He was no longer able to speak. I held his hands, and told him how much I and others treasured his work and loved him. He nodded towards a copy of his McGinley Lectures, a final gift to me. Before leaving I asked: 'May I have your blessing?' He nodded agreement, struggled to raise his hand, and blessed me.

[This obituary appeared in *The Tablet* for 20/27 December 2008, and is reproduced with permission.]

James ('Jim') Sturrock Peters (1913-2010)

The dust jacket of a history of sport at the University of Melbourne shows Jim Peters hitting a six into the grounds of Ormond College. The only other player visible in the photograph is Manning Clark, the Trinity College wicket keeper and a future historian of Australia. Also a footballer, Jim captained the Newman College team and in his last intercollegiate game kicked eighteen goals in a match against Queen's College. A freshman blue in 1931, he played with the University Blacks and in 1935 captained them to an A Grade premiership. That year he also captained three other winning teams: the medical students, Newman, and the Victorian Amateurs in the interstate competition. He was named captain of the All-Australian Amateurs. As an outstanding player of the 1930s, the Victorian Amateur Football Association inducted him in 2007 as a 'legend' of the game.

Jim grew up in country towns of Victoria where his father Victor taught at several state primary schools. As a boarder (on a scholarship) at St Patrick's College, Ballarat, Jim kicked 141 goals as full forward in the 1930 championship football team. Again on a scholarship (a Donovan Bursary), he started at Newman as a commerce student in 1931 but after a year followed his sister Sheila by studying medicine. He graduated MB BS at the University of Melbourne in 1937, the year in which he was also President of the Newman College Students Club.

Even if there was little money available during those depression years, Jim enjoyed the company of many friends at the University and, in particular, fellow medical students at Newman like Ray Gurry and Mark O'Brien. He shared fully in college life, not only flourishing at football but also playing for the XI and being on the athletics team

When the Second World War broke out, Jim enlisted and was posted to North Africa with the Sixth Division of the AIF. He served with the Ninth Division at the siege of Tobruk and the Battle of El Alamein, where he was mentioned in dispatches.

In 1945 Jim left the army as a lieutenant colonel and became a Resident Medical Officer at Royal Melbourne Hospital. He completed his MS and in 1946 married Moira O'Collins, my eldest sister, in the Newman chapel. Shortly after the wedding they sailed for England, where he became a Resident Surgical Officer at St James's Hospital (London) and, with hard work, quickly secured his FRCS.

Returning to Australia in 1948, he received his FRACS and became an honorary urological surgeon at Prince Henry's Hospital and the founding specialist in urology at the Repatriation General Hospital, Heidelberg (now the Austin Hospital). When he died, the Austin Health Urology Unit recalled how Jim had 'championed the training of Australian urologists within Australia. His immense contribution is commemorated by the Jim Peters Fellowship for Urological Research.' With rooms in Collins Street, he built up a large practice and was appointed to the editorial committee of the British and Italian journals of urology. He served as President of the Australasian Urological Society (1961-62) and as an Australasian delegate to the International Society of Urology (1967-73).

Jim and Moira had eight children (five sons and three daughters), all university graduates. He constantly encouraged his children and was immensely proud of them: the doctors (Marion and Justin), the lawyers (Stewart, Joanna and James), the veterinarian (Bronwen), the banker (Mark) and the engineer (Stephen). Stewart, Justin, James and Stephen all attended Newman College. Justin was also elected President of the Students Club in 1975. Jim instilled in his children the values of hard work, fair play and the importance of being able to relax occasionally. He took a great interest in their family lives and careers right to the time when he passed away.

Jim and Moira enjoyed trips overseas, often to urological conferences in Brazil, Japan, South Africa and the United States. During the Cold War they even visited Moscow. Travel brought them a team of international friends, some of whom would stay at their home in Orrong Road on visits to Melbourne.

Jim loved his golf, playing off five in his younger days. He was a keen member of Peninsula and Metropolitan Golf Clubs. At Metro he became the longest serving member, being a member for 73 years. At Peninsula he won several Service Trophies; at Metro he twice won the Umphelby Cup. He also won the Knox Trophy and the Captain's Trophy in the same year, a feat never achieved before or repeated since.

Horse racing was also a passion. With his good friend Sir Maurice Nathan, Jim had much success with Penny Edition, including a win at the Toorak Handicap. He and Moira regularly attended the Caulfield and Melbourne Cup Carnivals, entertaining members of their family and guests from interstate and overseas.

Jim and Moira loved life on the land. For years, helped by their children, they ran a station at Bunns Springs, just across the border in South Australia. In 1983 they took up a property ('Laurel Vale') near Kilmore and bred Angus cattle.

The epitome of cheerful affability, Jim shone at family and social occasions: at home, at Metropolitan Golf Club, Peninsula Country Golf Club and other clubs, and at Ballarat, where one of Moira's uncles, Bishop Sir James O'Collins, regularly entertained his whole clan. Jim was a very handsome man, and on such occasions his beaming smile and charm enhanced his good looks.

Even in his later years, Jim remained very strong. At 'Laurel Vale' he drove a tractor, fed the cattle and checked fences well into his nineties; He loved sitting on the verandah, enjoying the evening view and sharing a drink with Moira.

When he slowed down and his health weakened, he would still regularly attend parties. Just eight weeks before he passed away, he attended a luncheon for the University Blacks. He kept climbing twenty stairs to go to bed each evening, right to the night before he died.

Jim always said that Moira was 'the best thing that ever happened' to him. Married for 64 years, their bond of love remained very strong, and they shared that love with their children, in-laws, and grandchildren. They always made sure that everyone felt welcome and respected for their achievements. Jim was very blessed in the way Moira cared for him over his last years. She enabled him to stay and die at home with dignity and close to all who loved him.

In the reminiscences he wrote for the Newman magazine of 2007, Jim showed how much the college meant to him and how deeply grateful he was for all the college had brought him. He studied at Newman; he was married at Newman; he had to be buried from Newman.

The Chapel of the Holy Spirit at Newman was packed for the funeral Mass on 6 October 2010 celebrated by Moira's cousin, Monsignor William McCarthy, and concelebrated by Fr Bill Uren, Fr Peter Steele, Fr Michael Stoney and the parish priest of Toorak, Fr Brendan Hayes, Jim's fourth son, James Peters, S.C., gave the eulogy. He summed up Jim's life this way: 'He came from humble beginnings and was very successful in many arenas: academic, sporting, military and, more importantly, as husband, father and friend. He loved celebrating life, and he always rose to the occasion for the challenges that life brings.'

Then James recalled the last night of Jim's life when he and his brother Mark shared dinner with their parents: 'Dad was in great form, laughing and sharing stories with us. He was the Dad of old. Afterwards I helped him climb those twenty stairs to bed. Halfway up he started to flag. I said to him, "Dad, I would have hated to be a backman chasing you around the forward line." With that, his chest puffed out, his legs started pushing, and he marched up the stairs, rising to the occasion one last time. We have all been the richer for knowing him. He was special to all of us in ways that cannot be said.' Then, recalling Jim's characteristic way of recognizing effort and achievement, James ended by saying: 'There's no doubt about you, Dad.'

When the funeral Mass ended, Jim's five sons and one of his grandsons bore his coffin out of the chapel, followed by two sons-in-law and the rest of the family. They lifted him high as they carried him out to burial like a Viking king of old. There's no doubt about you, Jim. May you rest in peace.

Peter Daniel Steele, SJ, AM (1939-2012)

'Publishing a poem', Peter Steele once said to me, 'is like dropping a feather down the Grand Canyon and waiting for the echo.' Yet, right to the end of his life, he never stopped delighting in words and sharing his poetry with friends and with anyone who, like him, relished the possibilities of language and rejoiced in the mysterious features of the world.

Born a week before the beginning of the Second World War, Peter grew up in Perth, Western Australia, the eldest in a family of three boys. His father had emigrated to Australia from England at the age of nineteen, and became a Catholic (and a serious one) when he married Peter's mother, an Australian of mixed English and Irish stock. A pious boy, Peter grew up intending to become a priest, and from his early teens showed himself, as he put it, 'bookish. As Marxists have wrath and kangaroos have grasslands, I had books. Few of them were at home, but the school library was generous in scale, and for years my Christmas present was a subscription to the Central Catholic Library.' What he called 'logophilia', a 'respectable form of gluttony, gorging on the printed word, took hold of me very early.'

Peter was educated by the Christian Brothers, one of whom

encouraged Peter to think of joining the Jesuits. He learned something about them and later recalled: 'What struck me was the sense that Jesuits knew what they were about. They seemed to be informed, intelligent, and dedicated, and they seemed to want to be useful on a generous scale.' Peter could have been talking about himself and the ideals that were to guide his own life.

In January 1957 Peter took two days and three nights to travel by train from Perth to Melbourne to join the Jesuits, of whom he remained a member until death. From studying at the University of Melbourne and completing his PhD there, he moved smoothly to making this campus a base for a lifetime of teaching and writing. In 1993 he was named to a personal chair in English. After retirement in 2005, he became Emeritus Professor and Hon. Professorial Fellow in 2006, and was awarded a honorary doctorate (DLitt) in 2008. Further honorary doctorates came from Notre Dame University (2010) and Australian Catholic University (2011).

The campus of the University of Melbourne and his residence at Newman College were his 'local habitation', to borrow the title of a collection of poems and sermons he published in 2010: *A Local Habitation: Poems and Homilies*. Generations of students flocked to the lectures and seminars of this soft-spoken priest. They learnt from his wise humanity, his loving eye for detail, and his unfailingly sharp imagination that found so much to appraise and rejoice in.

Peter published major works on the Irish satirist and Anglican cleric, Jonathan Swift: first, *An Air of Truth Apparent: A Study of Gulliver's Travels* (1968) and then a longer book with the Clarendon Press, *Jonathan Swift: Preacher and Jester* (1978). He also wrote studies of contemporary poets, both Australians and others, *Expatriates: Reflections on Modern Poetry* (1985) and *Peter Porter* (1992), as well as a short study of Samuel Johnson and Dante Alighieri, *Flights of the Mind: Johnson and Dante* (1997).

A fellow of the Australian Academy of the Humanities, Peter held visiting chairs at Georgetown University (Washington, DC), the University of Alberta (Canada), and Loyola University in Chicago. He delivered the Martin D'Arcy Lectures at the University of Oxford, and later published them as *The Autobiographical Passion: Studies in the Self on Show* (1989).

Peter wrote two illustrated books of poems prompted by works of art: *Plenty: Art into Poetry* (2003) and *The Whispering Gallery: Art into Poetry* (2006). Patrick McCaughey, a former Director of the National Gallery of Victoria, wrote an introduction to the first volume, and Gerard Vaughan, also a Director of the National Gallery of Victoria, wrote a foreword to the second.

Peter published other volumes of poetry: *Words from Lilliput* (1973), *Marching on Paradise* (1984), *Invisible Riders* (1999), and *The Gossip and the Wine* (2010). *White Knight with Bee-Box: New and Selected Poems*, which appeared in 2008, was awarded the Philip Hodgins Medal for poetry in that year. In April 2011 he received the Christopher Brennan Award, given by the Fellowship of Writers for 'Lifetime Achievement in Poetry'.

From 1985 to 1990, Peter was provincial superior of the Australian Jesuits. When he finished that term of office, he recalled: 'the Irish joke, that when a man becomes a bishop he will never again eat a bad meal or be told the truth, is exactly reversed when it comes to being a provincial. He eats, on his peregrinations, a lot of very strange food, and he is told more truth than he can easily deal with.' As for the peregrinations, 'my predecessor told me that he had travelled half a million miles in his six years' stint, and I would have done all of that, within Australia and beyond it.'

For many years Peter preached the Sunday homily, whether at Newman College within the University of Melbourne, at Georgetown University, or wherever else he found himself in the world.

Meticulously crafted, these homilies offered a feast of insight, tackling universal questions and issues. They introduce an extraordinary range of subjects: from Robert Bolt's *A Man for All Seasons* to Shakespeare's *Richard II*, from the story of the Prodigal Son to the image of Neil Armstrong stepping onto the moon, from a travel agency named *Please Go Away* to reflections on the nature of heaven. Peter published 86 of these homilies in *Bread for the Journey* (2002).

Diagnosed with liver cancer in late 2006, Peter faced operations, chemotherapy, and blood transfusions with gentle courage, realism, and never a touch of self-pity. He moved with calm faith to a very peaceful death. A final book, a collection of poems and essays entitled *Braiding the Voices: Essays in Poetry*, was launched at Newman College on 12 June, the day after Peter was awarded an AM (Member in the General Division of the Order of Australia) in the Queen's Birthday Honours. In a wheel chair, he was present at the launch to receive long and repeated applause from a large crowd but could speak very little. A friend of 45 years, Professor Chris Wallace-Crabbe, read two of the poems from the new collection. Peter died quietly fifteen days later in Caritas Christi Hospice (Kew), with his only surviving brother at his bedside.

Peter was cherished and loved by his family, students, fellow Jesuits, academic colleagues, and fellow poets—not least by the Nobel laureate Seamus Heaney. Since he was born in the same year but a few months before Peter, Heaney called him 'young Steele'. As poet, priest, and preacher, Peter Steele touched the lives of those who met him in academic settings and beyond. He never failed in his affable concern for others, insatiable curiosity about all things human and divine, and restless delight in words.

[This obituary was published in *The Age* for 3 July 2012, and reprinted in the 2013 edition of *Swift Studies* (Münster, Germany).]

.Cardinal Carlo Maria Martini: the Pope that Never Was (1927-2012).

If Pope John Paul II had died in the 1990s, Cardinal Martini would have succeeded him. Even after Martini developed Parkinson's disease, a sizable block of cardinals voted for him at the first ballot in the conclave on the afternoon of 18 April 2005. Reportedly he drew their attention to his physical condition, and the way was clear the following day for Cardinal Joseph Ratzinger to be elected and take the name of Benedict XVI.

Martini will be remembered as an outstanding Archbishop of Milan (1980-2002), a world leader in encouraging believers to live their Christian lives in a more biblical manner, a major contributor in providing the most accurate text of the Greek New Testament, and a revered rector of two major Jesuit institutions: the Pontifical Biblical Institute (where he served as rector 1969-78) and the Pontifical Gregorian University (where his role as rector 1978-79 was cut short by his appointment as Archbishop of Milan).

The son of an engineer, Martini was born in Turin on 15 February 1927 (just two months before Joseph Ratzinger was born), attended a Jesuit high school and entered the Jesuit novitiate in September 1944. After studies in philosophy and theology at two centres in Northern Italy (Gallarate and Chieri), he was ordained a priest on 13 July 1952. To be ordained at the age of twenty-five was and remains remarkably young for a Jesuit, but shows the high regard and hopes superiors held for Martini.

In 1958 at the Gregorian University Martini was awarded a doctorate (*summa cum laude*) for a dissertation on some historical aspects of the resurrection of Jesus. After teaching for several years at Chieri, he was awarded a second doctorate (also *summa cum laude*) at the Biblical Institute for a thesis on some questions about the text of Luke's Gospel in the light of the *Codex Vaticanus* and the *Bodmer*

Papyrus XIV. From 1962 he held a chair in textual criticism at the Biblical Institute.

From the 1960s, as the only Roman Catholic on the team, Martini worked with an elite group of scholars headed by Professor Kurt Aland at the Institute for New Testament Textual Research at Münster (Westphalia). They produced their first edition of *The Greek New Testament* in 1966. He was still on the team when their fourth, revised edition appeared in 1993. This is unquestionably the most scientific edition of the New Testament in its original Greek ever produced.

One of his students at the Biblical Institute recalled a course on text criticism with Martini in the early 1970s: 'Carlo would walk into the classroom and, just as he arrived at the podium, the bell would ring to begin class. He would kneel down, say a prayer in Latin, and then teach (in Latin) for the next fifty minutes. (The other professors were already teaching in Italian.) At the end of class he would take questions, and then kneel down to say the closing prayer. Usually the bell would ring just as he was making the sign of the cross. The timing was perfect!' This former student added: 'His course was memorable. He brought into the classroom various editions of the Bible and would comment on aspects of each edition—unlike other professors who merely lectured. I continue to use his material today when explaining the different "families" of biblical texts.'

By then Martini was already known as an outstanding preacher of retreats. He would draw on the *Spiritual Exercises* of St Ignatius Loyola and subtly apply the Ignatian insights by reflecting on such biblical figures as Abraham, Job and Moses. Many of these retreats were subsequently published: for instance, four volumes of reflections in the light of Matthew, Mark, Luke and John. In 1978 Pope Paul VI invited Martini to preach the annual retreat offered during Lent at the Vatican for the papal collaborators. A few months later, on 31 July 1978, Paul VI signed the document appointing Martini 'rector magnificus' of the Gregorian University—apparently the last official act of Paul VI, who died a few days later on 6 August.

Martini lived and breathed the teaching of the Second Vatican Council (1962-65). That meant being constantly open to relations with Jews, other Christians, and those of other faiths. He cultivated connections, for instance, with the Hebrew University of Jerusalem, which eventually conferred on him an honorary doctorate in 2006. Archbishop George Carey invited him to preach in Canterbury Cathedral. Work together towards producing *The Greek New Testament* endeared him for life to Gordon Fee, a Pentecostal who became one of the world's leading interpreters of St Paul's letters.

Martini's life took a new turn when on 29 December 1979 he was appointed Archbishop of Milan, one of the largest and most prominent Catholic dioceses in the world. He was created a cardinal in 1983. Italian wits instantly fastened onto the red robes of a cardinal and the white robes of a pope to speak of 'Martini rosso' who would become one day 'Martini bianco'.

During his years in Milan, Martini constantly supported a wider role for the ministry of women, social justice (especially for immigrants, refugees, and other minorities), more qualified positions in matters of human sexuality and the right to be allowed to die, and more collegiality or shared decision-making at every level in the Church. He reached out famously to young people through meeting them each month for biblical reflection in the Milan cathedral. Long before he left Rome for Milan, his devotion to young people had been constantly shown not only to his students at the Biblicum and the Gregorian but also to such groups as the San Egidio Community, a lay-led organization founded in 1968.

The press cherished him, not least the Milan daily, *Corriere della Sera*. That paper carried a remarkable exchange of letters between Martini and Professor Umberto Eco on ecological, political, social and religious challenges to the Church and the whole world. (This exchange was published as *Belief or Non-Belief* (New York, 2000).) They began with the future of our race and planet. Eco had no difficulty in listing some ecological and other threats, and even entertained the thought of humanity's 'necessary suicide': we must 'perish in order to rescue not only those species' that we have 'almost obliterated' but even 'Mother Earth' herself who is 'denatured and suffocating'. Without minimizing the terrifying portents listed by Eco, Martini insisted that no human or satanic power can destroy the hope of believers: the virtue of hope is, after all, a gift from God.

Without neglecting his ministry for the Archdiocese of Milan, Martini accepted invitations to visit Africa, India, Japan, the United States and some other countries. In 1997, he was among the cardinals who preached at Westminster Cathedral, London, for the centenary of its foundation. In its spiritual and biblical brilliance, Martini's sermon stood out. Those who heard him speak on that occasion knew later that the Catholic Church had lost a pope who would have ranked among the greatest papal preachers—with Leo the Great and Gregory the Great.

Martini shone on his visit to Australia in 1996. At a Melbourne luncheon for a thousand people, the largest gathering of business leaders ever organized by the Institute for Company Directors, he encouraged better ethical practices. This was followed by a comparable gathering in Sydney, chaired by Malcolm Turnbull. At a meeting in St Mary's Church, West Melbourne, his audience included the retiring archbishop, Sir Frank Little and his successor, Archbishop George Pell. Addressing them, Martini remarked that Little, with his vision and hospitality, reminded him of Abraham. Then he told Pell: 'You remind me of Moses, a leader and the meekest of men. I wish for you the gift of meekness.'

A tall, aristocratic man, Martini spoke with gentle and measured authority. On official occasions he had to dress in the full regalia of a cardinal, but preferred to wear simple, clerical dress. He took his distance from *Dominus Iesus*, a document produced by Cardinal Ratzinger's office in 2000 that characterized many Christian communities as not being 'proper churches' and that proposed, against the explicit teaching of Vatican II, that members of non-Christian religions may reach 'belief' in God but not genuine 'faith'. Martini called the document 'theologically rather dense, peppered with quotations, and not easy to read'. In his exchange with Umberto Eco he had this to say on the question of women and the ordained ministry within the Catholic Church: 'On the one hand, the role and presence of women in all aspects of church life and society must be realized, far beyond the degree to which it has been previously. On the other hand, our understanding of the nature of the priesthood and ordained ministers must be more profound than ever before.' He ended by quoting a conviction that St Thomas Aquinas had taken over from St Augustine: 'the liberation of the human being should show itself in both sexes.'

After his retirement at age seventy-five from the See of Milan, Cardinal Martini spent as much time as he could in Jerusalem, the city that mattered most to him in the world. Increasing frailty meant that eventually he had to live full time to Italy. On 31 August 2012 he died at Gallarate (near Milan).

[This obituary appeared in *The Age* for 4 September 2012]

Appendix 9

The Living Word, the Living Tradition

It's a delight being home in Adelaide, to celebrate the publication of the Australian Lutheran-Roman Catholic Dialogue's latest work, *Living Word, Living Tradition*. For nearly twenty years here in South Australia, my maternal grandfather represented in the federal parliament an electorate that was heavily and devoutly Lutheran. So, from that point of view also, it's a real homecoming being with you this evening. Let me extend my warm congratulations to the members of the dialogue, both Lutheran and Roman Catholic, for their work and not least for their happy choice of a title for the document: *Living Word, Living Tradition*. This joint work has led them to affirm eleven points of agreement that concern the relationship of Scripture and Tradition, as well as to identify two points of difference in their interpretation of Scripture. I feel privileged and honored to take part in welcoming their document.

Let limit myself to three particular issues: two are comments on the Roman Catholic contribution to the document; and the third is a question for all members of the dialogue.

(1) My first comment concerns discerning the traditions or, as the text puts it, 'testing' traditions. Roman Catholics, we read, should test human traditions in the light of the whole people of God's 'sense of faith', of the teaching authority of the Church, and of 'the good news of Jesus Christ found in the biblical word of God' (no. 58). Here we need to look beyond Vatican II's Dogmatic Constitution on Divine Revelation (*Dei Verbum*). Let me explain. Other documents from the Second Vatican Council offer some illuminating examples of traditions being tested. On the issue of testing human traditions,

some other texts from the Council provide striking cases of traditions being tested, modified or dropped. I think, for instance, of the Constitution on the Divine Liturgy (*Sacrosanctum Concilium*, the Decree on the Renewal of Religious Life (*Perfectae Caritatis*), and the Decree on the Formation of Priests (*Optatam Totius*). In these three texts we observe the Council at work testing, modifying and changing some traditions, and doing so in the areas of the liturgy, the life of vowed religious, and seminary training, respectively. One could cite further documents from Vatican II to illustrate what testing human traditions involves. But these three are enough to establish my case. What the Constitution on the Divine Liturgy mandates about the reform of liturgy exemplifies all that testing, modifying, and changing some liturgical traditions can entail. The Decree on the Formation of Priests shows us the Council turning away from various entrenched traditions of seminary training to encourage approaches centred on the study of the Sacred Scripture as the 'soul of theology' (OT 16; see DV 24). The Decree on the Renewal of Religious Life aims to reform and renew the life of religious by revising and even suppressing various traditions and practices (PC 3), and doing so, above all, in the light of the Gospel, 'the supreme rule' for all religious institutes (PC 2; see 6). In short, as regards 'testing' traditions, Roman Catholics need to look beyond the Constitution on Divine Revelation to see specific examples of the Second Vatican Council at work discerning, renewing, and dismantling such traditions. Where particular traditions no longer provide life coming from the Holy Spirit, the Spirit can lead us in new and unexpected directions.

(2) My second comment on *Living Word, Living Tradition* bears on the closing sentence of no. 35 in the section on 'A Roman Catholic Perspective'. Apropos of Scripture and Tradition, it is said that 'they are both the word of God'. Beyond question, Scripture is the word of God. But can one simply say that Tradition *is* the word of God? Later

the document cites the Second Vatican Council and its Dogmatic Constitution on Divine Revelation, *Dei Verbum*, to describe Tradition through a series of verbs: it 'preserves', 'transmits', 'expounds', and 'disseminates' the word of God (no. 54). I've always been happy with this language: without wanting to say that Tradition *is* the word of God, over the years I have described Tradition as transmitting, interpreting, and applying the word of God. But, when we speak of Tradition in upper case or the presence at the heart of Church life of the living Christ, a presence effected and supported by the Holy Spirit, then we can also say that Tradition *is* the word of God. But we need to make it clear that we are taking Tradition as the dynamic presence of the risen and glorified Christ. In that sense, Tradition is identical with the living Word of God. We need to explain this point a little further.

The document being celebrated this evening takes over from the US Lutheran and Catholic dialogue the distinction between tradition as *process* and tradition as *content*—a distinction which, incidentally, I made more than a decade earlier.[33] That distinction can support speaking of tradition as being the living Word of God. The dialogue in the United States called tradition as *process* 'the Word of God precisely as it is handed on in the church' or *verbum Dei traditum*', while the dialogue referred tradition as *content* to 'the totality of the gracious presence of Christ passed on in history through the power of the Spirit, in the life, teaching, and worship of the church' (no. 48).

To make it even clearer that we can rightly say, 'Tradition is the Word of God', we need to adjust slightly our description of the process and the content. Tradition as process is the Word of God handing himself on in the church, the *Verbum Dei seipsum tradens*. The content *is* the totality of his presence that he passes on through the power of the Spirit, the *Verbum Dei a seipso traditum*. The process *is*

---

33 G. O'Collins, *Fundamental Theology* (New York: Paulist Press, 1981), pp. 202-04.

the living Christ acting in the church; the content is all that he is in himself and for us. In short, the risen Lord is both *tradens* and *traditum*. That allows us to say that tradition *is* the Word of God.

(3) Finally, I would like to put a specific question to all members of the dialogue. They have been reflecting on Scripture and Tradition not only in terms of past teaching but also in the light of the post-Vatican II situation (no. 60). This means, for instance, that they have also attended to the US Lutheran-Roman Catholic Dialogue and what it published in 1994 (footnote 8). Since the closing of Vatican II in 1965, one notable shift has occurred in the language used of tradition in theology and also in official documents. We now read texts that speak of tradition as 'the collective memory of the Church'.

Even before the Council ended, Yves Congar had already associated tradition and memory, and could even say: 'Tradition is memory.'[34] Despite his being closely associated with the drafting of the Dogmatic Constitution on Divine Revelation, he and the bishops who valued his theological contribution did not introduce the language of collective memory into the text of that document. But this language has come to be used in characterizing the nature of living tradition. In his 1979 apostolic exhortation on 'Catechesis in Our Time (*Catechesi Tradendae*)', Pope John Paul II described the divine self-revelation in Jesus as 'a revelation stored in the depths of the Church's *memory* and in Sacred Scripture, and constantly communicated from one generation to the next by a living, active *traditio*' (no. 22; emphasis mine). In an influential book, Jean-Marie-Roger Tillard argued that 'as the memory of the Church, Tradition represents the permanence of a word which is always alive'.[35] After Vatican II closed, George Tavard developed the theme of tradition as memory and could write: 'one

---

34 Y. Congar, *The Meaning of Tradition* (New York: Hawthorn, 1964), p. 2.
35 J.-M.-R. Tillard, *Church of Churches: The Ecclesiology of Communion*, trans. R. C. De Peaux (Collegeville, Minn.: Liturgical Press, 1992), p. 141.

could analyze tradition from the point of view of memory and define it as the Church's memory'.[36]

This is to make of the Church a collective subject that 'stores' revelation in its memory, 'communicates' it, and ensures that the revealed word remains 'always alive'. How should we understand a collective subject that 'remembers'? We are obviously dealing with an extended, metaphorical use of language, when we take memory, which is properly attributed to an individual person, and apply it to a collectivity or community like the Church.

But in this particular case, are we meant to hear a hint of various things that St Paul says about the Holy Spirit? It is through the Spirit that God reveals and the Spirit 'searches everything, even the depths of God' (1 Cor 2:10). It is that kind of language which could have encouraged the 1993 *Catechism of the Catholic Church* to describe the Holy Spirit as 'the Church's living memory' (no. 1099). This attributes memory to an individual subject: the Holy Spirit. How then does the Spirit as individual 'living memory' interact with the community that is the Church and its collective memory?

Obviously applying to tradition the language of collective memory means taking on board attractively personal terminology. Thinking of the collective memory of the Church helps us to appreciate the work of the Holy Spirit, who indwells the whole Church, lives within the baptized, and maintains Christians in unity. Yet the language of memory may also bring to mind how memory and memories can be selective, forgetful and, one must add, misleadingly 'creative'. Through our memory, we may give a shape to a past that never really was. We also know how people can suppress memories.

On the one hand, I welcome calling tradition the collective memory of the Church. But, on the other hand, there is clearly a need

---

36 G. H. Tavard, 'Tradition in Theology: a Problematic Approach', in J. F. Kelly (ed.), *Perspectives on Scripture and Tradition* (Notre Dame, Ind.: Fides, 1976), p. 92.

for theologians who use this metaphorical language to reflect more deeply on what it involves and where it meets its limits.

These then are my two comments and one question prompted by the latest fine text to come from the Lutheran-Roman Catholic Dialogue in Australia. First, Vatican II documents other than the Constitution on Divine Revelation can show us the Council at work in updating, renewing, or abandoning various traditions that have affected such areas as the liturgy, seminary training, and the practice of religious life. Second, if we are going to say that tradition *is* the word of God, we need to make it clear that we intend here to speak of tradition as the living presence of the glorious Christ. Third, recent developments in the theology of tradition leave us with the question: what is involved in calling tradition 'the collective memory of the Church'?

[This is a lecture delivered on 1 December 2011 in St Francis Xavier Cathedral, Adelaide, on the occasion of the launch of the latest document produced by the Australian Lutheran-Roman Catholic Dialogue.]

Index of Names

Abbas, Mahmoud, political leader 201

Adorno, Theodor, philosopher 171, 174

Afanas'ev, Nikolai, theologian 15

Aland, Kurt, biblical scholar 221

Alberigo, Giuseppe, historian 180

Alfaro, Juan, theologian 91–92

Alford, Stuart, barrister 101

Allen, William, cardinal 78

Ambrose of Milan, saint 173

Antonelli, Ennio, cardinal 34

Aristotle, philosopher 36

Armstrong, Neil, astronaut 219

Asquith, Julian, earl 81

Auden, W. H., poet 178

Augustine of Hippo, saint 36–37, 168–69, 174, 224

Bacon, Francis, philosopher 172, 174

Baigent, Michael, writer 17, 20–21

Bakhita, Josephine, saint 173

Balasuriya, Tissa, priest 87–88

Barnes, Edward Shippen, composer 176

Barrett, Joseph, prison chaplain 10–11, 13

Bartlett, Michael, classical scholar 132–33

Basile, Fiona, journalist ix

Batt, John, judge ix, 130–32

Bauckham, Richard, biblical scholar 32

Becker, Karl Josef, cardinal 180

Bede, the Venerable, saint 83

Beilby, James K., theologian 101

Benedict XVI, pope *passim*

Benedict of Nursia, saint 34

Benelli, Giovanni, cardinal 162

Benson, Edward White, archbishop 176

Bergoglio, Jorge, cardinal *see* Francis, Pope

Bernard of Clairvaux, saint 173

Bertone, Tarcisio, cardinal 41–42, 163

Biko, Steve, murdered activist 109

Billington, Philomena, educationalist 125

Bizet, Georges, composer 97

Blainey, Geoffrey, historian ix, 124, 136

Blair, Tony, prime minister 76, 89

Boff, Leonardo, theologian 182, 187

Bolotov, Vasilij, theologian 15

Bolt, Robert, writer 219

Borgia, Francis, saint vii

Boucher, Bruce, art historian 18–19

Boulding, Mary C., translator 160 n. 30

Braithwaite, David, Jesuit 129, n. 17
Brenk, Fred, Jesuit ix
Brett, Mark, biblical scholar 128
Brookes, Sir Norman, tennis champion 55–56
Brooks, Phillips, bishop 176
Brown, Abigail, social worker 205
Brown, Dan, novelist 16–25
Brown, Raymond, biblical scholar 32
Bulgakov, Sergii, theologian 15
Bull, George, writer 206
Burke, Robert O'Hara, explorer 132
Burke, William, murderer 77
Burns, Tom, editor 91
Burrows, William, theologian 114–15
Byrne, Brendan, biblical scholar 32
Byron, Lord, poet 54

Caear, Julius, general 23, 55
Capriati, Jennifer, tennis champion 131
Carey, Eileen, wife of George ix, 110–11
Carey, George, archbishop ix, 110–11, 208, 222
Carnley, Peter, archbishop 127
Casaroli, Agostino, cardinal 4
Casey, Tom, priest 33–34
Caswall, Edward, composer 177
Chadwick, Henry, theologian 91
Chadwick, Priscilla, daughter of Henry 91

Charles, Prince, heir to throne 127
Chavez, Hugo, politician 38
Chong, Fiona, writer 137
Christie, Agatha, novelist 73–74
Clark, Manning, historian 212
Clooney, Francis, theologian 97, 114
Columba, saint 82
Congar, Yves, theologian 27, 99, 145, 160, 228
Constantine I, emperor 19, 32
Cornille, Catherine, theologian 63
Cornwell, Peter, writer 29 n. 7
Court, Margaret, tennis champion 60
Cowen, Sir Zelman, governor general 1–2
Cronin, Daniel, canon 65
Cuthert, saint 83
Cyprian of Carthage, saint 149

Dagobert II, king 23
Dalai Lama, head of Tibetan Buddhism 102
Dalton, William, biblical scholar 93–94
Daniélou, Jean, cardinal 99
Dante Alighieri, poet 167, 217
Dawkins, Richard, atheist 86–87, 168
Day, Dorothy, social activist 53
D'Costa, Gavin, theologian 114–15
De Bertodano, Frederick Ramon, marquis 84
De Bertodano, Martin, lawyer 110

Index of Names

De Bertodano, Sylvia, judge 110
De Bertodano, Tessa, wife of Martin 110
De Gray, Richard, crusader 79
De Lubac, Henri, cardinal 99, 173
De Mello, Anthony, writer 69–71
Descartes, René, philosopher 36
Divall, Richard, knight of Malta 95–97
Dolan, Timothy, cardinal 104
Donne, John, poet 174
Doogue, Geraldine, TV presenter 130
Doria Pamphilj, Filippo Andrea, prince 2, 206–07
Doria Pamphilj, Frank Pogson, prince 2, 143, 195, 204–09
Doria Pamphilj, Gesine, daughter of Frank and Orietta 205
Doria Pamphilj, Jonathan, son of Frank and Orietta 205
Doria Pamphilj, Orietta, princess 2–3, 26, 143, 195–96, 204–09
Dostoyevsky, Fyodor, novelist 15, 174
Dugdale, Rose, revolutionary 76
Dulles, Avery, cardinal 143, 209–11.
Dulles, Allen, director of the CIA 211
Dulles, John Foster, secretary of state 210
Dunn, James, biblical scholar 32, 73

Dupuis, Jacques, theologian 7–8, 16, 26, 62–63, 85, 113–15, 128, 210–11

Eco, Umberto, novelist 222–24
Eddy, Paul, theologian 101
Egan, Edward, cardinal 104
Egan, Philip, bishop 110
Einstein, Albert, genius 172
Eisenhower, Dwight David, president 210
Eliot, T. S., poet 200
Elizabeth II, queen 209
Elliott, Charles, son of Chris and Luisa 60
Elliott, Chris, doctor 60
Elliott, Luisa, wife of Chris 60
Elizabeth I, queen 23
Elizabeth II, queen 209
Ellison, John, husband of Monica 56–57
Ellison, Monica, cousin 56–57
Emerson, Roy, tennis champion 60
Engels, Friedrich, political philosopher 172
Estévez, Jorge Medina, cardinal 145–48
Evans, Steve, philosopher 97
Evdokimov, Paul, theologian 15

Faggioli, Massimo, historian 112, 160 n. 29

Farrugia, Edward G., theologian 15, 63, 100
Farrugia, Mario, theologian 99, 124
Fee, Gordon, biblical scholar 222
Fischer, Tim, ambassador ix, 34, 130, 134
Fitzgerald, Michael, archbishop 41
Fitzmyer, Joseph, biblical scholar 32
Flood, Alison, journalist 100
Florenskij, George, theologian 15
Flynn, Gabriel, theologian 99
Foley, Edward, liturgical scholar 148
Follay, Bernard, bishop 43
Francis, Pope 37–38, 125, 127, 139, 145, 163–66, 201–02
Francis of Assisi, saint 164
Fraser, Malcolm, prime minister 131
Fraser, Neale, tennis player 60
Freier, Philip, archbishop ix, 135
Frings, Josef, cardinal 27

Gabriele, Paolo, papal butler 163
Gahizi, Patrick, martyr 10
Gallagher, Paul, archbishop 138
Gantin, Bernardin, cardinal 162
Gassendi, Pierre, astronomer 36
Gibson, Mel, actor 6, 10–11, 13
Gifford, David, Jewish executive 46
Gilbert, Hugh, bishop 75
Glynn, Patrick McMahon, parliamentarian 129–30, 225

Gobbo, James, Sir, governor ix, 95, 141
Goolagong Cawley, Evonne, tennis champion 60
Goss, Sir John, composer 177
Graves, Robert, novelist 56
Greer, Germaine, writer 64–65
Gregory the Great, pope 21–22, 36, 223
Grocholewski, Zenon, cardinal 162
Groer, Hans Hermann, cardinal 9
Gurry, Ray, doctor 212

Haas, Wolfgang, archbishop 9
Haig, Douglas, field marshal 2
Hall, Catherine, archivist ix
Hammond, Joan, soprano 96
Hammond, Richard, TV personality 24–25
Handel, George Frederick, composer 176–77
Hanrahan, Brian, TV presenter 5–6, 33–34
Harbert, Bruce, monsignor, 147, 149
Hare, William, murderer 77
Harrington, Daniel, biblical scholar 32
Harrison, Carol, historian 37 n. 9
Hart, Kevin, poet and philosopher 97
Hayes, Brendan, parish priest 215
Hayes, Michael, priest 53, 59, 61, 65–66, 98

Head, Michael, educator ix
Heaney, Seamus, poet 219
Hengel, Martin, biblical scholar 29
Henry VIII, king 79
Hirsch, Eric Donald, literary critic 148, 199–200
Hoffman, Dustin, actor 74
Hogg, Quintin, lord chancellor 80–81
Homer, Greek poet 133
Horace, Latin poet 133
Horkheimer, Max, philosopher 171, 174
Howells, Edward, writer 71
Hünermann, Peter, theologian 44
Hunt, Anne, theologian 97–98
Hylton, Raymond, lord 80–82

Iemma, Maurice, premier ix, ii
Ignatius Loyola, saint viii, 221
Isaacs, Isaac, governor general 1
Isouard, Nicolò, composer 96

James, Clive, writer 167
Januarius, saint 86
Jansen, Gary, publisher 70
Jeffrey, Peter, musicologist 146
Joan of Arc, saint 53
John of Austria, don 42
John XXIII, saint 44–45, 55, 160, 228

John Paul I, pope 7 n. 2
John Paul II, saint *passim*
Johnson, Boris, mayor 133
Johnson, Luke Timothy, biblical scholar 32
Johnson, Samuel, writer 217
Jolliffe, Emily, daughter of Raymond Hylton 82
Jones, Michael Keenan, parish priest ix, 64, 76, 102–03, 105
Jung, Carl Gustav, psychologist 194

Kant, Immanuel, philosopher 174
Kasper, Walter, cardinal 27–29, 189–81
Keating, Thomas, abbot 198
Kendall, Daniel, biblical scholar 17 n. 3, 67, 69–70, 101–02, 128
Kennedy, Ethel, wife of Robert Kennedy 196
Kennedy, John, president 196
Kennedy, Robert, brother of John 196
Kleinberg, Aviad, historian 22–23
Knox, Ronald, apologist 81, 146, 159
König, Franz, cardinal 7
Korda, Petr, tennis player 131
Klinkostroem, Maximilian, missionary 121
Kranewitter, Aloysius, missionary 121
Krauth, Lothar, translator 151 n. 24

Le-Bao-Tinh, Paul, martyr 170
LaBelle, Jeffrey, Jesuit 67, 69–70
Lee, Dorothy, biblical scholar 128, 130
Lefebvre, Marcel, archbishop 43–44
Lehmann, Karl, cardinal 28
Leigh, Richard, writer 17, 20–21
Leigh, Vivien, actress 84
Leo the Great, pope 21–22, 223
Leonardo da Vinci, genius 18–19, 24
Levi, Carlo, writer 60
Lincoln, Henry, writer 17, 20–21
Little, Frank, archbishop 223
Livingstone, Ken, mayor 133
Lohse, Eduard, bishop 195
Lossky, Vladimir, theologian 15

McAdam, Jane, writer 137
McCarthy, Eugene, doctor 104, 193–98
McCarthy, John, son of Eugene and Maureen 194
McCarthy, Joseph, son of Eugene and Maureen 193–94
McCarthy, Maureen, wife of Eugene 104, 193–98
McCarthy, Paul, son of Eugene and Maureen 194
McCarthy, William, monsignor 215
McCaughey, Davis, church leader 93–94
McCaughey, Patrick, art critic 218

McGinn, Bernard, expert in mysticism 71
Maciel, Marcial Delgollado, sex abuser 9–10
Mackerras, Sir Charles, conductor 96
MacKillop, Donald, brother of Mary 120
MacKillop, Mary, saint 120–22
Mahoney, Roger, cardinal 148
Malachy, saint 34
Mandela, Nelson, statesman 109
Mannin, Ethel, novelist 56
Manuel II Palaeologus, emperor 41
Mark, Kevin, publisher ix
Marshall, John, neurologist 55, 59
Martin de Porres, saint 109
Martínez Somalo, Eduardo, cardinal 162
Martini, Carlo Maria, cardinal 3, 143, 220–24
Marx, Karl, political philosopher 172
Maximus the Confessor, saint 173
May, John, Jesuit winemaker 121
Meier, John, biblical scholar 32
Meister, Chad, theologian 101
Melloni, Alberto, historian 97
Mendelssohn, Felix, composer 176
Menezes, Albert, Jesuit 69
Merry del Val, Rafael, cardinal 162
Metz, Johann Baptist, theologian 26
Meyers, Mary Ann, Templeton fellow 102

Michelangelo Buonarroti, genius 19
Moloney, Francis, biblical scholar 27, 29
Monaghan, Christopher, biblical scholar 27 n. 5
Moltmann, Jürgen, theologian 95
Morant, 'Breaker' Harry, horseman 84
More, Thomas, saint 78
Moreton, Cole, journalist 99
Mostert, Christiaan, theologian 95
Muhammad, prophet 41
Murdoch, Rupert, media baron 127
Murphy-O'Connor, Cormac, cardinal 88–90, 180
Murray, Paul, theologian 99
Murray II, William, publisher 54
Mussolini, Benito, dictator 207

Nathan, Sir Maurice, business man 214
Napier, Wilfrid, cardinal 138
Neale, John Mason, composer 178
Neusner, Jacob, rabbi 31
Newman, Carey, biblical scholar 100
Newman, John Henry, blessed 1–2, 177
Nguyen Van Thuan, cardinal 168–69
Nichols, Vincent, cardinal 65
Nicholson, Ernest, biblical scholar 1–2
Nietzsche, Friedrich, philosopher 36

Ninham, Sally, historian 137–39

Obama, Barack, president 153
O'Brien, Mark, biblical scholar 27 n. 5
O'Brien, Mark, doctor 212
O'Collins, James, bishop 214
O'Collins, James, son of Jim and 'Posey' 2
O'Collins, Jim, surgeon 1–3, 39
O'Collins, Joan, my mother 22
O'Collins, Moira *see* Peters, Moira
O'Collins, Rosemary ('Posey'), wife of Jim ix, 39
O'Collins, Victoria ('Tori'), daughter of Jim and Posey 2–3
Odasso, Giovanni, biblical scholar 62
O'Flaherty, Hugh, monsignor 206
O'Kelly, Gregory, bishop 120
O'Malley, John, historian 76
O'Sullivan, Maureen, actress 84

Paisley, Ian, political leader 208
Pallhuber, John, missionary 121–22
Pannenberg, Wolfhart, theologian 95
Parker, Elizabeth, archivist ix
Parolin, Pietro, cardinal 163 n. 32
Patrick, saint 87
Patte, Daniel, biblical scholar 33
Paul VI, blessed 8, 45, 55, 160–62, 208, 221–22

Pavarotti, Luciano, tenor 96
Pell, George, cardinal 223
Penrose, Amber, wife of Charles Elliott 60
Penrose, Beryl, aunt of Amber 60
Pepinster, Catherine, editor ix, 91–92
Peres, Shimon, president 201
Peters, Bronwen, veterinarian 213
Peters, James Sturrock, surgeon 143, 212–16
Peters, James W. S., barrister 137, 213, 215–16
Peters, Joanna, lawyer 213
Peters, Justin, surgeon 213
Peters, Marion, hepatologist 213
Peters, Mark, banker 213
Peters, Moira, wife of James Sturrock Peters ix, 135, 213–15
Peters, Sheila, doctor 212
Peters, Stephen, engineer 213
Peters, Stewart, solicitor 213
Peters, Victor, father of James Sturrock Peters 212
Phan, Peter, theologian 63
Philip II, king 23
Pieper, Josef, philosopher 151 n. 24
Pironio, Eduardo, cardinal 13–14
Pitt the Younger, William, prime minister 54
Pius V, saint 44
Pius XII, pope 64, 190, 201, 207–08
Plantard, Pierre, confidence trickster 20

Plato, philosopher 36, 174
Plunkett, Anne, ambassador vii, ix, 11
Porter, Peter, poet 217
Pseudo-Dionysius the Areopagite, church father 36
Pugh, Jonathan, cartoonist 13
Pullman, Philip, writer 99–100

Radcliffe, Timothy, Dominican master general 65
Rahner, Karl, theologian 5, 99, 114, 190
Ramsey, Michael, archbishop 208
Ratzinger, Joseph, *see* Benedict XVI
Ratzinger, Maria, sister of Joseph 26
Redgrave, Vanessa, actress 74
Ricciarelli, Katia, soprano 96
Richardson, David, canon 130
Richardson, Margie, wife of David 130
Riordan, Jean, writer 148
Ronayne, Mary, translator 160 n. 30
Rosen, David, rabbi 47
Runcie, Robert, archbishop 26
Rutagambwa, Innocent, martyr 10
Ryan, Michael, priest 150

Sallust, Roman historian 36
Samson, Allisia, wife of Scott ix
Samson, Scott, knight of Malta ix

Index of Names

Samuels, Digby, parish priest 84
Schumann, Robert, composer 200
Shakespeare, William, genius 108
Shigi, Evarist, Jesuit ix, 136
Skinner, Gerard, priest 35
Smith, Graham, priest ix, 135
Smith, Peter, judge 17
Sobrino, Jon, theologian 15, 91, 189, 191–92
Solov'iev, Vladimir, theologian 15
Steele, Peter, priest and poet 143, 215–19
Steiner, George, literary critic 146, 148 n. 20
Stewart, Mary, friend 84–85
Stoney, Michael, Jesuit 215
Stump, Eleonore, philosopher 97
Suess, Paulo, missionary expert 38
Sullivan, Francis A., theologian 180, 183
Swift, Jonathan, satirist 217

Tagore, Rabindranath, writer 204
Tate, Nahum, composer 177
Tavard, George, theologian 228–29
Taylor, Maurice, bishop 147
Teilhard de Chardin, Pierre, palaeontologist 173
Teresa of Avila, saint 194
Teresa of Calcutta, blessed 1, 3–6
Teuffenbach, Alexandra von, theologian 183

Thomas Aquinas, saint 37, 173, 190–92, 224
Thompson, Ross, educationalist 82
Tillard, Jean-Marie-Roger, theologian 228
Todd, John, publisher 80
Tolkien, J. R. R., writer 23, 53
Tolstoy, Leo 15, 36
Tomko, Jozef, cardinal 162
Torrance, Thomas, theologian 75
Tromp, Sebastian, theologian 183
Turnbull, Malcolm, politician ix, 11, 223
Tutu, Desmond, bishop 109
Tyler, Peter, expert in spirituality 61, 71

Uren, William, Jesuit 215

Vaughan, Gerard, gallery director 218
Vianney, Jean-Baptiste Marie, saint 79–80
Villot, Jean-Marie, cardinal 161
Virgil, poet 36
Vorgrimler, Herbert, theologian 27

Wadding, Luke, bishop 177
Wade, John Francis, composer 176
Wallace-Crabbe, Chris, poet 219
Walpole, Horace, art historian 61
Watts, Isaac, hymn writer 176

Wayte, Simon, theologian 95
Webb, David, surgeon 134
Wesley, Charles, composer 176
White, Carnie, wife of Denis 131
White, Denis, philosopher 131
Wicks, Jared, theologian 27, 66, 76, 99
Widgery, John, chief justice 80
Wilberforce, William, philanthropist 54
Wilding, Tony, tennis champion 56
Wilkins, John, editor 6–8, 148
Williams, Ralph Vaughan, composer 176–77
Williams, Rowan, archbishop 33, 133
Williamson, Richard, bishop 28, 43–44
Wills, William John, explorer 132
Winning, Thomas, cardinal 147
Winter, Sean, biblical scholar 95
Wojtyla, Karol, *see* John Paul II, saint
Woods, Julian Tenison, priest 121
Woodward, George Ratcliffe, religious poet 177
Woodward, Kenneth, journalist 196
Wright, N. T., bishop and biblical scholar 32, 73

Yeats, W. B., poet 56
Young, Norman, theologian 94–95

www.ingramcontent.com/pod-product-compliance
Ingram Content Group UK Ltd.
Pitfield, Milton Keynes, MK11 3LW, UK
UKHW021324180426
11947UKWH00017B/1427